TM

References for the Rest of Us!®

BESTSELLING BOOK SERIES

Do you find that traditional reference books are overloaded with technical details and advice you'll never use? Do you postpone important life decisions because you just don't want to deal with them? Then our *For Dummies*® business and general reference book series is for you.

For Dummies business and general reference books are written for those frustrated and hard-working souls who know they aren't dumb, but find that the myriad of personal and business issues and the accompanying horror stories make them feel helpless. *For Dummies* books use a lighthearted approach, a down-to-earth style, and even cartoons and humorous icons to dispel fears and build confidence. Lighthearted but not lightweight, these books are perfect survival guides to solve your everyday personal and business problems.

> *"More than a publishing phenomenon, 'Dummies' is a sign of the times."*
>
> — The New York Times

> *"A world of detailed and authoritative information is packed into them..."*
>
> — U.S. News and World Report

> *"...you won't go wrong buying them."*
>
> — Walter Mossberg, Wall Street Journal, on For Dummies books

Already, millions of satisfied readers agree. They have made For Dummies the #1 introductory level computer book series and a best-selling business book series. They have written asking for more. So, if you're looking for the best and easiest way to learn about business and other general reference topics, look to For Dummies to give you a helping hand.

Wiley Publishing, Inc.

Stock Investing For Dummies®

The Ten Most Important Points about Stock Investing

1. You're not buying a stock; you're buying a company.

2. The only reason why you buy a stock is because the company is making a profit.

3. If you buy a stock that isn't making a profit, then you're not investing; you're speculating.

4. A stock (or stocks in general) should never be 100 percent of your assets.

5. In some cases (such as a severe bear market), stocks are not a good investment at all.

6. A stock's price is dependent on the company, which in turn is dependent on its environment, which includes its customer base, its industry, the general economy, and politics.

7. Your common sense and logic can be just as important in choosing a good stock as the advice of any investment expert.

8. Always have well-reasoned answers to questions such as "Why are you investing in stocks?" and "Why are you investing in a particular stock?"

9. If you have no idea about the prospects of a company (and sometimes even if you think you do), always use stop-loss orders.

10. Even if your philosophy is "buy and hold for the long term," continue to monitor your stocks and consider selling them if they're not appreciating in value.

Mandatory Reading List for Investors

- The company's annual report
- The 10K and 10Q reports that the company files with the SEC
- *Standard & Poor's Stock Guide*
- *The Wall Street Journal* and/or *Investor's Business Daily*

Important Things to Look at in a Company's Fundamentals

- **Earnings:** The number should be higher than the year before.
- **Sales:** The number should be higher than the year before.
- **Debt:** The number should be lower than or about the same as the year before.
- **Equity:** The number should be higher than the year before.

The Best Financial Measures

- **Price to earnings ratio:** For large cap stocks, the ratio should be under 20. For all stocks (including growth, small cap, and speculative issues), it should not exceed 40.
- **Price to sales ratio:** The PSR should be as close to 1 as possible.
- **Return on equity (ROE):** ROE should be going up by at least 10 percent.
- **Earnings growth:** Earnings should be at least 10 percent higher than the year before. This rate should be maintained over several years.
- **Debt to asset ratio:** Debt should be half or less compared to assets.

Eight Events That Could Spell Trouble for Your Stock

- A bear market
- Heavy insider selling
- A lawsuit by the government
- Excessive government taxation
- Excessive government regulation
- An SEC investigation
- An economic slowdown or decline in the industry or sector
- National or international conflict (such as war or acts of terrorism)

Best Internet Sources for Alternative Views on the Stock Market

- Fall Street (www.fallstreet.com)
- Prudent Bear (www.prudentbear.com)
- Le Metro Pole Café (www.lemetropolecafe.com)
- Financial Sense (www.financialsense.com)

Best Internet Tools for Investors

- Stock screening tools available at Web sites such as www.amex.com
- Insider trading monitoring at Web sites such as www.marketwatch.com
- Earnings reports and estimates at www.firstcall.com
- Public document databases such as EDGAR at www.sec.gov
- Sources such as www.iexchange.com that monitor analysts' views and track records
- Great stock investing books at www.amazon.com

Top Ten Web Sites for Investors

- www.bloomberg.com
- www.nyse.com
- www.nasdaq.com
- www.sec.gov
- www.marketwatch.com
- www.forbes.com
- www.smartmoney.com
- www.dowjones.com
- www.aaii.org
- www.dismal.com

For Dummies: Bestselling Book Series for Beginners

Stock Investing
FOR
DUMMIES®

by Paul Mladjenovic

Wiley Publishing, Inc.

Stock Investing For Dummies®

Published by
Wiley Publishing, Inc.
909 Third Avenue
New York, NY 10022
www.wiley.com

Copyright © 2002 by Wiley Publishing, Inc., Indianapolis, Indiana

Published simultaneously in Canada

For general information on our other products and services or to obtain technical support, please contact our Customer Care Department within the U.S. at 800-762-2974, outside the U.S. at 317-572-3993, or fax 317-572-4002.

Wiley also publishes its books in a variety of electronic formats. Some content that appears in print may not be available in electronic books.

Library of Congress Cataloging-in-Publication Data:

Library of Congress Control Number: 2002103279

ISBN: 0-7645-5411-5

Manufactured in the United States of America

10 9 8 7 6 5 4 3 2

1O/TR/QZ/QS/IN

About the Author

Paul Mladjenovic is a certified financial planner practitioner, financial consultant, writer, and public speaker who has a Web site at www.mladjenovic.com. His business, PM Financial Services, has helped people with financial and business concerns since 1981. He achieved his CFP designation in 1985 and his BA degree from Seton Hall University in 1981. Since 1986, Paul has taught thousands of budding investors through popular national seminars such as "The $50 Wealthbuilder" and "Stock Investing like a Pro." Paul has been quoted or referenced by many media outlets such as Bloomberg, CNBC, and many financial and business publications and Web sites. As an author, he has written the books *The Unofficial Guide to Picking Stocks* (Wiley, 2000) and *Zero-Cost Marketing* (Todd Publications, 1995) and reports such as "1,001 Stocks with Dividend Reinvestment Plans." In addition, he has authored the software kit *Internet Wealth-Building Tools for Investors* and the forthcoming CD *The Financial Mega-Kit*. In recent years, he has achieved attention as a result of his economic forecasting. In 1999, he forecast the bear market of 2000 and the recession of 2001.

Dedication

Author's Acknowledgments

First and foremost, I offer my appreciation and gratitude to the wonderful people at Wiley. It has been a pleasure to work with such a top-notch organization that works so hard to create products that offer readers tremendous value and information. I wish all of you continued success! There are some notables there whom I want to single out.

The first person is Marcia Johnson (my editor), a true publishing professional who has been extremely helpful, understanding, and patient. Those words are not enough to express my thanks for her fantastic guidance.

A special (and I mean very special) note of thanks to Cynthia Kitchel, another magnificent professional at Wiley. Her forbearance and foresight at a critical juncture became instrumental in making this book a reality.

Tina Sims is yet another Wiley pro whom I am grateful to work with. She has been wonderful in helping shape my muddled prose into the type of writing that is worthy of the *For Dummies* tradition.

I also want to thank Kevin Thornton and Mark Butler who championed this book from the beginning.

Fran, Lipa Zyenska, you helped make those late nights at the computer more tolerable, and you helped me focus on the important things. Te amo and I thank God that you are by my side. With you and the rest of my loving family, I know that the future will be bright.

My deepest thanks to Murray Sabrin, professor of finance at Ramapo College in New Jersey who is also a fantastic author and writer. As the technical consultant to this book, you have offered expertise and feedback that have been very valuable and most appreciated.

Lastly, I want to acknowledge you, the reader. Over the years, you have made the *For Dummies* books what they are today. Your devotion to these wonderful books created a foundation that played a big part in the creation of this book and many more yet to come. Thank you!

Publisher's Acknowledgments

We're proud of this book; please send us your comments through our online registration form located at www.dummies.com/register.

Some of the people who helped bring this book to market include the following:

Acquisitions, Editorial, and Media Development

Project Editor: Marcia L. Johnson

Acquisitions Editor: Pam Mourouzis

Copy Editor: Tina Sims

Technical Editor: Murray Sabrin

Editorial Manager: Jennifer Ehrlich

Editorial Assistant: Nivea C. Strickland

Cover Photos: © Corbis/Stockmarket/ Alan Schein

Production

Project Coordinator: Nancee Reeves

Layout and Graphics: Stephanie D. Jumper, Tiffany Muth, Brent Savage, Jeremey Unger, Mary J. Virgin

Proofreaders: John Greenough, Andy Hollandbeck, Carl Pierce, TECHBOOKS Production Services

Indexer: TECHBOOKS Production Services

Publishing and Editorial for Consumer Dummies

Diane Graves Steele, Vice President and Publisher, Consumer Dummies
Joyce Pepple, Acquisitions Director, Consumer Dummies
Kristin A. Cocks, Product Development Director, Consumer Dummies
Michael Spring, Vice President and Publisher, Travel
Brice Gosnell, Publishing Director, Travel
Suzanne Jannetta, Editorial Director, Travel

Publishing for Technology Dummies

Richard Swadley, Vice President and Executive Group Publisher
Andy Cummings, Vice President and Publisher

Composition Services

Gerry Fahey, Vice President of Production Services
Debbie Stailey, Director of Composition Services

Contents at a Glance

Cartoons at a Glance

By Rich Tennant

page 131

page 187

page 7

page 261

page 71

Cartoon Information:
Fax: 978-546-7747
E-Mail: richtennant@the5thwave.com
World Wide Web: www.the5thwave.com

Table of Contents

Introduction

Stock Investing For Dummies has been an honor for me to write. I'm grateful that I can share my thoughts, information, and experience with such a large and devoted group of readers.

Stock investing is a great topic that has fascinated me for years, so I welcome the chance to invite you to join me in that pursuit, and to guide you along the way. Although the stock market has served millions of investors for nearly a century, recent years have shown me that a great investing vehicle such as stocks can be easily be misunderstood, misused, and even abused. The great bull market of 1982–1999 came to a screeching halt in 2000. During 2000 and 2001, millions of investors lost a total of 5 trillion dollars. What bothers me is that much of that loss was easily avoidable. Investors at the tail end of a bull market often think that stock investing is an easy, carefree, mindless way to make a quick fortune. How wrong they are! The countless stories of investors who lost tremendous amounts of money speculating in tech stocks, dot-coms, and other flashy stocks are lessons for all of us. Successful stock investing takes diligent work and knowledge like any other meaningful pursuit. This book will definitely help you avoid the mistakes others have made and can point you in the right direction.

I thank you again for considering Stock Investing For Dummies. I hope you explore the pages to find the topics that most interest you regarding the world of stock investing. Let me assure you that I have squeezed two decades of experience, education, and expertise between these covers. In all the years that I have counseled and educated investors, the single difference between success and failure, between gain and loss, boils down to one word: knowledge. Take this book as your first step in a lifelong learning adventure.

Why This Book?

The stock market has been a centerpiece of the American scene in recent years. In the late 1990s, stock investing seemed to replace baseball as the national pastime. Yet, even though a record 55 percent of all households in 1999 had at least a portion of their wealth in the stock market, very few actually understood stocks. All they knew was what the talking heads on TV and their broker were telling them. Sadly, even the so-called experts did not understand stocks. How else do you explain that the majority of stock analysts and market pundits did not see the bear market of 2000 coming even though the evidence of a pending decline was obvious?

Investors have, to put it bluntly, heard a lot of garbage about economics in general and stock investing in particular. They heard misguided economists in 1999 proclaim that recessions are now obsolete and economic growth and stocks will continue to rise forever (actual words!). Then they heard celebrated investment experts say that you should buy Internet stocks even though these companies were loaded with debt, losing tons of money, and showing no realistic economic potential.

This book is designed to give you a realistic approach to making money in stocks. It provides the essence of sound, practical stock investing strategies and insights that have been market tested and proven from nearly a hundred years of stock market history.

Stock Investing For Dummies is also a book that is quite different from the torrents of "get rich with stocks" and "Dow 87,000" titles that have crammed the bookshelves in recent years. It doesn't take a standard approach to the topic; it doesn't assume that stocks are a sure thing and the be-all and end-all of wealth building. At times in this book, I tell you *not* to invest in stocks. This book can help you succeed not only in up markets but also in down markets. Bull markets and bear markets come and go, but the informed investor can keep making money no matter what. This book also gives you strategies for avoiding losses, which is important information during tough economic times.

This book is valuable for several reasons:

- If you are a beginner and want a crash course on stock investing that is also an easy and humorous read, this book is for you. This book is not written in a cloggy, academic style (thank God!). The book is meant for everyday people (like the author himself).

- If you're already a stock investor, the book is laid out so that you don't have to read everything; each chapter is a stand-alone read. You can read only those chapters that cover specific stock investing topics of interest to you.

- Review your own situation with the information in the book. Did you miss anything when you invested in that hot stock that your brother-in-law recommended? The book gives you an easy way to make sure that you're not blindsided by your stock choices.

- It's a great gift idea! When Uncle Mo is upset over his Enron or Global Crossing stock picks, this book can help him get back on his financial feet. Be sure to get a copy for your broker, too. (Odds are that the broker was the one who made those recommendations to begin with.)

How This Book Is Organized

The information is laid out in a straightforward format. The parts progress in a logical approach that any investor interested in stocks can follow very easily.

Part 1: The Essentials of Stock Investing

This section is for everyone. Understanding the essentials of stock investing and investing in general will only help you, especially in uncertain economic times. Stocks may even touch your finances in ways not readily apparent. For example, stocks are not only in individual accounts; they're also in mutual funds and pension plans.

An important point is that stocks are really financial tools that are a means to an end. Investors should be able to answer the question "Why am I considering stocks at all?" Stocks are a great vehicle for wealth building, but only if investors realize what they can accomplish and how to use them.

One of the essentials of stock investing is understanding risk. Most people are clueless about risk. The chapter on risk is one of the most important chapters that serious stock investors should read. You can't avoid every type of risk out there. (Life itself embodies risk.) However, this chapter can help you recognize it and find ways to minimize it in your stock investing program.

Part II: Before You Get Started

Once you're ready to embark on your career as a stock investor, you'll need to use some resources to gather information about the stocks you're interested in. Fortunately, we live in the information age. I pity the investors from the 1920s, who didn't have access to so many resources, but today's investors are in an enviable position. This part tells you where to find information and how to use it to be a more knowledgeable investor (a rarity in recent years!). For example, I explain that stocks can be used for both growth and income purposes, and I discuss the characteristics of each.

When you're ready to invest, you'll invariably have to turn to a broker. There are several types, so you should know which is which. The wrong broker could make you . . . uh . . . broker. Part II helps you choose.

Part III: Picking Winners

Part III is about picking good stocks by using microeconomics, meaning that you look at the stocks of individual companies. I explain how to evaluate a company's products, services, and other factors so that you can determine whether a company is strong and healthy.

Where do you turn to find about the company's financial health? I show you the documents you should review to make a more informed decision. Once you find the information, you'll discover how to make sense of that data as well.

I compare buying stock to picking goldfish. If you look at a bunch of goldfish to choose which ones to buy, you want to make sure that you pick the healthiest ones. With stocks, you also need to pick companies that are healthy.

Part IV: Investment Strategies and Tactics

Even the stocks of great companies can fall in a bad investing environment. This is where you should be aware of the "macro." If stocks were goldfish, the macro would be the pond or goldfish bowl. In that case, even healthy goldfish can die if the water is toxic. Therefore, you should monitor the investing environment for stocks. Part IV reveals tips, strategies, and resources that you shouldn't ignore.

As a matter of fact, the macro picture is the one major area where most stock investing pros go wrong. Fortunately, you have right in your hands the information to understand the investing environment! You may even want to consider quoting some of my advice to your broker.

Once you understand stocks and the economic environment in which they operate, choose the strategy and the tactics to help steer you to your wealth-building objectives. Part IV reveals some of my all-time favorite techniques for building wealth and holding on to your stock investment gains. (Definitely check it out.)

You may be an investor, but that doesn't mean that you have deep pockets. This part tells you how to buy stocks with lower (or no) transaction costs. If you're going to buy the stock anyway, why not save on commissions and other costs?

As an investor, you must keep an eye on what the company insiders are doing. In this part, I explain what it may mean if the company's management is buying or selling the same stock that you're considering.

After you spend all your time, money, and effort to grow your money in the world of stocks, you have yet another concern: holding on to your hard-earned gains. This challenge is summarized in one word: taxes. Sound tax planning is crucial for everyone who works hard. After all, taxes are the biggest expense in your lifetime.

Part V: The Part of Tens

I wrap up the book with a hallmark of *For Dummies* books — the Part of Tens. These chapters give you a mini crash course in stock investing, including the ten things you should be aware of before you invest in your first stock.

What's that? You already bought stock? Then check out the chapter on what you should be aware of after you invest. You just might save a bundle. Find out about the steps to avoid fraud. To make this part complete, I offer some clues to choosing a winning stock and how to recognize the warning signs of a stock poised to fall.

Appendixes

Don't overlook the appendixes. I pride myself on the resources I can provide my students and readers so that they can make informed investment decisions. Whether the topic is stock investing terminology, economics, or avoiding capital gains taxes, I include a treasure trove of resources to help you. Whether you go to a bookstore, the library, or the Internet, Appendix A gives you some great places to turn to for help. In Appendix B, I explain financial ratios, which can help you better determine whether to invest in a particular company's stock.

Icons Used in This Book

This icon flags a particular bit of advice that just may give you an edge over other investors.

When you see this icon, I'm reminding you about some information that you should always keep stashed in your memory, no matter whether you're new to investing or an old pro.

Pay special attention to this icon because the advice can prevent headaches, heartaches, and financial aches.

The text attached to this icon may not be crucial to your success as an investor, but it may enable you to talk shop with investing gurus and better understand the financial pages of your favorite business publication or Web site.

Part I

The Essentials of Stock Investing

The 5th Wave   By Rich Tennant

In this part . . .

You need to know a lot before you invest your first dollar in stocks. Most investors don't realize that they should be scrutinizing their own situations and financial goals at least as much as they scrutinize stocks. But how else can you know which stocks are right for you? Too many people risk too much simply because they don't take stock of their current needs, goals, and risk tolerance before they invest. The chapters in this part tell you what you need to know to choose the stocks that best suit you. Additionally, they introduce you to the major stock indexes and concepts so that you can invest like a pro.

Chapter 1

Exploring the Basics

. . . .

. . . .

Stock investing became all the rage during the 1990s. Investors watched their stock portfolios and mutual funds skyrocket as the stock market experienced an 18-year rising market (or bull market). Investment activity in the United States is a great example of the popularity that stocks experienced during that time period. By 1999, over half of U.S. households became participants in the stock market. Yet millions lost money during the stock market's decline in 2000. People invested. Yet they really didn't know exactly what they were investing in. If they had a rudimentary understanding of what stock really is, perhaps they could have avoided some expensive mistakes. The purpose of this book is not only to tell you about the basics of stock investing but also to let you in on some sharp tactics that can help you profit from the stock market. Before you invest your first dollar, you need to understand the basics of stock investing.

Heading to the Store

The stock market is a market of stocks; it is a market like any other market, such as a grocery store or a flea market. A grocery store, for instance, is a place that offers soup to nuts along with numerous other things for shoppers to buy. The stock market is an established market where people (investors) can freely buy and sell millions of shares issued by thousands of companies. Investors buy stocks because they seek gain in the form of appreciation (their stock, if held long enough, goes up in value) or income (some stocks pay income in the form of dividends) or both. Those who already own stock may sell it to cash in and use the money for other purposes. Companies issue stock because they want money for a particular purpose.

Understanding why companies sell stock

The first time a company sells stock to the public is known as an *initial public offering* (IPO), sometimes referred to as "going public." The most prominent new stock IPOs are usually reported in the pages of financial publications such as *The Wall Street Journal* and *Investor's Business Daily*.

Generally, two types of companies go public by issuing stock:

- ✔ **An existing private company:** A company is currently in operation as a private corporation, but it wants to expand.

- ✔ **A start-up company:** A company is just starting up and decides to go public immediately to raise the capital necessary to establish itself.

Between the two, the safer situation for investors is the first type.

Why does a company go public? It goes public because it needs to raise the money necessary for its financial success. More specifically, the money raised through a public offering of stock can be used for the following purposes:

- ✔ **To raise capital for expansion.** If XYZ Corporation wants to increase its production capacity, it needs a new manufacturing facility. In order to raise the capital needed to build and operate the new facility, it may decide to sell stock to the public.

- ✔ **To finance product (or service) development.** Maybe the company needs money for research and development for a new invention or innovation.

- ✔ **To pay off debt.** The company may want to use the proceeds of a stock sale to pay off debt.

- ✔ **Miscellaneous reasons.** The company may need money for other reasons that are important for the health and growth of the enterprise, such as payroll or retail operations.

Start-ups can be risky business

In recent years, investors have lost a lot of money by investing in brand-new companies offering growth opportunities in high-tech and Internet businesses. Pets.com and eToys.com are examples of Internet start-ups that went bankrupt within three years of going public. However, investors found more assured opportunities for growth in well-established private companies that went public. A good example is Krispy Kreme Doughnuts. It was a proven, profitable company when it was private, and it proved increasingly profitable when it went public. The stock premiered in April 2000 at just under $10 per share, and it hit $40 by March 2002.

Keep in mind that a stock offering doesn't always have to be in first-time situations. Many companies issue stock in secondary offerings to gain the capital they need for expansion or other purposes.

Going public: It's no secret

When a private company wants to offer its stock to the general public, it usually asks a stock underwriter to help. An *underwriter* is a financial company that acts as an intermediary between stock investors and public companies. The underwriter is usually an investment banking company or the investment banking division of a major brokerage firm. The underwriter may put together a group of several investment banking companies and brokers. This group is also referred to as the *syndicate.* Usually the main underwriter is called the *primary underwriter,* and others in the group are referred to as *subsidiary underwriters.*

Before a company can sell stock to the public, a couple things have to happen:

✔ The underwriter or syndicate agrees to pay the company a predetermined price for a minimum number of shares and then must resell those shares to buyers such as their own clients (which could be you or me), mutual funds, and other commercial brokerages. Each member of the syndicate agrees to resell a portion of the issued stock. The underwriters earn a fee for their underwriting services.

✔ The underwriter sets a time frame to start selling the issued stock (the window of time that the primary market is taking place). The underwriter also helps the company prepare a preliminary prospectus that details the required financial and business information for investors, such as the amount of money being sought in the IPO and who is seeking the money and why. (For details, see the section "The watchdog role of the SEC," later in this chapter.)

The preliminary prospectus is referred to as the "red herring" because it usually comes stamped with a warning in red letters that identifies this as preliminary — a kind of disclaimer that the stock's price may or may not be changed as the final issue price.

The IPO stock usually isn't available directly to the public. Interested investors must purchase the initial shares through the underwriters authorized to sell the IPO shares during the primary market. After the primary market period — at the start of the secondary market — you can ask your own stockbroker to buy you shares of that stock. The *secondary market* is more familiar to the public and includes established, orderly public markets such as the New York Stock Exchange, the American Stock Exchange, and Nasdaq.

Proceed with caution when considering an IPO

Many people think of getting into IPOs as "getting in on the ground floor." However, the record shows that the price of the stock usually goes down during the first 12 months in the life of that stock. Depending on market and economic conditions, the majority of IPOs in some years fall in price during the opening months that the stock is in the secondary market. Investors have no reason to rush in when the IPO first becomes available. The better route for investors (especially beginning investors) is to search out established companies with proven track records that can be bought at reasonable stock prices and held for the long term.

Sometimes, you may not have to find the IPO; sometimes it finds you! If you get calls from brokers offering you a ground-floor opportunity in an IPO, your best advice is to avoid this investment. Many investors have been burned by brokers with hard-sell approaches in unproven opportunities.

The watchdog role of the SEC

The market for IPOs and all public stocks is regulated by the Securities and Exchange Commission (SEC) under the Securities Act of 1933, also known as the Full Disclosure Act. The SEC sets the standard for disclosure and governs the creation of the prospectus. The prospectus must contain information such as the description of the issuer's business, names and addresses of the key company officers, key information relating to the company's financial condition, and how the proceeds from the stock offering will be used. For more on the SEC — what reports companies must file and how investors can benefit from this information — see Chapters 6 and 11.

SEC approval of the sale of stock doesn't mean that the SEC recommends the stock. SEC approval only means that the sale of stock can go forward legally. The SEC ensures only that all necessary information and documentation have been filed and are available to the public.

Knowing What You're Buying: Defining Stock

Stock represents ownership in a corporation (or company). Just like the owner of a car has a title that says he has ownership of a car, a stock certificate shows that you own a piece of a company. If a company issues stock of, say, 1 million shares and you own 100 shares, this means you have ownership equivalent to 1/10,000th of the company.

The physical evidence of ownership is a stock certificate that shows what stock you own and how many shares. These days, investors rarely get the certificates in hand, direct from the company; instead, they simply trade through brokerage accounts (see Chapter 7 for tons of information on brokers) and shareholder service departments that hold the stock. Your brokerage statements tell you what you have — kind of like a bank statement. Such statements are sufficient today, when producing the actual stock certificate has become less necessary in our modern technological era than in the early days of stock investing.

There is a real distinction between the stock and the company. The company is what you invest in, and the stock is the means by which you invest. Many investors get confused and think that the company and its stock act as one entity.

Adjusting to your role as a stockholder

When you own stock, you become a *stockholder* (also known as a *shareholder*). The benefit of owning stock in a corporation is that whenever the corporation profits, you profit as well. For example, if you buy stock in General Electric and it comes out with an exciting new consumer electronics product that the public buys in massive quantities, not only does the company succeed, but so do you, depending on how much stock you own.

Just because you own a piece of that company, don't expect to go to the company's headquarters and say, "Hi! I'm a part owner. I'd like to pick up some office supplies since I'm running low. Thank you and keep up the good work." No, it's not quite like that.

As a regular stockholder, you generally do not have the privilege of intervening in the company's day-to-day operations. Instead, you participate in the company's overall performance at a distance.

As an owner, you participate in the overall success (or failure) of a given company along with thousands or millions of others who are *co-owners* (other investors who own stock in the company). The flip side is that if the company is sued or gets on the wrong side of the law, you won't be in trouble — at least not directly. The company's stock will be negatively affected and you'd most likely see a decline in the value of your stock, but you won't go to jail.

Exerting your stockholder's influence

A stock also gives you the right to make decisions that may influence the company, such as determining the stock price. Each stock you own has a little bit of voting power, so the more shares of stock you own, the more decision-making power you have.

In order to vote, you must either attend a corporate meeting or fill out a proxy ballot. (See Chapter 11 for information about participating in these meetings — in person or by proxy.) The ballot contains a series of proposals that you may either vote for or against. Common questions concern who should be on the board of directors, whether to issue additional stock, and whether the stock should split. (See Chapter 18 for more on stock splits.)

Recognizing stock value

Imagine that you like eggs and you're willing to buy them at the grocery store. In this example, the eggs are like companies, and the prices represent the prices that you would pay for the companies' stock. The grocery store is the stock market. What if two brands of eggs are very similar, but one costs 50 cents while the other costs 75 cents? Which would you choose? Odds are that you would look at both brands, judge their quality, and, if they were indeed similar, take the cheaper eggs. The eggs at 75 cents are overpriced. The same with stocks. What if you compare two companies that are similar in every respect but have different share prices? All things being equal, the cheaper price has greater value for the investor. But there is another side to the egg example.

What if the quality of the two brands of eggs is significantly different but their prices are the same? If one brand of eggs is stale and poor quality and priced at 50 cents and the other brand is fresh and superior quality and also priced at 50 cents, which would you get? I'd take the good brand because they're better eggs. Perhaps the lesser eggs might make an acceptable purchase at 10 cents. However, the inferior eggs are definitely overpriced at 50 cents. The same example works with stocks. A badly run company isn't a good choice if a better company in the marketplace can be bought at the same — or a better — price.

Comparing the value of eggs may seem overly simplistic, but doing so does cut to the heart of stock investing. Eggs and egg prices can be as varied as companies and stock prices. As an investor, you must make it your job to find the best value for your investment dollars.

Understanding how market capitalization affects stock value

You can determine the value of a company (and thus the value of its stock) in many ways. The most basic way to measure this is to look at a company's market value, also known as market capitalization (or market cap). *Market capitalization* is simply the value you get when you multiply all the outstanding shares of a stock by the price of a single share.

Calculating the market cap is easy. It is the number of shares outstanding multiplied by the current share price. If the company has 1 million shares outstanding and its share price is $10, the market cap is $10 million.

Small cap, mid cap, and large cap aren't references to headgear; they're references to how large the company is as measured by its market value. Here are the five basic stock categories of market capitalization:

- **Micro cap (under $250 million):** These are the smallest and hence the riskiest stocks available.

- **Small cap ($250 million to $1 billion):** These stocks fare better than the microcaps and still have plenty of growth potential. The key word here is "potential."

- **Mid cap ($1 billion to $5 billion):** For many investors, this category offers a good compromise between small caps and large caps. These stocks have some of the safety of large caps while retaining some of the growth potential of small caps.

- **Large cap ($5 billion to $25 billion):** This category is usually best reserved for conservative stock investors who want steady appreciation with greater safety. Stocks in this category are frequently referred to as "blue chips."

- **Ultra cap (over $25 billion):** These stocks are also called "mega caps" and obviously refer to companies that are the biggest of the big. Stocks such as General Electric and Exxon Mobil are examples.

From a point of view of safety, the company's size and market value do matter. All things being equal, large cap stocks are considered safer than small cap stocks. However, small cap stocks have greater potential for growth. Compare these stocks to trees: Which tree is sturdier — a giant California redwood or a small oak tree that is just a year old? In a great storm, the redwood would hold up well, while the smaller tree would have a rough time. But you also have to ask yourself which tree has more opportunity for growth. The redwood may not have much growth left, but the small oak tree has plenty of growth to look forward to.

For beginning investors, comparing market cap to trees is not so far-fetched. You want your money to branch out without becoming a sap.

Although market capitalization is important to consider, don't invest (or not invest) just because of it. It is just one measure of value. As a serious investor, you need to look at numerous factors that can help you determine whether any given stock is a good investment. Keep reading — this book is full of information to help you decide.

Sharpening Your Investment Skills

Investors who analyze the company can better judge the value of the stock and profit from buying and selling it. Your greatest asset in stock investing is knowledge (and a little common sense). To succeed in the world of stock investing, keep in mind these key success factors:

- ✔ Analyze yourself. What do you want to accomplish with your stock investing? What are your investment goals? Chapter 2 can help you.

- ✔ Know where to get information. The decisions you make about your money and what stocks to invest in require quality information. If you want help with information sources, turn to Chapter 3.

- ✔ Understand why you want to invest in stocks. Are you seeking appreciation (capital gains) or income (dividends)? Look at Chapters 8 and 9 for information on this topic.

- ✔ Do some research. Look at the company whose stock you are considering to see whether it's a profitable company worthy of your investment dollars. Chapters 10 and 11 help you scrutinize the company.

- ✔ Understand how the world affects your stock. Stocks succeed or fail in large part due to the environment in which they operate. Economics and politics make up that world, so you should know something about them. Chapter 13 covers these topics.

- ✔ Use investing strategies like the pros do. In other words, how you go about investing can be just as important as what you invest in. Chapter 15 highlights techniques for investing to help you make more money from your stocks.

- ✔ Keep more of the money you earn. After all your great work in getting the right stocks and making the big bucks, you should know about keeping more of the fruits of your investing. I cover tax implications of stock investing in Chapter 19.

Actually, every chapter in the book offers you valuable guidance on some essential aspect of the fantastic world of stocks. The knowledge you pick up and apply from these pages has been tested over nearly a century of stock picking. The investment experience of the past — the good, the bad, and some of the ugly — is here for your benefit. Use this information to make a lot of money (and make me proud!).

Stock market schizophrenia

Have you ever noticed a stock going up even though the company is reporting terrible results? How about seeing a stock nosedive despite the fact that the company is doing well? What gives? Well, judging the direction of a stock in a short-term period — over the next few days or weeks — is almost impossible.

Yes, in the short term, stock investing is irrational. The price of a stock and the value of its company seem disconnected and almost schizophrenic. The key phrase to remember is "short term." A stock's price and the company's value become more logical over an extended period of time. The longer a stock is in the public's view, the more rational the performance of the stock's price. In other words, a good company will continue to draw attention to itself; hence, more people will want its stock, and the share price will rise to better match the value of the company. Conversely, a bad company won't hold up to continued scrutiny over time. As more and more people see that it's not a good investment, the share price will fall. Over the long run, a stock's share price and the value of the company become equal for the most part.

Chapter 2

Taking Stock of Your Current Financial Situation and Goals

. . . .

In This Chapter

▶ Preparing your personal balance sheet

▶ Looking at your cash flow statement

▶ Determining your financial goals

. . . .

*Y*es, you want to make the big bucks. Yes, you want to succeed in the stock market and retire rich! But before you make reservations for your Caribbean cruise, you have to map out your action plan for getting there. Stocks can be a great component of most wealth-building programs, but you must first do some homework on a topic that you should be very familiar with — yourself. That's right. Understanding your current financial situation and clearly defining financial goals are the first steps in successful investing.

This chapter is undoubtedly one of the most important chapters in this book. It may at first seem to be a chapter more suitable for some general book on personal finance. Wrong! The greatest weakness of unsuccessful investors is in not understanding their financial situation and how stocks fit in. More times than not, I have counseled people to stay out of the stock market because they were unprepared for the responsibilities of stock investing — they hadn't been regularly reviewing the company's financial statements or tracking the company's progress.

Investing in stocks requires balance. Investors sometimes tie up too much money in stocks and therefore put themselves at risk of losing a significant portion of their wealth should the market plunge. Then again, other investors place little or no money in stocks and therefore miss out on excellent opportunities to grow their wealth. Stocks should be a part of most investors' portfolios, but the operative word is *part*. Stocks should take up only a *portion* of your money. A disciplined investor also has money in bank accounts, bonds, mutual funds, and other assets that offer growth or income opportunities. Diversification is key to minimizing risk. (For more on risk, see Chapter 4.)

Establishing a Starting Point

The first step for budding investors is to know where you stand with your money right now. Whether you're already in stocks or you're looking to get into stocks, you'll need the funds to do so. However, no matter what you hope to accomplish, you need to establish where you stand with your current finances. To do this, the first thing you need to prepare and review is your personal balance sheet. A *balance sheet* is simply a list of your assets and your liabilities and what each item is currently worth at a specific time. I know that it sounds like accounting mumbo jumbo, but knowing your net worth is important to your future financial success, so just do it.

Composing your balance sheet is simple. Pull out a pencil and a piece of paper. For the computer savvy, a spreadsheet software program accomplishes the same task. Gather up all your financial documents, such as bank and brokerage statements and other such paperwork — you need figures from these documents. Then follow the steps that I outline in the following sections. Update your balance sheet and income statement at least once a year to monitor your financial progress.

Your personal balance sheet is really no different from balance sheets that giant companies prepare. (The main difference is a few zeros, but I help you work on that.) In fact, the more you find out about your own balance sheet, the easier it will be to understand the balance sheet of companies in which you're seeking to invest.

Step 1: List your assets in liquidity order

Liquid assets aren't references to beer or cola (unless you're Anheuser-Busch). No, *liquidity* in a financial context essentially means how quickly you can convert that particular asset (something you own that has value) into cash. Liquidity is important to your financial picture because ultimately you need cash for wants and needs that may present themselves. If you have to pay for a medical procedure or you find a good investment, having liquid assets can save the day.

Knowing the liquidity of an asset (such as an investment) is important for those moments when you need cash to buy some stock (or pay some bill). All too often, people have too little cash and too much wealth tied up in *illiquid investments* such as real estate, leading to what Alan Greenspan, the Federal Reserve Board chairman, would call a "liquidity crisis." Being *illiquid* is just a fancy way of saying that you don't have the immediate cash to meet a pressing need. (Hey, we've all had those moments!) Review your assets and take measures to ensure that you have enough of both types of assets.

Listing your assets in order of liquidity gives you an immediate picture of which assets you can quickly convert to cash and which ones you can't. If you say, "I need money, and I need it now to pay X," you can see that cash in hand, your checking account, and your savings account are at the top of the list. The items last in order of liquidity become obvious; they're things like real estate and other assets that could take a long time to convert to cash. Real estate, even in a seller's market, can take months to sell. Investors who don't have adequate liquid assets run the danger of selling assets quickly and possibly at a loss as they scramble to accumulate the cash necessary to meet their short-term financial obligations. For stock investors, it may mean prematurely selling stocks that were originally intended as long-term investments.

The first asset on your list should be cash. You should have an amount equal to at least three to six months' worth of your gross living expenses. This time frame is important because it gives you cushion during the most common forms of financial disruption in your life. A good example is the loss of your job. Finding a new job can take anywhere from three to six months (depending on the economy).

If your monthly expenses (or *outgo*) are $2,000, you should have at least $6,000, and probably closer to $12,000, in a secure, FDIC-insured, interest-bearing bank account. Consider this an emergency fund and not an investment. Establish this amount in a bank account and leave it there. Don't use it to buy stocks.

Too many Americans don't have an emergency fund, meaning that they put themselves at risk. Walking across a busy street while wearing a blindfold is a great example of putting yourself at risk, and in recent years, investors have done the financial equivalent. Investors piled on tremendous debt, put too much into investments (such as stocks) that they didn't understand, and had little or no savings. Being unaware of financial pitfalls such as these certainly creates more risk of financial problems.

Resist the urge to start thinking of your investment in stocks as a savings account generating over 20 percent per year. This is dangerous thinking! If your investments tank, or if you lose your job, you certainly will have your own "liquidity crisis."

Table 2-1 shows a typical listing of assets. Use it as a guide for making your own asset list.

Table 2-1	John Q. Investor: Personal Assets as of December 31, 2001	
Asset Item	*Market Value*	*Annual Growth Rate %*
Current Assets		
Cash on hand and in checking	$150	0
Bank savings accounts and certificates of deposit	$500	2%
Stocks	$2,000	11%
Mutual funds	$2,400	9%
Other financial assets	$240	
Total current assets	**$5,290**	
Long-term assets		
Auto	$1,800	–10%
Residence	$150,000	5%
Real estate investment	$125,000	6%
Personal stuff (such as jewelry)	$4,000	
Total long-term assets	**$280,800**	
Total assets	**$286,090**	

The first column of Table 2-1 describes the asset (a *current asset* means that you can quickly and conveniently convert it to cash).

The second column gives the most current market value for that item. Keep in mind that this is not the purchase or original amount; it reflects the amount you would realistically get if you sell it in the current market.

The third column tells you how well that investment did from one year ago. If the percentage rate is 5 percent, that means that item increased in value by 5 percent from a year ago. You need to know how well all your assets are doing.

Figuring the annual growth rate (in the third column) as a percentage is not difficult. Say that you bought 100 shares of the stock Gro-A-Lot Corp. (GAL) and its market value on December 31, 2000, was $50 per share for a total market value of $5,000 (100 shares × $50 per share). When you checked its value on December 31, 2001, you found out it was at $60 per share. (Make believe that no dividends were paid during the year.) The annual growth rate is 20 percent. You calculate this by taking the amount of the gain ($60 – $50 = $10) and dividing it by the value at the beginning of the time period ($5,000). In this case, you get 20 percent, or $1,000 divided by $5,000.

What if GAL also generated a dividend of $2 per share during that period; now what? In that case, GAL would have generated a total return of 24 percent. Total return would take both the appreciation ($10 per share) and the dividend income ($2 per share) and divided the total return ($10 + $2, or $12) by the value at the beginning of the year ($50 per share). This works out as a total of $1,200 ($1,000 of appreciation and $200 total dividends), or 24 percent ($1,200 ÷ $5,000).

Long-term assets are basically items that aren't very liquid. They certainly have value, but you can't necessarily convert them to cash quickly. Notice that the Auto category has a negative percentage in the third column. This reflects the fact that an automobile is generally a depreciating asset and should be reflected as such. You need to know which of your assets are going down in value as well as which ones are going up.

The last line lists the total for all the assets and their current market value. The third column answers the question "How well did your total assets grow from a year ago?"

Step 2: List your liabilities

Liabilities are simply the bills that you're obligated to pay. Whether it's a credit card bill or a mortgage payment, it's an amount of money you have to pay back eventually (with interest). If you don't keep track of your liabilities, you may end up thinking that you have more money than you really do.

Table 2-2 lists some common liabilities. Use it as a model when you list your own.

Table 2-2	Listing Personal Liabilities	
Liabilities	*Amount*	*Paying Rate %*
Credit cards	$4,000	15%
Personal loans	$13,000	10%
Mortgage	$100,000	8%
Total liabilities	$117,000	

The first column in Table 2-2 names the type of debt. Don't forget to include student loans and auto loans if you have any of these. Never avoid listing a liability because you're embarrassed to see how much you really owe. Be honest with yourself — doing so will help you improve your financial health.

The second column shows the current value (or current balance) of your liabilities. You should list the most current balance to see where you stand with your creditors. If you compare your liabilities and your personal assets, you may find opportunities to reduce the amount you pay for interest. Say, for example, that you pay 15 percent on a credit card balance of $4,000 but also have as a personal asset $5,000 in a bank savings account earning 2 percent in interest. In that case, you may want to consider taking $4,000 out of the savings account and paying off the credit card balance. Doing so would save you $520; the $4,000 in the bank was earning only $80 (2 percent of $4,000), while you were paying $600 on the credit card balance (15 percent of $4,000).

The third column reflects how much interest you're paying for carrying that debt. This information should be an important reminder to you about how debt can be a wealth zapper. Credit card debt can have an interest rate of 18 percent or more, and to add insult to injury, it isn't even tax deductible. Using a credit card to make even a small purchase can cost you if you maintain a balance. A $50 sweater at 18 percent can easily end up costing $59 when you add in the potential interest you would pay.

If you can't pay off high-interest debt, at least look for ways to minimize the cost of carrying the debt. The most obvious ways include the following:

- Replacing high-interest cards with low interest cards. Many companies offer incentives to consumers to sign up with favorable rates that can be used to pay-off high-interest cards.

- Replacing unsecured debt with secured debt. Credit cards and personal loans are *unsecured* (meaning that there's no collateral or other asset to secure the debt); therefore, they have higher interest rates because this type of debt is considered riskier for the credit card company. Sources of secured debt (such as home equity line accounts and brokerage accounts) provide you with a means to replace your high-interest debt with lower-interest debt. Secured debt has lower interest rates because it's less risky for the creditor — the debt is backed up by collateral (your home or your stocks).

The year 2001 is the fifth consecutive year that personal bankruptcies have surpassed the million mark in the United States. Corporate bankruptcies are also at record levels. Make a diligent effort to control and reduce your debt, or your wealth will be wiped out during periods of economic decline. If you don't, you'll probably have to sell off your stocks just to stay solvent. Remember, Murphy's Law states that you *will* sell your stock at the worst possible moment! Don't go there.

Robbing Peter to pay Paul

In recent years, there has been tremendous activity in the world of home equity financing and mortgage refinancing. Millions of people have borrowed more and more money secured by the rising equity in their homes. People are using this money both for good reasons (to pay off high-interest debt) and for not-so-good reasons (to finance an extravagant lifestyle or to speculate in risky investments).

Step 3: Calculate your net worth

Your *net worth* is an indication of your total wealth. The basic equation for calculating net worth is total assets (Table 2-1) less total liabilities (Table 2-2) equals net worth (net assets).

Table 2-3 shows this equation in action with a net worth of $169,000 — a very respectable number. For many investors, just having a net worth is great news. Use Table 2-3 as a model to analyze your own financial situation. Your mission (if you choose to accept it — and you should) is to ensure that your net worth increases from year to year as you progress toward your financial goal.

Table 2-3	Figuring Out Your Personal Net Worth	
Totals	*Amounts ($)*	*Increase from Year Before*
Total assets (from Table 2-1)	$286,090	+5%
Total liabilities (from Table 2-2)	($117,000)	–2%
Net worth (total assets less total liabilities)	$169,090	+3%

Step 4: Analyze your balance sheet

Create a balance sheet to illustrate your current finances. Take a close look at it and try to identify any changes you can make to increase your wealth. Sometimes reaching your financial goals can be as simple as refocusing the items on your balance sheet. Here are some brief points to consider:

✔ For the items that constitute your emergency (or rainy day) fund, is the money sitting in an ultra-safe account and earning the highest interest available? Bank money market accounts or money market funds are recommended. The safest type of account is a U.S. Treasury money market fund.

✔ Can you replace depreciating assets with appreciating assets? Say that you have two stereo systems. Why not sell one and invest the proceeds? You may say, "But I bought that unit two years ago for $500, and if I sell it now, I'll only get $300." That's your choice. You need to decide what will help your financial situation more — a $500 item that keeps shrinking in value (a *depreciating asset*) or $300 that can grow in value when invested (an *appreciating asset*).

✔ Can you replace low-yield investments with high-yield investments? Maybe you have $5,000 in a bank certificate of deposit earning 3 percent. You can certainly shop around for a better rate at another bank, but you can also seek alternatives that can offer a higher yield, such as U.S. savings bonds or short-term bond funds.

✔ Can you pay off any high-interest debt with funds from low-interest assets? If, for example, you have $5,000 earning 2 percent in a taxable bank account and you maintain $2,500 in a credit card account paying 18 percent (nondeductible), you may as well pay off the credit card balance and save on the interest.

✔ If you're carrying debt, is that money being used to give you an investment return that is greater than the interest you're paying? Carrying a loan with an interest rate of 8 percent is acceptable if that borrowed money is yielding more than 8 percent elsewhere. Suppose that you have $6,000 in cash in a brokerage account. If you qualify, you can actually make a stock purchase greater than $6,000 by using margin (essentially a loan from the broker). You can buy $12,000 of stock using your $6,000 in cash, with the remainder financed by the broker. Of course, you pay interest on that margin loan. But what if the interest rate is 6 percent and the stock you're about to invest in has a dividend that yields 9 percent? In that case, the dividend can help you pay off the margin loan, and you keep the additional income. (For more on buying on margin, see Chapter 16.)

✔ Can you sell any personal stuff for cash? Garage sales and auction Web sites can help you replace unproductive assets with investable cash.

✔ Can you use your home equity to pay off consumer debt? Borrowing against your home has more favorable interest rates, and this interest is still tax deductible.

Paying off consumer debt by using funds borrowed against your home is a great way to wipe the slate clean. What a relief to get rid of your credit card balances! Just don't be the type of borrower who runs up the consumer debt again. You could get overburdened and experience financial ruin (not to mention homelessness). Not a pretty picture.

I owe, I owe, so off to work I go

One reason that you continue to work is probably so that you can pay off your bills. But many people today are getting laid off because their company owes, too!

Debt is one of the biggest financial problems in America today. Excessive debt held by companies and individuals was a primary culprit in the stock market's massive decline in 2000 and in the U.S. economic slowdown in 2001. If individuals managed their personal liabilities more responsibly, the general economy would be much better off.

One of the biggest reasons the United States appeared to be doing so well during the late 1990s was the fact that individuals and organizations went on an unprecedented spending binge, financed mostly by excessive debt. The economy looked unstoppable. However, sooner or later you have to pay the piper. Stock prices may go up and down, but debt stays up until it is either paid down or the debtor files for bankruptcy.

The important point to remember is that you can take control of your finances with discipline (and with the advice I offer in this book).

Funding Your Stock Program

If you're going to invest money in stocks, the first thing you need is . . . money! Where is that money going to come from? If you're waiting for that inheritance to come through, you may have to wait a long time, considering all the advances being made in healthcare lately. What's that? You were going to invest in healthcare stocks? How ironic. Yet, the challenge still comes down to how to fund your stock investing program.

For many investors, reallocating their investments and assets does the trick. *Reallocating* simply means selling some investments or other assets and reinvesting that money into stocks. It boils down to deciding what investment or asset you should sell or liquidate. Generally, you probably want to consider those investments and assets that give you a low return on your money (or no return at all). If you have a complicated mix of investments and assets, you may want to consider reviewing your options with a financial planner. Reallocation is just part of the answer; your cash flow is the other part.

Ever wonder why there's so much month left at the end of the money? Consider your cash flow. Your *cash flow* refers to what money is coming in (income) and what money is being spent or disbursed (outgo). The net result is either a positive cash flow or a negative cash flow, depending on your cash management skills. Maintaining a positive cash flow (more money coming in than going out) helps you to increase your net worth (mo' money, mo' money, mo' money!). A negative cash flow ultimately depletes your wealth and wipes out your net worth if you don't turn it around immediately. The following sections show you how to analyze your cash flow. The first step is to do a cash flow statement.

Don't confuse a cash flow statement with an income statement (also called a "profit and loss statement" or an "income and expense statement"). A cash flow statement is simple to calculate because you can easily track what goes in and what goes out.

With a cash flow statement (see Table 2-6), you ask yourself three questions:

- ✔ **What money is coming in?** In your cash flow statement, jot down all sources of income. Calculate it for the month and then for the year. Include everything, including salary, wages, interest, dividends, and so on. Add them all up and get your grand total for income.

- ✔ **What is your outgo?** Jot down all the things that you spend money on. List all your expenses. If possible, categorize them into essential and nonessential. You should have an idea of all the expenses that you could reduce without affecting your lifestyle. But before you do that, make as complete a list as possible of what you spend your money on.

- ✔ **What's left?** If your income is greater than your outgo, then you should have money ready and available for stock investing. No matter how small it may seem, it will definitely help. I've seen fortunes built when people started to diligently invest as little as $25 to $50 per week or per month. If your outgo is greater than your income, then you better sharpen your pencil. Cut down on nonessential spending and/or increase your income. If your budget is a little tight, hold off on your stock investing until your cash flow improves.

Step 1: Tallying up your income

Using Table 2-4 as a worksheet, list and calculate the money you have coming in. The first column describes the source of the money, the second column indicates the monthly amount from each respective source, and the last column indicates the amount projected for a full year. Include all income, such as wages, business income, dividends, interest income, and so on. Then project these amounts for a year (multiply by 12) and enter those amounts in the third column.

Dot-com-and-go

If there were to be a book about negative cash flow, any one of a hundred dot-com companies that flew sky-high in 1999 and crashed in 2000 and 2001 would be qualified to write it. Companies such as eToys.com, Pets.com, and DrKoop.com were given millions, yet they couldn't turn a profit and eventually closed for business. You may as well call them "dot-com-and-go." You can learn from their mistakes. (Actually, they could have learned from you.) In the same way that profit is the most essential single element in a business, a positive cash flow is important for your finances in general and for funding your stock investment program in particular.

Table 2-4	Listing Your Income	
Item	*Monthly $ Amount*	*Yearly $ Amount*
Salary and wages		
Interest income and dividends		
Business net (after taxes) income		
Other income		
Total income		

This is the amount of money you have to work with. To ensure your financial health, don't spend more than this. Always be aware of and carefully manage your income.

Step 2: Adding up your outgo

Using Table 2-5 as a worksheet, list and calculate the money that's going out. What are you spending and on what? The first column describes the source of the expense, the second column indicates the monthly amount, and the third column shows the amount projected for a full year. Include all the money you spend, including credit card and other debt payments; household expenses, such as food, utility bills, and medical expenses; and money spent for nonessential expenses such as video games and elephant-foot umbrella stands.

Table 2-5	Listing Your Expenses (Outgo)	
Item	*Monthly $ Amount*	*Yearly $ Amount*
Payroll taxes		
Rent or mortgage		
Utilities		
Food		
Clothing		
Insurance (medical, auto, homeowners, and so on)		
Telephone		
Real estate taxes		
Auto expenses		
Charity		
Recreation		
Credit card payments		
Loan payments		
Other		
Total		

Payroll taxes is just a category in which to lump all the various taxes that are taken out of your paycheck. Feel free to put each individual tax on its own line if you prefer. The important thing is that you create a comprehensive list that is meaningful to you. You may notice that the outgo doesn't include items such as payments to a 401(k) plan and other savings vehicles. Yes, these do impact your cash flow, but they're not expenses; the amounts that you invest (or have invested for you by your employer) are essentially an asset that benefits your financial situation versus an expense that doesn't have value that helps you build wealth.

Step 3: Creating a cash flow statement

Okay, you're almost to the end. The last step is creating a cash flow statement so that you can see (all in one place) how your money moves — how much comes in and how much goes out and where it goes.

Plug the amount of your total income (from Table 2-4) and the amount of your total expenses (from Table 2-5) into the Table 2-6 worksheet to see your *cash flow*. Is it positive or negative?

Table 2-6	Looking at Your Cash Flow	
Item	*Monthly $ Amount*	*Yearly $ Amount*
Total income (from Table 2-4)		
Total outgo (from Table 2-5)		
Net inflow/outflow		

The bottom line for you comes down to this: Is your cash flow good or not? Do you have positive cash flow — more coming in than going out — so that you can start investing in stocks (or other investments), or are expenses overpowering your income? Doing a cash flow statement isn't just about finding money in your financial situation to fund your stock investing program. First and foremost, it's about your financial well-being. Are you managing your finances well or not?

As I write this chapter, an ominous economic statistic was just announced: The year 2001 was a record year for personal and business bankruptcies. Personal debt and expenses far exceeded whatever income they generated. That announcement should serve as another reminder to all of you to watch your cash flow; keep your income growing and your expenses and debt as low as possible.

Step 4: Analyzing your cash flow

Use your cash flow statement to identify sources of funds for your investment program. The more you can increase your income and the more you can decrease your outgo, the better. Scrutinize your data. Where can you improve the results? Here are some questions to ask yourself:

- How can you increase your income? Do you have hobbies, interests, or skills that can generate extra cash for you?
- Can you get more paid overtime at work? How about a promotion or a job change?
- Where can you cut expenses?
- Have you categorized your expenses as either "necessary" or "nonessential"?

- ✔ Can you lower your debt payments by refinancing or consolidating loans and credit card balances?

- ✔ Have you shopped around for lower insurance or telephone rates?

- ✔ Have you analyzed your taxes to see whether you can lower the amount withheld from your pay?

Finding investment money in tax savings

According to the Tax Foundation, the average U.S. citizen pays more in taxes than in food, clothing, and shelter combined. Sit down with your tax advisor and try to find ways to reduce your taxes. A home-based business, for example, is a great way to gain new income and increase your tax deductions, resulting in a lower tax burden. Your tax advisor can make recommendations that will work for you.

One tax strategy to consider is doing your stock investing in a tax-sheltered account such as a traditional Individual Retirement Account (IRA) or a Roth Individual Retirement Account (Roth IRA). Again, check with your tax advisor for deductions and strategies available to you. For more on the tax implications of stock investing, see Chapter 19.

Setting Your Sights on Your Financial Goals

Consider stocks as tools for living, just like any other investment — no more, no less. Stocks are the tools you use (one of many) to accomplish something — to achieve a goal. Yes, successfully investing in stocks is the goal that you're probably shooting for if you're reading this book. However, you as the reader must complete the following sentence: "I want to be successful in my stock investing program to accomplish _____." You must consider stock investing as a means to an end. When people buy a computer, they don't (or shouldn't) think of buying a computer just to have a computer. People buy a computer because doing so will help them achieve a particular result, such as being more efficient in business, playing fun games, or having a nifty paperweight (tsk, tsk).

Know the difference between long-term, intermediate-term, and short-term goals and then set some of each. Long-term is a reference to projects or financial goals that will need funding five or more years from now. Intermediate-term refers to financial goals that will need funding two to five years from now, while short-term is under two years.

Stocks, in general, are best suited for long-term goals such as these:

- ✔ Achieving financial independence (think retirement funding)
- ✔ Paying for future college costs
- ✔ Paying for any long-term expenditure or project

Some categories of stock (such as conservative or blue-chip) may be suitable for intermediate-term financial goals. An intermediate-term goal is any event that you will need money for within two to five years. If, for example, you will retire four years from now, conservative stocks are appropriate. If you're optimistic about the stock market and confident that stock prices will rise, then go ahead and invest. However, if you're negative about the market ("bearish," or you believe that stock prices will decline), you may want to wait until the economy starts to forge a clear path. For more on investing in bull or bear markets, see Chapter 14.

Stocks generally aren't suitable for short-term investing goals — when you plan to use the money within one or two years — because stock prices can behave irrationally in a short period of time. Stocks fluctuate from day to day, so you won't know what the stock will be worth in the near future. You may end up with less money than you thought. For investors seeking to reliably accrue money for short-term needs, short-term bank certificates of deposit or money market funds are more appropriate.

In recent years, investors have sought quick, short-term profits by trading and speculating in stocks. Lured by the fantastic returns generated by the stock market in the late 1990s, investors saw stocks as a get-rich-quick scheme. It is very important for you to understand the difference between *investing, saving,* and *speculating.* Which one do you want to do? Knowing the answer to this question is crucial to your goals and aspirations. Investors who don't know the difference tend to get burned. Here's some information to help you distinguish among these three actions:

- ✔ *Investing* is the act of putting your money into securities or tangible assets for the purpose of gaining appreciation, income, or both. Investing requires time, knowledge, and discipline. The investment can fluctuate in price but has been chosen for long-term potential.

- ✔ *Saving* is the safe accumulation of funds for a future use. Savings don't fluctuate and are generally free of financial risk. The emphasis is on safety and liquidity.

- ✔ *Speculating* is the financial world's equivalent of gambling. An investor who speculates is seeking quick profits gained from short-term price movements in that particular asset or investment.

These distinctly different concepts are often confused even among so-called financial experts. I know of one financial advisor who actually put a child's college fund money into an Internet stock fund only to lose over $17,000 in less than ten months! This advisor thought she was investing, but in reality, she was speculating. I know of another advisor who told a client to avoid savings accounts altogether because the client had a 401(k) plan. This particular advisor didn't catch the crucial difference between "saving" and "investing." The client eventually found out the difference; his 401(k) fell by 40 percent when the bear market of 2000 arrived.

Chapter 3

Defining Common Approaches to Stock Investing

*R*ead this chapter carefully. Millions of investors are at risk as you read this because there is as much misinvesting activity in stocks as there is investing. I know it sounds weird, but it's similar to your Uncle Bill using the accelerator rather than the brakes when heading right toward the Grand Canyon — he knows that he needs to be doing something, but he chooses the wrong mechanism. Stocks are tools you can use to build your wealth. When used wisely and for the right purpose, they do a great job. But when improperly applied, they can lead to disaster.

There are various kinds of stocks, as well as various kinds of investment approaches. The key to success in the stock market is matching the right kind of stock with the right kind of investment situation. You have to choose the approach that matches your goals. (See Chapter 2 for more on defining your financial goals.)

Before investing in stocks, ask yourself, "When do I want to reach my financial goal?" Stocks are a means to an end. Your job is to figure out what that end is — or really when it is. Are you seeking to retire in ten years, or next year? Are you paying for your kid's college education next year, or 18 years from now? The length of time you have before you need the money that you hope to earn from stock investing determines what stocks you should buy. Table 3-1 gives you some guidelines for choosing the kind of stock best suited for your goals.

Table 3-1	Matching Stock Types to Financial Goals and Investor Types	
Type of Investor	Time Frame for Your Financial Goal	Type of Stock Most Suitable
Conservative (worries about risk)	Long term (over five years)	Large cap stocks and mid cap stocks
Aggressive (high tolerance to risk)	Long term (over five years)	Small cap stocks and mid cap stocks
Conservative (worries about risk)	Intermediate term (two to five years)	Large cap stocks, preferably with dividends
Aggressive (high tolerance to risk)	Intermediate term (two to five years)	Small cap stocks and mid cap stocks
Short term	One to two years	Don't even think about a stock investment!

Table 3-1 gives general guidelines, but keep in mind that not everyone can neatly fit into a particular profile. Every investor has a different situation, set of goals, and level of risk tolerance. Remember that *large cap, mid cap,* and *small cap* just refer to the size (or market capitalization, also known as market cap) of the company. All things being equal, large companies are safer (less risky) than small companies. For more on market caps, see the section "Investing by Style," later in this chapter.

Investing by Term

Are your goals long term or short term? Answering this question is important because individual stocks can be either great or horrible choices, depending on the term you're looking at. Generally, the term can be short term, intermediate term, or long term. The following sections outline what kinds of stocks are most appropriate for each term length.

Investing in stocks become less risky as the necessary time frame lengthens. Stock prices tend to fluctuate on a daily basis, but they do have a tendency to trend up or down over an extended period of time. Even if you invest in a stock that goes down in the short term, you're likely to see it rise and even go above your investment if you have the patience to wait it out and let the stock price appreciate.

Looking at the short term

Short term generally means one year or less, although some people say that short term means two years or less. You get the point.

All of us have short-term goals. Some are modest, such as setting aside money for a vacation next month or paying for medical bills. Other short-term goals are more ambitious, such as accruing funds for a down payment for a new home purchase within six months. Whatever the expense or purchase, you need a predictable accumulation of cash soon. If this sounds like your situation, stay away from the stock market!

Because stocks can be so unpredictable in the short term, they're a bad choice for short-term considerations. I get a kick out of market analysts on TV saying things such as "At $25 a share, XYZ is a solid investment, and we feel that its stock should hit our target price of $40 within six to nine months." You know that someone hears that and says, "Gee, why bother with 3 percent at the bank when this stock will rise by more than 50 percent? I better call my broker." It may hit that target amount (it may even surpass that price), or it may not. Most of the time, the target price is not reached, and the investor is disappointed. The stock could even go down! But what if the money invested was meant to be used for an important short-term need? Remember, short-term stock investing is very unpredictable, and your short-term goals are better served with stable, interest-bearing investments (like bank CDs) instead.

During the raging bull market of the late 1990s, investors watched as some high-profile stocks went up 20 to 50 percent in a matter of months. Hey, who needs a savings account earning a measly &$#% interest when stocks grow like that! Of course, when the bear market hit in 2000 and those same stocks fell 50 to 70 percent, all of a sudden, a savings account earning a measly &$#% interest rate didn't seem so bad.

Stocks, even the best ones, will fluctuate in the short term. No one can really predict the price movement accurately (unless they have some inside information), so stocks are definitely not appropriate for any financial goal that you need to reach within one year.

Considering intermediate-term goals

Intermediate term refers to your financial goals that need to be reached within five years. If, for example, you need to accumulate funds to put money down for investment real estate property four years from now, some growth-oriented investments may be suitable.

Short-term investing = speculating

If you look at a period of a single year, stocks have had a mixed performance record compared with other investments, such as bonds or bank investments, in the same 12-month span. In 1999, big-company stocks grew an average of 25 percent, and small-company stocks averaged a blistering 50 to 70 percent, while bank accounts and various bonds ranged from 1.5 to 7 percent. In the year 2000, the picture was much different.

Stock investors lost their shirts, and conservative investors who put their money in bank certificates of deposit and treasury bonds saw their money grow.

The bottom line is that investing in stocks for the short term is nothing more than speculating, and your only possible strategy is luck.

Although *some* stocks *may* be appropriate for a two- or three-year period, not all stocks are good intermediate-term investments. There are different types and categories of stocks. Some stocks are fairly stable and hold their value well, such as the stock of much larger or established companies. Other stocks have prices that go all over the place, such as the stocks of untested companies that are just starting out and haven't been in existence long enough to develop a consistent track record.

If you plan to invest in the stock market to meet intermediate-term goals, large, established companies or dividend-paying companies in much-needed industries (like food and beverage or electric utilities, for instance) are good choices for you. *Dividends* are payments made to an owner (unlike *interest,* which is payment to a creditor). Dividends are a great form of income, and companies that issue dividends tend to have more stable stock prices as well. For more information on dividend-paying stocks, see Chapter 9.

Investing for the long term

Stock investing is best suited for making money over a long period of time. When you measure stocks against other investments in terms of five or (preferably) ten or more years, they excel. Even investors who bought stocks in the depths of the Great Depression saw profitable growth in their stock portfolios over a 10-year period.

In fact, if you take any 10-year period over the past 75 years, you'll see that stocks beat out other financial investments (such as bonds or bank investments) in every single 10-year period when measured by total return (taking into account reinvesting and compounding of capital gains and dividends)! As you can see, long term is where stocks shine. Of course, it doesn't stop there. You still have to do your homework and choose stocks wisely because, even in good times, you can lose money if you invest in companies that go out of business. The chapters in Part III show you how to evaluate specific companies and industries, and they alert you to factors in the general economy that can affect stock behavior.

Because there are many different types and categories of stocks, virtually any investor with a long-term perspective should add stocks to his investment portfolio. Whether you're saving for a young child's college fund or for future retirement goals, carefully selected stocks have proven to be a superior long-term investment.

Investing for a Purpose

When the lady was asked why she bungee-jumped off the bridge that spanned a massive ravine, she answered, "Because it's fun!" When someone asked the fellow why he went in a pool that was chock-full of alligators and snakes, he responded, "Because someone pushed me." Your investment in stocks should not happen for any other reason except a purpose that you understand. Even if you invest because some advisor told you to, be sure that you get an explanation of how that stock choice fits your purpose.

I know a very nice, elderly lady who had a portfolio brimming with aggressive growth stocks because she had an overbearing stockbroker. Her purpose should have been conservative, and she should have chosen investments to preserve her wealth rather than to grow it. Obviously, the broker's purpose got in the way. Stocks are just a means to an end. Figure out your desired ends and then match the means.

Making lots of money quickly: Growth investing

When investors want their money to grow, they're looking for investments that appreciate in value. *Appreciate* is just another way of saying "growth." If you have a stock that you bought for $8 per share and now it's $30 per share, your investment has grown by $22 per share — that's appreciation. I know I would appreciate it.

Appreciation (also known as *growth* or *capital gain*) is probably the number one reason why people invest in stocks. Few investments have the potential to grow your wealth as conveniently as stocks. If you're looking to the stock market to make lots of money relatively quickly (and you can assume some risk), Chapter 8 takes an in-depth look at investing for growth.

Stocks are a great way to grow your wealth, but they're not the only way. Many investors seek alternate ways to make money, but many of them are more aggressive and carry significantly more risk. You've probably heard about people who made a quick fortune in areas such as commodities (like wheat, pork bellies, or precious metals), options, and other more sophisticated investment vehicles. Keep in mind that you should limit risky investments to only a portion of your portfolio, such as 10 percent of your investable funds. Experienced investors, however, can go as high as 20 percent.

Making some money steadily: Income investing

Not all investors want to make a killing. Some people just want to invest in the stock market as a means of providing themselves with a steady income. They don't need stock values to go through the ceiling. Instead, they need stocks that perform well consistently.

If your purpose for investing in stocks is to provide you with current income, you need to choose stocks that pay dividends. Dividends are paid quarterly to stockholders on record.

Distinguishing between dividends and interest

Don't confuse dividends with interest. Most people are familiar with interest because that's how their money has grown for years in the bank. The important difference is that *interest* is paid to creditors, while *dividends* are paid to owners. (Owners are shareholders — and if you own stock, you're a shareholder because stocks represent shares in a publicly traded company.)

When you buy stock, you're buying a piece of that company. When you put money in a bank (or when you buy bonds), you're really loaning your money. You become a creditor, and the bank or bond issuer is the debtor, and as such, it must eventually pay your money back to you with interest.

Recognizing the importance of an income stock's yield

Investing for income means that you have to consider that investment's yield. If you're seeking income from a stock investment, you must compare the yield from that particular stock with alternatives. Looking at the yield is a way to compare the income you would receive from one investment with that from others. Table 3-2 shows some comparative yields.

Table 3-2	Comparing the Yields of Various Investments				
Investment	*Type*	*Amount*	*Pay Type*	*Payout*	*Yield*
Smith Co.	Stock	$50/share	Dividend	$2.50	5%
Jones Co.	Stock	$100/share	Dividend	$4	4%
Acme Bank	Bank CD	$500	Interest	$25	5%
Acme Bank	Bank CD	$2,500	Interest	$131.25	5.25%
Acme Bank	Bank CD	$5,000	Interest	$287.50	5.75%
Brown Co.	Bond	$5,000	Interest	$300	6%

To understand how to calculate yield, you need the following formula:

Yield = payout ÷ investment amount

Yield enables you to compare how much income you would get for a prospective investment compared with the income you would get from other investments.

Jones Co. and Smith Co. are both typical dividend-paying stocks, and in this example, presume that both companies are similar in most respects. But these two stocks have different dividends. How can you tell whether a $50 stock with a $2.50 annual dividend is better (or worse) than a $100 stock with a $4 dividend? The yield tells you.

Even though Jones Co. pays a higher dividend ($4), Smith Co. has a higher yield (5 percent). Therefore, if I had to choose between those two stocks as an income investor, I would choose Smith Co. Of course, if I truly wanted to maximize my income and didn't really need my investment to appreciate a lot, I would probably choose Brown Co.'s bond because it offers a yield of 6 percent.

Dividend-paying stocks do have the ability to increase in value. They may not have the same growth potential as growth stocks, but at the very least, they have a greater potential for capital gain than bank CDs or bonds.

Investing by Style

Your investing style isn't a blue-jeans-versus-three-piece-suit debate. It refers to your approach to stocks. Do you want to be conservative or aggressive? Would you rather be the tortoise or the hare? Although the investment style you attribute to yourself depends on your purpose and the term over which you're planning to invest, the following sections outline the two most general investment styles.

Conservative investing

Conservative investing isn't necessarily a reference to growth or income. It's not even a reference to the type of investor you are, although the type of investment you invest in does generally describe you as well. Conservative investing means that you put your money in something proven, tried, and true. Conservative investing in general means putting your money in safe and secure places such as banks and government-backed securities, but how does that apply to stocks?

Conservative stock investors want to invest their money in companies that have exhibited some of the following qualities:

- **Proven performance:** Conservative investors want companies that have shown, year after year, increasing sales and earnings. They don't demand anything spectacular, just a strong and steady performance.

- **Market size:** Companies should be "large cap" (short for large capitalization). In other words, companies should have a market value exceeding $10 billion in size. Conservative investors surmise that bigger is safer.

- **Market leadership:** Companies should be leaders in their industries.

- **Perceived staying power:** Conservative investors want companies with the financial clout and market position to weather uncertain market and economic conditions, no matter what happens in the economy or who gets elected.

Conservative investors don't mind if their share prices jump (who wouldn't?), but they're more concerned with growth over the long term.

Aggressive investing

Aggressive investors can be long term or intermediate term, but in any case, they want stocks that are jack rabbits — those that have the potential to break out of the pack.

Aggressive stock investors want to invest their money in companies that have exhibited some of the following qualities:

- ✔ **Great potential:** The company must have goods, service, ideas, or ways of doing business that are better than the competition.

- ✔ **Capital gains possibility:** Aggressive investors don't consider dividends. If anything, aggressive investors dislike dividends. They feel that the money that would have been dispensed as dividends is better reinvested in the company. This, in turn, can spur greater growth.

- ✔ **Innovation:** Companies should have technologies, ideas, or innovative methods that make them stand apart from other companies.

Aggressive investors usually seek out small capitalization stocks, known as *small caps,* because they have plenty of potential for growth. It's similar to the idea of trees: A giant redwood may be strong but may not grow much more, whereas a brand-new sapling has a lot of growth to look forward to. Why invest in stodgy, big companies when you can invest in smaller enterprises that could become tomorrow's leaders? Aggressive investors have no problem investing in obscure companies because they hope that such companies will become another IBM or McDonald's.

Chapter 4

Recognizing the Risks

*I*nvestors face many risks, most of which I cover in this chapter. The simplest definition of risk for investors is "the possibility that your investment will lose some (or all) of its value." Yet risk is not something to fear but something to understand and plan for. You need to get familiar with the concept of risk. You must understand the oldest equation in the world of investing: risk versus return. This equation states the following:

> If you want a greater return on your money, you need to tolerate more risk. If you don't want to tolerate more risk, you must tolerate a lower rate of return.

This point about risk is best illustrated from a moment in one of my investment seminars. One of the attendees told me that he had his money in the bank but was dissatisfied with the rate of return. He lamented, "The yield on my money is pitiful! I want to put my money somewhere where it can grow." I asked him, "How about investing in common stocks? Or what about growth mutual funds? They have a solid, long-term growth track record." He responded, "Stocks? I don't want to put my money there. It's too risky!" Okay, then. If you don't want to tolerate more risk, then don't complain about earning less on your money. Risk (in all its forms) has a bearing on all your money concerns and goals. That's why it's so important that you understand risk before you invest.

This man — as well as all of us — needs to remember that risk is not a four-letter word. Well, it does have four letters, but you know what I mean. Risk is present no matter where you put your money. Even if you simply stick your money in your mattress, risk is involved — several kinds of risk, in fact.

There is the risk of fire. What if your house burns down? There is the risk of theft. What if burglars find your stash of cash? There is also relative risk. (In other words, what if your relatives find it?)

Be aware of the different kinds of risk, and you can easily plan around them to keep your money growing.

Exploring Different Kinds of Risk

Think about all the ways that an investment can lose money. You can list all sorts of possibilities. It might make you think, "Holy cow! Why invest at all?"

Don't let risk frighten you. After all, life itself is risky. Just make sure that you understand the different kinds of risk before you start navigating the investment world. Be mindful of risk and find out about the effects of risk on your investments and personal financial goals.

Financial risk

The financial risk of stock investing is that you can lose your money if the company whose stock you purchase loses money or goes belly up. This type of risk is the most obvious because companies do go bankrupt.

You can greatly enhance the chances that your financial risk will pay off by doing an adequate amount of research and choosing your stocks carefully (which this book helps you do). Financial risk is a real concern even when the economy is doing well. Some diligent research, a little planning, and a dose of common sense will help you reduce your financial risk.

In the stock investing mania of the late 1990s, millions of investors (along with many financial show pundits and commentators) ignored some financial risks that were obvious problems with many popular stocks during that time. Investors blindly plunked their money into stocks that were bad choices. Consider investors who put their money in DrKoop.com, a health information Web site, in 1999 and held on during 2000. Despite the fact that DrKoop.com never earned a penny of profit, it hit a high of $45 a share as the great rush toward Internet stocks became a bloated, speculative investment bubble. But the bubble popped in 2000. DrKoop.com needed intensive care as its mounting losses pushed the stock to below $2!

Similarly, investors saw their money in eToys vanish as its losses and excessive debt drove it into the ground. The eToys stock, which flew higher than a kite in 1999, eventually went the way of Cabbage Patch dolls as the company filed for bankruptcy in early 2001. The stock fell from $85 in late 1999 to literally zero in March 2001. Although eToys reemerged from the ashes as a new company, the damage to investors had already been done. Is the new eToys a good investment? Time will tell, but as of early 2002, don't even consider it as an investment; it is best suited for speculators. (*Now* you're talking risk!)

Another good example is Amazon.com. As of the first quarter of 2001, it had yet to generate a profit. Its debt ballooned to $3 billion. If it doesn't start making money soon, it may not have a future. One of my favorite commentators called Amazon.com the "river of no returns." The stock, after hitting a high in 1999 of $113, plummeted to under $10 per share by January 2001. Although Amazon.com finally reported a profitable quarter (it earned a questionable one penny per share in the fourth quarter of 2001), the expectation for a profitable 2002 is very dubious, and it hasn't made any progress in decreasing its tremendous debt load. Amazon.com's stock price continued to languish in the low teens at the end of February 2002. The bottom line for the company: Financial risk is alive and well, but Amazon may be up the river without a paddle.

Investors who did their homework regarding the financial conditions of these companies discovered that these companies had the hallmarks of financial risk — high debt and low (or no) earnings and plenty of competition. They steered clear, avoiding tremendous financial loss. Investors who didn't do their homework were lured by the status of these companies — the poster children of booming Internet fortunes — and lost their shirts.

I don't believe that the individual investors who lost money by investing in these trendy, high-profile companies deserve all the responsibility for their tremendous financial losses; some high-profile analysts and media sources also should have known better. The late 1990s will be a case study of how euphoria and the herd mentality rather than good, old-fashioned research and common sense won the day (temporarily). The excitement of making potential fortunes can get the best of people sometimes, and they throw caution to the wind. Historians will look back at those days and say, "What *were* they thinking?" Achieving true wealth takes diligent work and careful analysis.

In terms of financial risk, the bottom line is . . . well . . . the bottom line! A healthy bottom line means that a company is making money. And if a company is making money, then you can make money by investing in its stock. However, if a company isn't making money, neither will you if you invest in it. Profit is the lifeblood of any company. (Are you listening, Dr. Koop?)

Interest rate risk

Interest rate risk may sound like an odd type of risk. In fact, interest rate risk is a common consideration for investors. This refers to the fact that interest rates change on a regular basis, causing some challenging moments. Interest rates are set by banks, and the primary institution that people watch closely is the Federal Reserve (the Fed), which is, in effect, the country's central bank. The Fed raises or lowers interest rates, actions that, in turn, cause banks to raise or lower interest rates accordingly. Interest rate changes affect consumers, businesses, and, of course, investors.

The scenario outlined in the following paragraphs gives you a generic introduction to the way fluctuating interest rates risk can affect investors in general.

Suppose that you buy a long-term, high-quality corporate bond and get a yield of 6 percent. Your money is safe, and your return is locked in at 6 percent. Whew! That's a guaranteed 6 percent. Not bad, huh? But what happens if, after you commit your money, interest rates increase to 8 percent? You lose the opportunity to get that extra 2 percent interest. The only way to get out of your 6 percent bond is to sell it at current market values and use the money to reinvest at the higher rate.

The only problem with this scenario is that the 6 percent bond is likely to drop in value because interest rates rose. Why? Say that the investor is Bob and the bond yielding 6 percent is a corporate bond issued by Lucin-Muny (LM). According to the bond agreement, LM must pay 6 percent (called the "face rate" or "nominal rate") during the life of the bond and then, upon maturity, pay the principal. If Bob buys $10,000 of LM bonds on the day they are issued, he gets $600 (of interest) every year for as long as he holds the bonds. If he holds on until maturity, he'll get back his $10,000 (the principal). So far so good, right? The plot thickens, however.

Say that he decides to sell the bond long before maturity and that, at the time of the sale, interest rates in the market rise to 8 percent. Now what? The reality is that no one would want his 6 percent bond if the market is offering bonds at 8 percent. What's Bob to do? He can't change the face rate of 6 percent, and he can't change the fact that only $600 will be paid each year for the life of the bond. What will have to change so that current investors get the *equivalent* yield of 8 percent? If you said, "The bond's value will have to go down," . . . bingo! In this example, the bond's market value needs to drop to $7,500 so that investors buying the bond would get an equivalent yield of 8 percent. Here's how that figures:

New investors would still get $600 annually. However, $600 is equal to 8 percent of $7,500. Therefore, even though investors would get the face rate of 6 percent, it equals a yield of 8 percent because the actual investment amount is $7,500. In this example, there is no financial risk, but it illustrates how interest rate risk can present itself. Bob finds out that you can have a good company with a good bond yet still lose $2,500 because of the change in the interest rate. Of course, if Bob doesn't sell, he won't realize that loss.

The lesson in all of this is that you can still lose money even in an apparently sound investment because of something that sounds as harmless as "interest rates have changed."

Rising and falling interest rates offer a special risk to stock investors. Historically, rising interest rates have had an adverse effect on stock prices. There are several reasons for this, and I outline them for you in the following sections.

Hurting a company's financial condition

Rising interest rates have a negative impact on companies that carry a large current debt load or that need to take on more debt, because when interest rates rise, the cost of borrowing money rises, too. This ultimately reduces the company's profitability and its ability to grow. When a company's profits (or earnings) drop, its stock becomes less desirable, and its stock price will fall.

Affecting a company's customers

Every company succeeds when it sells its products or services. But what happens if its customers (specifically, other companies that buy from it) are negatively impacted by increased interest rates? The financial health of its customers will directly affect the company's ability to grow sales and earnings.

For a good example of this situation, consider what happened to Cisco Systems in 2000. Because a huge part of its sales went to the telecommunications industry, the health of that entire industry was vital to Cisco's profitability. The telecom industry's debt ballooned to $700 billion. This debt became the telecom industry's financial Achilles heel, which, in turn, became a pain in the neck to Cisco. As telecom companies bought less (especially from Cisco), Cisco's profits shrank. From March 2000 to March 2001, Cisco's stock fell by nearly 70 percent! As of September 2001, Cisco's stock price continued to decline because the companies that were Cisco's customers were hurting financially.

Affecting investors' decision-making considerations

When interest rates rise, investors start to rethink their investment strategies. This can result in one of two outcomes:

> ✔ Investors may sell any shares in interest-sensitive stocks that they hold. Interest-sensitive industries include electric utilities, real estate, and the financial sector. Although increased interest rates can hurt these sectors, the reverse is also generally true: Falling interest rates boost the same industries. Keep in mind that interest rate changes affect some industries more than others.

> ✔ Investors who favor increased current income (versus waiting for the investment to grow in value to sell for a gain later on) are definitely attracted to investment vehicles that offer a higher rate of return. Higher interest rates can cause investors to switch from stocks to bonds or bank certificates of deposit.

Hurting stock prices indirectly

High or rising interest rates can have a negative impact on any investor's total financial picture. What happens when an investor struggles with burdensome debt, such as a second mortgage, credit card debt, or *margin debt* (debt you incur from borrowing against stock in a brokerage account)? He may sell some stock in order to pay off some of his high-interest debt. Selling stock to service debt is a common practice that, when taken collectively, can hurt stock prices.

The late 1990s saw a tremendous explosion of personal, mortgage, and corporate debt in the U.S. economy. These record-setting levels of debt subsequently resulted in record levels of personal bankruptcies and loan defaults for both consumers and corporations. Many investors sold their stock to pay for their debt. This action in turn forced stocks to fall farther. Debt considerations played an instrumental role in the decline of stock prices during 2000.

Because of the effects of interest rates on stock portfolios, both direct and indirect, investors should regularly monitor interest rates in both the general economy and in their personal situations. Although stocks have proven to be a superior long-term investment (the longer the term, the better), every investor should maintain a balanced portfolio that includes other investment vehicles, such as money market funds, savings bonds, and/or bank investments.

A diversified investor should have some money in vehicles that do well when interest rates rise. These include such things as money market funds, U.S. savings bonds (EE), and other variable-rate investments whose interest rates rise when market rates rise. These types of investments add a measure of safety from interest rate risk to your stock portfolio.

Market risk

When people talk about *the market* and how it goes up or down, it sounds like a monolithic entity instead of what it really is — a group of millions of individuals making daily decisions to buy or sell stock. No matter how modern our society and economic system, you can't escape the laws of supply and demand. When masses of people want to buy a particular stock, it becomes in demand, and its value rises. That value rises higher if the supply is limited. Conversely, if no one's interested in buying a stock, its value falls. This is the nature of market risk. The value of your stock can rise and fall on the fickle whim of market demand.

Millions of investors buying and selling each minute of every trading day affect the share price of your stock. This fact makes it impossible to judge which way your stock will move tomorrow or next week. This unpredictability is why stocks aren't appropriate for short-term financial growth.

In April 2001, a news program reported that in 2000, a fellow with $80,000 in the bank decided to invest it in the stock market. Because he was getting married in 2001, he wanted his money to grow faster and higher so that he could afford a nice wedding and a down payment on the couple's future home. What happened? His money shrank to $11,000, and he had to change his plans.

Losing money is only one headache you face when you lose money this way; the idea of postponing a joyful event, such as a wedding or a home purchase, just adds to the pain. The gent in the preceding story could have easily minimized his losses with some knowledge and discipline.

Markets are by their nature volatile; they go up and down, and investments need time to grow. This poor guy (literally, now) should have been aware of the fact that stocks in general aren't suitable for short-term (one year or less) goals. Despite the fact that the companies he invested in may have been fundamentally sound, all stock prices are subject to the gyrations of the marketplace and need time to trend upward.

Investing requires diligent work and research before putting your money in quality investments with a long-term perspective. Speculating is making a relatively quick profit by monitoring the short-term price movements of a particular investment. Investors seek to minimize risk, whereas speculators don't mind risk, because it can also magnify profits. There is a clear difference between speculating and investing, and investors frequently become speculators and ultimately put themselves and their wealth at risk. Don't go there!

Consider the married couple nearing retirement who decided to play with their money to see about making their pending retirement more comfortable. They borrowed a sizable sum by tapping into their home equity to invest in the stock market. (Their home, which they had paid off, had enough equity to qualify for this loan.) What did they do with these funds? You guessed it; they invested in the high-flying stocks of the day, which were high-tech and Internet stocks. Within eight months, they lost almost all their money.

Understanding market risk is especially important for people who are tempted to put their nest eggs or emergency funds into volatile investments such as growth stocks (or mutual funds that invest in growth stocks or similar aggressive investment vehicles). Remember, you can lose everything.

Inflation risk

Inflation is the artificial expansion of the quantity of money so that too much money is used in exchange for goods and services. To consumers, inflation shows up in the form of higher prices for goods and services. Inflation risk frequently is also referred to as "purchasing power risk." This just means that your money doesn't buy as much as it used to. For example, a dollar that bought you a sandwich in 1980 can barely buy you a candy bar a few years later. For you, the investor, this means that the value of your investment (a stock, for example) may not keep up with inflation.

Say that you have money in a bank savings account currently earning 4 percent. This account has flexibility in that if the market interest rate goes up, the rate you earn in your account goes up. Your account is safe from both financial risk and interest rate risk. But what if inflation is running at 5 percent?

In an inflationary economy, 5 percent inflation means that if your money is earning 4 percent, you're actually losing money. The purchasing power of your money decreases, so that you end up buying less instead of more with the same amount of money.

Tax risk

Taxes (such as income tax or capital gains tax) don't affect your stock investment directly, but they can affect how much of your money you get to keep. Because the entire point of stock investing is to build wealth, you need to understand that taxes take away a portion of the wealth that you're trying to build. Taxes can be risky because, if you make the wrong move with your stocks (selling them at the wrong time, for example), you can end up paying higher taxes than you need to. Because tax laws change so frequently, tax risk is part of the risk-versus-return equation, as well.

Many investors set up their wealth in tax-advantaged instruments such as municipal bonds and tax shelters only to have their plans thwarted by changes in the tax laws. In the mid-1980s, real estate was a booming investment market. However, the Tax Reform Act of 1986 significantly changed the rules of real estate investing. Subsequently, it played an important role in the decline of the real estate market in 1987. It pays to gain knowledge about how taxes can impact your wealth-building program before you make your investment decisions. Chapter 19 covers in greater detail the impact of taxes.

Political and governmental risks

If companies were fish, politics and government policies (such as taxes, laws, and regulations) would be the pond. In the same way that fish die in a toxic or polluted pond, politics and government policies can kill companies. Of course, if you own stock in a company exposed to political and governmental risks, you should be aware of this. For some companies, a single new regulation or law is enough to send it into bankruptcy. For other companies, a new law could help them increase sales and profits.

What if your money is in oil futures and you find out that Saudi Arabia's policy toward oil exports has changed drastically because of a political revolution? What if you invest in gold options and the federal government passes new laws restricting gold transactions? These actions would have a significant impact on your investment.

Similarly, what if you invest in companies or industries that become political targets? For example, tobacco companies were the targets of political firestorms that battered their stock prices. Whether one agrees or disagrees with the political machinations of our day is not the issue. As an investor, you have to ask yourself, "How does politics affect the market value and prospects of my chosen investment?" (See Chapter 13 for more on how politics can affect the stock market.)

Personal risks

Frequently, the risk involved with investing in the stock market may not be directly involved with the investment or factors directly related to the investment; sometimes the risk is with the investor's circumstances.

Suppose that investor Ralph Snodgrass puts $15,000 into a portfolio of common stocks. Imagine that the market experiences a drop in prices that week and Ralph's stocks drop to a market value of $14,000.

Because stocks are good for the long term, this type of decrease is usually not an alarming incident. Odds are that this dip is temporary, especially if Ralph carefully chose high-quality companies. Incidentally, if a portfolio of high-quality stocks *does* experience a temporary drop in price, it can be a great opportunity to get more shares at a good price.

Over the long term, Ralph would probably see the value of his investment grow substantially. But, what if during a period when his stocks are declining, Ralph experiences financial difficulty and needs quick cash? He may have to sell his stock to get some money.

This problem occurs frequently for investors who don't have an emergency fund or a rainy day fund to handle large, sudden expenses. You never know when your company may lay you off or when your basement may flood, leaving you with a huge repair bill. Car accidents, medical emergencies, and other unforeseen events are part of life's bag of surprises — for anyone. Be sure to set money aside for sudden expenses before you buy stocks. Then you won't be forced to prematurely liquidate your stock investments to pay emergency bills.

You probably won't get much comfort from knowing that stock losses are tax deductible — a loss is a loss. However, you can avoid the kind of loss that results from prematurely having to sell your stocks if you maintain an emergency cash fund. A good place for your emergency cash fund is in either a bank savings account or money market fund.

Emotional risk

Huh? What does emotional risk have to do with stocks? Emotions are important risk considerations because the main decision makers are human beings. Logic and discipline are critical factors in investment success, but even the best investor can let emotions take over the reins of money management and cause loss. For stock investing, the main emotions that can sidetrack you are fear and greed. You need to understand your emotions and what kinds of risk they can expose you to.

Paying the price for greed

In the 1998–2000 period, millions of investors threw caution to the wind and chased highly dubious, risky dot-com stocks. The dollar signs popped up in their eyes (just like slot machines) when they saw that easy street was lined with dot-com stocks that were doubling and tripling in a very short time. Who cares about price/earnings (P/E) ratios and earnings when you can just buy stock, make a fortune, and get out with millions? (Of course, *you* care about making money with stocks, so you can flip to Chapter 10 and Appendix B to find out more about P/E ratios.)

Unfortunately, the lure of the easy buck can easily turn healthy attitudes about growing wealth into unhealthy greed that blinds investors and discards common sense.

Recognizing the role of fear

Greed can be a problem, but fear is the other extreme. People who are fearful of loss frequently avoid suitable investments and end up settling for a low rate of return. If you have to succumb to one of these emotions, at least fear exposes you to less loss.

Looking for love in all the wrong places

Tina Turner might ask, "What's love got to do with it?" Stocks are dispassionate, inanimate vehicles, but people can look for love in the strangest places. Emotional risk occurs when investors fall in love with a stock and refuse to sell it even when the stock is plummeting and shows all the symptoms of getting worse. Emotional risk also occurs when investors are drawn to bad investment choices just because they sound good, are popular, or are pushed by family or friends.

You can just see the promo for a television talk show: "Investors and their stocks: Has romance shrunk to codependency?" Or you can imagine Dr. Laura's next caller: "My XYZ stock is dissatisfying, yet I can't let go!" Ugh. People have lost tons of money because of an unhealthy attachment to an investment.

Love and attachment are great in relationships with people but are horrible with investments. Keep in mind that stocks (as with any investment) are tools for building wealth to improve your life. No more, no less. If the stock isn't performing, get rid of it.

Investment lessons from September 11

September 11, 2001, is a horrific day that is burned in our minds and won't be forgotten in our lifetime. The acts of terrorism that day took over 3,000 lives and caused untold pain and grief. A much less important aftereffect were the hard lessons that investors learned that day. It reminds us that risk is more real than ever and that we should never let our guard down. What lessons should investors learn from the worst acts of terrorism to ever happen on U.S. soil? Here are a few pointers:

✔ **Diversify your portfolio.** Of course, the events of September 11 were certainly surreal and unexpected. But before the events occurred, investors should have made it a habit to assess their situations and see whether they had any vulnerabilities. Stock investors with no money outside the stock market will always be more at risk. Keeping your portfolio diversified is a time-tested strategy that is more relevant than ever before.

✔ **Regularly review your portfolio.** September 11 triggered declines in the overall market, but specific industries, such as airlines and hotels, were hit particularly hard. In addition, some industries, such as defense and food, saw stock prices rise. Monitor your portfolio and ask yourself whether it is overly reliant on or exposed to events in specific sectors. If so, reallocate your investments to decrease your risk exposure.

✔ **Check for signs of trouble.** Techniques such as trailing stops (which I explain in Chapter 16) come in very handy when unexpected events cause your stocks to plummet. Even if you don't use them, you should make it a regular habit to analyze your stocks and check for signs of trouble, such as debts or P/E ratios that are too high. If so, consider selling anyway.

Minimizing Your Risk

Now, before you go crazy thinking that stock investing carries so much risk that you may as well not get out of bed, take a breath. Minimizing your risk in stock investing is easier than you think. Although wealth building through the stock market doesn't take place without some amount of risk, you can take steps to maximize your profits and still keep your money secure.

Gaining knowledge

The more familiar you are with the stock market — how it works, factors that affect stock value, and so on — the better you can navigate around its pitfalls and maximize your profits. Diminishing risk starts with gaining knowledge. You've probably heard the cliché "The more you know, you more you grow." The same knowledge that enables you grow your wealth also enables you to minimize your risk. Before you put your money anywhere, you want to know as much as you can. (This book is a great place to start.)

Lack of knowledge constitutes the greatest risk of all to new investors. But it's a needless risk because if you take the time and trouble to educate yourself about stock investing, you can avoid the biggest — and most expensive — mistakes. Check out Chapter 6 for a rundown of the kinds of information you should know before you buy stocks, as well as the resources that can give you the information you need to invest successfully.

Oddly enough, some people spend more time analyzing a restaurant menu to buy a $10 meal than researching where to put their next $5,000. In the past few years, millions of investors lost trillions of dollars simply because they didn't know what they were getting into. I met an investor who lost a lot of money on an Internet stock. When I asked him simple questions about the stock, such as "How much money does the company make?" and "What is the company's price/earnings ratio?" I got blank stares.

In this book, I squeeze as much information as possible between the covers in order to steer you in the right direction, but you're responsible for getting as much information as possible and staying on top of changes and developments.

Staying out . . . for now

If you don't understand stocks, don't invest! Yeah, I know this book is about stock investing, and I think that some measure of stock investing is a good idea for most people. But that doesn't mean you should be 100 percent invested 100 percent of the time. If you don't understand a particular stock (or don't understand stocks, period), stay away from them. Instead, I urge you to follow certain stocks for a while without investing your money. Pick a few stocks that you think will increase in value and then track them for a while and see how they perform. As you find out more and more about stock investing, you'll get better and better at picking individual stocks, and you won't have risked — or lost — any money during your learning period.

As you're getting started, give yourself an imaginary sum of money, such as $100,000, and make your best choices for stocks. Give yourself reasons to invest and just make believe. Follow your chosen stocks for a few weeks or even a few months. Understand how the price of a stock goes up and down. Watch what happens to the stocks you chose when various events take place. How are share prices affected when the president makes a major speech? How about when earnings are reported? Seeing how stock prices behave is important for beginners. It's like putting your toes in the shallow end of the pool before you wade into deeper water.

Getting your financial house in order

Believe it or not, some people out there have $13,987 in consumer debt and $1.38 in their bank account and barely make ends meet, yet they think, "Gee, the stock market could make me rich!" Many such people have no business investing in stocks.

Before you buy your first stock, do the following things to get your finances in order:

- ✔ Have a cushion of money somewhere safe, such as in a bank account or treasury money market fund, in case you suddenly need cash for an emergency. A minimum amount to set aside is at least three months' worth of your gross living expenses when times seem good. If the times are uncertain, you should have at least four or five months' worth of gross living expenses.

- ✔ Reduce your debt. Overindulging in debt was the worst personal economic problem for many Americans in the late 1990s. Consumer spending along with job layoffs and speculative investment choices drove the bankruptcy rate in America to over 1 million personal cases per year starting in 1997. The year 2001 was a record year, with nearly 1.5 million people filing for bankruptcy. (Incidentally, corporate bankruptcies hit a record high as well.)

- ✔ Make sure that your job is as secure as you can make it. Are you keeping your skills up to date? Is the company you work for strong and growing? Is the industry that you work in strong and growing?

- ✔ Make sure that you have adequate insurance to cover you and your family's needs in case of illness, death, disability, and so on.

I don't want to get into a long laundry list of tips here. Advice on what to do before you invest could be a whole book all by itself. The bottom line is that you want to make sure that you are, first and foremost, financially secure before you take the plunge into the stock market. If you're not sure about your financial security, look over your situation with a financial planner. (You can find more on financial planners in Appendix A.)

Diversifying your investments

When you talk to any astute financial advisor about risk in the stock market, the first piece of advice you're likely to hear is, "You can reduce your risk with proper diversification." Fair enough. But what does that mean?

Diversification is a strategy for reducing risk by spreading your money across different investments. It's a fancy way of saying, "Don't have all your eggs in one basket." For most people, that advice is generally true. Having a little bit in this investment and a little bit in that investment means never having to say, "I lost all my money!" But how do you go about divvying up your money and distributing it among different investments? The easiest way to understand proper diversification may be to look at what you should *not* do:

- ✔ **Don't put all your money in just one stock.** Sure, if you choose wisely and select a hot stock, you may make a bundle, but the odds are tremendously against you. Unless you're a real expert on that particular company, it behooves you to have only a small portion of your money in any one stock. As a general rule, the money you tie up in a single stock should be money you can do without.

- ✔ **Don't put all your money in one industry.** I know people who own several stocks, but the stocks are all in the same industry. Again, if you're an expert in that particular industry, it could work out. But just understand that you're not properly diversified. If a problem hits an entire industry, you'll get hurt.

- ✔ **Don't put all your money in just one type of investment.** Stocks may be a great investment, but you should have money elsewhere. Bonds, mutual funds, bank accounts, treasury securities, real estate, and precious metals are perennial alternatives to complement your stock portfolio.

Okay, now that you know what you *shouldn't* do, what *should* you do? Until you become more knowledgeable, follow this advice:

- ✔ **Don't put any more than 25 percent of your investment money directly into stocks.**

✔ **Invest in four or five different stocks that are in different industries.** Which industries? Choose industries that offer products and services that have shown strong, growing demand. To make this decision, use your common sense (which isn't as common as it used to be). Think about the industries that people will need no matter what happens in the general economy, such as food, energy, and other consumer necessities. See Chapter 12 for more information about analyzing industries.

Weighing Risk against Return

How much risk is appropriate for you, and how do you handle it? Before you try to figure out what risks accompany your investment choices, you should first analyze the one topic you should be an expert on — yourself. What are you all about? What are you trying to accomplish? What are your goals? What is your investor profile? Are you comfortable with taking chances with your money, or are you very concerned about risk? Here are some points to keep in mind when weighing risk versus return in your situation:

✔ **Your financial goal:** In five minutes with a financial calculator, you can easily see how much money you're going to need to become financially independent (presuming that this is your goal). Say that you need $500,000 in ten years for a worry-free retirement and that your financial assets (such as stocks, bonds, and so on) are currently worth $400,000. In this scenario, your assets would need to grow by only 2.5 percent to hit your target. Getting investments that grow by 2.5 percent safely is easy to do because that is a relatively low rate of return.

The important point is that you don't have to knock yourself out trying to double your money with risky, high-flying investments; some run-of-the-mill bank investments will do just fine. All too often, investors take on more risk than is necessary. Figure out what your financial goal is so that you know what kind of return you realistically need.

✔ **Your investor profile:** Are you nearing retirement, or are you fresh out of college? Your life situation matters when it comes to looking at risk versus return. If you're just beginning your working years, you can certainly tolerate greater risk than someone facing retirement. This is true because even if you lose big time, you still have a long time horizon in which to recoup your money and get back on track. However, if you're approaching retirement, risky or aggressive investments will do much more harm than good. If you lose money, you don't have as much time to recoup your investment, and the odds are that you'll need the investment money (and its income-generating capacity) to cover your living expenses once you are no longer employed.

✔ **Asset allocation:** I never tell retirees to put a large portion of their retirement money into a high-tech stock or other volatile investment. But if they still want to speculate, I don't see a problem as long as they limit such investments to 5 percent of their total assets. As long as the bulk of their money is safe and sound in secure investments (such as U.S. treasury bonds), I know I can sleep well (knowing that *they* can sleep well!).

Asset allocation beckons back to diversification. For people in their 20s and 30s, having 75 percent of their money in a diversified portfolio of growth stocks (such as mid cap and small cap stocks) is acceptable. For people in their 60s and 70s, it's not acceptable. They may, instead, consider investing no more than 20 percent of their money in stocks (mid caps and large caps are preferable). Check with your financial advisor to find the right mix for your particular situation.

Better luck next time

A little knowledge can be very risky. Consider the true story of one "lucky" fellow who played the California lottery in 1987. He discovered that he had a winning ticket, with the first prize of $412,000. He immediately ordered a Porsche, booked a lavish trip to Hawaii for his family, and treated his wife and friends to a champagne dinner at a posh Hollywood restaurant. When he finally went to collect his prize, he found out that he had to share first prize with over 9,000 other lottery players who also had the same winning numbers. His share of the prize was actually only $45! Hopefully, he invested that tidy sum based on his increased knowledge about risk.

Chapter 5

Say Cheese: Getting a Snapshot of the Market

"*H*ow's the market doing today?" is the most common question that interested parties ask about the stock market. "What did the Dow do?" "How about Nasdaq?" Invariably, people asking those questions are expecting the performance number of an index. "Well, the Dow fell 57 points to 9500, while Nasdaq was unchanged at 1882." Indexes can be useful, general gauges of stock market activity. They give the investor a basic idea of how well (or how poorly) the overall market is doing.

An *index* is a statistical measure that represents the value of a batch of stocks. This measure is used like a barometer to track the overall progress of the market (or a segment of it). There are indexes for all sorts of markets, but in this chapter, I focus the attention on stock market indexes.

Knowing How Indexes Are Measured

The oldest stock market index is the Dow Jones Industrial Average. It was created in 1896 by Charles Dow (of Dow Jones fame), and it covered only 12 stocks (the number increased to 30 stocks in 1928, and it has remained the same to this day). Because this was long before the age of computers, calculating a stock market index was kept simple and was done arithmetically by hand. Dow would add up the stock prices of the 12 companies and then divide it by 12. Technically, this was an *average* and not an index. Nowadays, the number gets tweaked to also account for things such as stock splits.

However, indexes get calculated differently. The primary difference between an "index" and an "average" is the concept of weighting. *Weighting* refers to the relative importance of the items when they are computed within the index. There are several kinds of indexes:

- ✔ **Price-weighted index:** This index tracks changes based on the change in the individual stock's price per share.

  To give you an example of this, suppose that you own two stocks: Stock A worth $20 per share and Stock B worth $40 per share. In a price-weighted index, the stock at $40 is allocated a greater proportion of the index than the one at $20. However, the market-value weighted index calculates the market capitalization (total shares times the share price).

- ✔ **Market-value weighted index:** This index tracks the proportion of a stock based on its market capitalization (or market value).

  Say that in your portfolio the $20 stock (Stock A) has 10 million shares and the $40 stock (Stock B) has only 1 million shares. Stock A's market cap is $200 million, while Stock B's market cap is $40 million. Therefore, in a market-value weighted index, Stock A represents 83 percent of the index's value because of its much larger market cap.

  This sample portfolio shows only two stocks — obviously not a good representative index. Most investing professionals (especially money managers and mutual fund firms) use a broad-based index as a benchmark to compare their progress. A *broad-based index* is an index that represents the performance of the entire market, such as the S&P 500. (See the section "Standard & Poor's 500," later in this chapter.)

- ✔ **Composite index:** This is an index or average that is a combination of several averages or indexes. An example is the New York Stock Exchange (NYSE) Composite, which tracks the entire exchange by combining all the stocks and indexes that are included in it.

The bottom line is that indexes give the investor an instant snapshot of how well the market is doing. They offer a quick way to compare the performance of one investor's stock portfolio or mutual funds with the rest of the market. If the Dow goes up 10 percent in a year and your portfolio shows a cumulative gain of 12 percent, then you know that you're doing well. Appendix A in the back of this book lists resources to help you keep up with various indexes.

The Dow Jones Industrial Average

The most famous stock market barometer is our first example — the Dow Jones Industrial Average (DJIA). The DJIA (simply referred to as "the Dow") is most frequently the index quoted when someone asks how the market is doing. The Dow is price weighted and tracks a basket of 30 of the largest and most influential public companies in the stock market. The following list shows the current roster of 30 stocks tracked on the DJIA.

Alcoa (AA)

American Express Co. (AXP)

AT&T (T)

Boeing (BA)

Caterpillar (CAT)

Citigroup (C)

Coca-Cola (KO)

Disney (DIS)

DuPont (DD)

Eastman Kodak (EK)

Exxon Mobil (XON)

General Electric (GE)

General Motors (GM)

Hewlett-Packard (HWP)

Home Depot (HD)

Honeywell International Inc. (HON)

Intel (INTC)

International Business Machines (IBM)

International Paper (IP)

Johnson & Johnson (JNJ)

J.P. Morgan Chase (JPM)

McDonald's (MCD)

Merck (MRK)

Microsoft (MSFT)

Minnesota Mining and Manufacturing (3M) (MMM)

Philip Morris (MO)

Procter & Gamble (PG)

SBC Communications (SBC)

United Technologies (UTX)

Wal-Mart Stores (WMT)

The Dow has survived as a popular gauge of stock market activity for over a century. Although it is an important indicator of the market's progress, it does have one major drawback: It tracks only 30 companies. Regardless of their status in the market, the companies in the Dow represent a limited number, so they don't communicate the true pulse of the market. For example, when the Dow surpassed the record 10,000 and 11,000 milestones during 1999 and 2000, the majority of (nonindex) companies showed lackluster or declining stock price movement.

The roster of the Dow has changed many times during the 100-plus years of its existence. The only original company from 1896 is General Electric. Most of the changes on the Dow have occurred for reasons such as mergers and bankruptcy. However, some changes were done to simply reflect the changing times. Microsoft, for example isn't an "industrial" company in the truest sense of the word, but it was added to the DJIA in 1999, while companies such as Union Carbide were dropped.

The Dow isn't a pure gauge of industrial activity because it also includes a hodgepodge of nonindustrial issues such as J.P. Morgan Chase and Citigroup (banks), Home Depot (retailing), and Microsoft (software). Because of these changes, it doesn't adequately reflect industrial activity. During the late 1990s and right up to 2001, true industrial sectors such as manufacturing had difficult times, yet the Dow rose to record levels.

Serious investors are better served by looking at the following:

- **Broad-based indexes:** Indexes such as the S&P 500 and the Wilshire 5000 are more realistic gauges of the stock market's performance.

- **Industry or sector indexes:** These are better gauges of the growth (or lack of growth) of specific industries and sectors. If you buy a gold stock, then you should track the index for the precious metals industry.

Dow Jones has several averages, including the Dow Jones Transportation Average (DJTA) and the Dow Jones Utilities Average (DJUA). Both of these are more strictly managed than the Dow. The DJUA sticks to utilities, so it tends to be a more accurate barometer of the market it represents. (The same goes for the DJTA.)

Nasdaq Indexes

Nasdaq became a formalized market in 1971. The name used to stand for "National Association of Securities Dealers Automated Quote" system, but now it is simply "Nasdaq" (as if it were a name like Ralph or Eddie). Nasdaq indexes are similar to other indexes in style and structure. The only difference is that, well, it covers Nasdaq. The Nasdaq has two indexes (both reported in the financial pages):

✔ **Nasdaq Composite Index:** Most frequently quoted on the news, the Nasdaq Composite Index covers the more than 5,000 companies that trade on Nasdaq. The companies encompass a variety of industries, but the index's concentration has primarily been technology, telecom, and Internet industries.

Because of the hypergrowth that these industries experienced during the late 1990s, the Nasdaq Composite even surpassed the Dow briefly in popularity. Because the Nasdaq Composite Index is market-value weighted, it soared to its all-time high of 5048 in March 2000. (That level is still its record high as of early March 2002.)

✔ **Nasdaq 100 Index:** The Nasdaq 100 tracks the 100 largest companies in Nasdaq. This index is for investors who want to concentrate on the largest companies, which tend to be especially weighted in technology issues.

In either case, the point that investors have to remember is that although these indexes track growth-oriented companies, these issues are also very volatile and carry commensurate risk. The indexes themselves bear this out; in the bear market of 2000 and 2001 (and even extending into 2002), they fell more than 60 percent.

Dow Jones milestones

This table shows when the Dow Jones Industrial Average reached each of eleven 1,000-point milestones and how long it took to reach that point:

Milestone	Date	How long it took
1,000	Nov. 14, 1972	76 years
2,000	Jan. 8, 1987	14 years
3,000	April 17, 1991	4 years
4,000	Feb. 23, 1995	4 years
5,000	Nov. 21, 1995	9 months
6,000	Oct. 14, 1996	11 months
7,000	Feb. 13, 1997	4 months
8,000	July 16, 1997	5 months
9,000	April 6, 1998	9 months
10,000	March 29, 1999	12 months
11,000	May 3, 1999	1 month

As you can see, the Dow took 76 years to hit its first milestone. But as each succeeding milestone came along, it took less and less time to hit the next one, due to the fact that the higher the Dow is in a relative sense, the easier it is to jump 1,000 points. For example, it went from 6,000 to 7,000 in only four months.

The Dow moved between 1,000 and 11,000 mostly during modern times. As the table indicates, most of the milestones happened during the 1982–1999 bull market. But notice that a new milestone wasn't reached during 2000 and 2001. That fact alone tells you that the Dow either stalled or declined as the bear market of 2000 arrived.

Standard & Poor's 500

The Standard & Poor's 500 (S&P 500) is an index that tracks the 500 largest (measured by market value) publicly traded companies. It was created by the publishing firm Standard & Poor's. (I bet you could have guessed that.) Because it contains 500 companies, the Standard & Poor's 500 is more representative of the overall market's performance than the DJIA's 30 companies. Money managers and financial advisors actually watch the Standard & Poor's 500 stock index more closely than the DJIA. Mutual funds especially like to measure their performance against the S&P 500 rather than against any other index.

The S&P 500 doesn't attempt to cover the 500 "biggest" companies. It instead includes companies that are widely held and widely followed. The companies are also industry leaders in a variety of industries, including energy, technology, healthcare, and finance. It is a market-value weighted index (which I explain in the section "Knowing How Indexes Are Measured," earlier in this chapter).

Although it is a reliable indicator of the market's overall status, the S&P 500 also has some limitations. Despite the fact that it tracks 500 companies, the top 50 companies encompass 50 percent of the index's market value. This situation can be a drawback because those 50 companies have a greater influence on the S&P 500 index's price movement than any other segment of companies. In other words, 10 percent of the companies have an equal impact to 90 percent of the companies on the same index. Therefore, the index may not offer an accurate representation of the general market.

These 500 companies are not set in stone. They can be added or removed as market conditions change. A company can be removed if it is not doing well or goes bankrupt. A company in the index can be replaced by another company that is doing better.

Other Indexes

Although the Dow, Nasdaq, and S&P 500 are the stars of the financial press, other indexes are equally important to follow because they cover other important facets of the market, such as small cap and mid cap stocks. The Russell 2000 and the Wilshire 5000 are useful because they cover a much broader range of publicly traded companies.

There are other less-sexy indexes that cover specific sectors and industries. If you're investing in an Internet stock, you should also check the Internet Stock Index to compare what your stock is doing as measured against the index. You can find indexes that cover industries such as transportation, brokerage firms, retailers, computer companies, and real estate firms. For a comprehensive list of indexes, go to www.djindexes.com (a Dow Jones & Co. Web site).

Russell 3000 Index

The Russell 3000 Index is mentioned here as a great example of an index that seeks more comprehensive inclusion of U.S. companies. It includes the 3,000 largest publicly traded companies (nearly 98 percent of publicly traded stocks). The Russell 3000 is important because it includes many mid cap and small cap stocks. Most companies covered in the Russell 3000 have an average market value of a billion dollars or less.

The Russell 3000 Index was created by the Frank Russell Company, which actually computes a series of indexes such as the Russell 1000 and the Russell 2000. The Russell 2000, for example, contains the smallest 2,000 companies from the Russell 3000, while the Russell 1000 contains the largest 1,000 companies. The Russell Indexes do not cover microcap stocks (companies with a market capitalization under $250 million).

Wilshire Total Market Index

The Wilshire 5000 Index, often referred to as the "Wilshire Total Market Index," is probably the largest stock index in the world. Created in 1980 by Wilshire Associates, it started out tracking 5,000 stocks and has ballooned to cover more than 7,500 stocks. The advantage of the Wilshire 5000 is that it's very comprehensive, covering nearly the entire market. (At the very least, the stocks tracked are the largest publicly traded stocks.) It includes all the stocks that are on the major stock exchanges (NYSE, AMEX, and the largest issues on Nasdaq), which by default also include all the stocks covered by the S&P 500. The Wilshire 5000 is a market-value weighted index, which I discuss in the section "Knowing How Indexes Are Measured," earlier in this chapter.

International indexes

Investors need to remember that the whole world is a vast marketplace that interacts with and exerts tremendous influence on individual national economies and markets. Whether you have one stock or a mutual fund, keep tabs on how your portfolio is affected by world markets. The best way to get a snapshot of international markets is, of course, with indexes. Here are some of the more widely followed international indexes:

- ✔ **Nikkei (Japan):** This is considered Japan's version of the Dow. If you're invested in Japanese stocks or in stocks that do business with Japan, you can bet that you want to know what's up with the Nikkei.

- ✔ **FTSE-100 (Great Britain):** Usually referred to as the "footsie," this is a market-value weighted index of the top 100 public companies in the United Kingdom.

- ✔ **CAC-40 (France):** This index tracks the 40 public stocks that trade on the Paris Stock Exchange.

- ✔ **DAX (Germany):** This index tracks the 30 largest and most active stocks that trade on the Frankfurt Exchange.

You can track these international indexes (among others) at major financial Web sites, such as www.bloomberg.com and www.marketwatch.com.

Failing to keep a watchful eye on the international market can cost you. What if you had stock in a company that had most of its customers in Argentina, for example? The year 2001 was terrible for Argentina's economy and its markets. If you had understood the interconnectedness of world markets, you could have sold your stock (or placed stop losses on it, as described in Chapter 16) before it got clobbered because of Argentina's economic woes.

Investing in Indexes

Is it possible to invest directly in indexes? I mean, if the market is doing well and your specific stock is not, why not find a way to invest in the index itself? With investments based on indexes, you can invest in the general market or a particular industry.

Say that you want to invest in the DJIA. To have a portfolio that mirrors the DJIA, is it practical to buy shares in each of the 30 stocks that make up this index? This approach sounds too expensive for the average investor, but there are practical alternatives. You may immediately think that the answer is a mutual fund, but in this case, you're only partially right. Although some great mutual funds are out there, this book is about stocks after all. A more appropriate vehicle for stock investors is the Exchange Traded Fund (ETF).

An ETF is a hybrid between a stock and an index. It has most of the usual features of a stock — shares are bought and sold through a broker, dividends are paid to stockholders, shares can be bought on margin, and so on — but it really reflects the performance of a specific index. ETFs are traded on the stock exchanges as regular stock. With ETFs, you have the ability to buy an entire portfolio of stocks as easily as buying a single stock. An ETF is similar in structure to a real estate investment trust (REIT). (For more on REITs, see Chapter 9.)

A REIT is a hybrid between a stock and a mutual fund. It is like a stock in most respects, but it's not a conventional company that sells goods or services. A REIT makes its money like a mutual fund in that it buys, sells, and manages a portfolio of real estate. An ETF is, in most respects, like a stock. However, it doesn't deal in goods, services, or real estate. It is a fixed portfolio of securities that mirror a particular index.

A good example of an ETF is Diamonds — Dow Jones Industrial Average Depository receipts — which is assigned the stock symbol DIA. When you buy DIA, it's like buying a piece of the portfolio of stocks that comprise the DJIA. Because it's like a stock, you can actually buy as little as one share.

When investing in DIAs (and most ETFs), here are some important points to keep in mind:

✔ **You can buy them through your broker.** Like any stock, the purchase or sale is easy, no matter whether you call up the broker or do the transaction at the broker's Web site.

✔ **You can short them.** If you think that the market (or a particular industry or foreign country) will decline, you can still profit by going short (see Chapter 16) in the same manner that you can with individual stocks. The same risks of going short are also present.

✔ **You can purchase ETFs on margin.** Again, just as with other stock, ETFs are marginable securities.

✔ **ETFs are inexpensive to buy.** Most ETFs can be purchased for as little as one share. Some types must be purchased in a round lot (100 shares or more). Find out from the exchange that lists them or through your broker.

✔ **Expect to pay management fees.** The institutions that package and sell the ETFs do charge fees for doing so. These charges are usually embedded in the cost structure of the ETF, so you don't pay these directly. The only fees that you may notice are the commissions that your broker charges you to buy and sell them. Keep in mind that all fees affect the return on your investment.

✔ **There will be tax implications.** Because the ETF doesn't actively manage the portfolio, there is less incidence of capital gains consequences. This makes ETFs more tax efficient. In addition, dividends may be issued, but that depends on the portfolio of stocks that are included. An ETF that covers the utilities sector probably issues dividends, while an ETF covering the tech sector does not.

✔ **You still need to diversify.** This point should be obvious, but it is important to mention here. Diversification is always an important issue for investors (especially small investors). ETFs are obviously more diversified than a single stock and have inherently less risk. However, ETFs will go up and down based on the stocks that are in the ETF. If the utilities industry is having difficulties, an ETF specializing in the utilities industry will go down in value.

✔ **The valuation is not precise.** An ETF strives to mirror the index as much as possible, but it may not always be 100 percent accurate. However, the difference is usually inconsequential.

Some other noteworthy ETFs that are very popular and worth some further investigation include the following:

✔ **QQQ:** This ETF mirrors the Nasdaq 100.

✔ **SPDRs:** Standard & Poor's Depository Receipts. There are a batch of these. The main SPDR tracks the S&P 500, but you can also invest in SPDRs that cover specific sectors, such as healthcare, energy, and other major segments of the S&P 500.

✔ **HOLDRS:** These are ETFs that are issued by Merrill Lynch and traded on the American Stock Exchange. HOLDRS give stock investors the ability to buy a portfolio of stocks in a single stock that covers a specific sector, such as energy or healthcare.

You can get updated information on ETFs through the Web sites of major exchanges. (See Appendix A for specific URLs.) However, most ETFs are traded through the American Stock Exchange, which offers complete information on ETFs at its Web site at www.amex.com.

ETFs generally have the same characteristics as the indexes themselves. Whether they move up or down, they give the investor the opportunity to do just as well as the market itself.

Part II
Before You Get Started

"Growth stock? Income stock? I say we stick the money in the ground like always, and then feed this guy to the sharks."

In this part . . .

As you're about to begin investing in stocks, you should know that there are different types of stocks for different objectives. In this part, you can find out where to start gathering information and discover what stockbrokers can do for you.

Chapter 6

Gathering Information

. . . .

In This Chapter

▶ Exploring financial issues you need to know about to be a well-informed investor

▶ Deciphering stock tables

▶ Interpreting dividend news

▶ Recognizing good (and bad) advice when you hear it

. . . .

Knowledge and information are two critical success factors in stock investing. (Isn't that true about most things in life?) People who plunge headlong into stocks without sufficient knowledge of the stock market in general, and current information in particular, quickly learn the lesson of the eager diver who didn't find out ahead of time that the pool was only an inch deep (ouch!). In their haste to avoid missing so-called golden investment opportunities, investors too often end up losing money.

Opportunities to *make* money in the stock market will always be there, no matter how well or how poorly the economy and the market are performing in general. There's no such thing as a single (and fleeting) magical moment, so don't feel that if you let an opportunity pass you by, you'll always regret that you missed your one big chance. The stock market is an entity that opens and closes every day. Tomorrow's opportunities may not even be imaginable today. Resist the urge to jump at what seem to be golden investment opportunities unless you really know what you're doing. A better approach is first building your knowledge and finding quality information. Then buy stocks and make your fortunes more assuredly. Where do you start and what kind of information should you acquire? Keep reading.

Figuring Out What You Need to Know

If you're just beginning to study the stock market and you still can't tell the difference between stock in your investment portfolio or stock in a warehouse, take this time to find out all you can. Beginners need to start with the nuts and bolts. Before you buy stock, you need to know that the company you're investing in is

- Financially sound and growing.
- Offering products and services that are in demand by consumers.
- In a strong and growing industry.
- Thriving in a strong and growing general economy.

Knowing where to look for answers

The adage "You've gotta learn to walk before you can run" applies to stock investing. Before you invest in stocks, you need to be completely familiar with the basics of stock investing. At its most fundamental, stock investing is about using your money to buy a piece of a company that will give you value in the form of appreciation or income. Fortunately, many resources are available to help you find out about stock investing. Some of my favorite places are the stock exchanges themselves.

Who knows better about the mechanics of stock investing than the New York Stock Exchange (NYSE)? Stock exchanges are organized marketplaces for the buying and selling of stocks (and other securities). The NYSE, as the premier stock exchange, provides a framework for stock buyers and sellers to make their transactions, and they make money not only from a piece of every transaction but also from fees charged to companies and brokers that are members of their exchanges. The main exchanges for most stock investors are the NYSE, the American Stock Exchange (AMEX), and Nasdaq. All three of these exchanges encourage and inform people about stock investing. They usually offer free tutorials at their Web sites and free investor publications for anyone who asks. Here's where to find that information:

- New York Stock Exchange: www.nyse.com
- American Stock Exchange: www.amex.com
- Nasdaq: www.nasdaq.com

They don't offer free information because they're so benevolent. Don't get me wrong — they are upstanding institutions — but their main interest is to see to it that stock investing grows in its acceptance and activity. After all, that's how they make money. Still, they provide terrific information resources for investors.

Understanding stocks and the companies they represent

Stocks represent ownership in companies. Before you buy individual stocks, you should understand the companies whose stock you're considering and find out about their operations. It may sound like a daunting task, but the point is easier to digest when you realize that companies work very similar to how you work and that they make decisions on a day-to-day basis just as you do.

Think about how you grow and prosper as an individual or as a family, and you see the same issues with companies and how they grow or prosper. Low earnings or high debt are examples of financial difficulties that can affect both people and companies. Understanding companies' finances is easier when you take some time to pick up some information in two basic disciplines: accounting and economics. These two disciplines play a significant role in understanding the performance of a company's stock.

Accounting for taste and a whole lot more

Accounting. Ugh! But face it: Accounting is the language of business, and believe it or not, you're already familiar with the most important accounting concepts! Just look at the following three essential principles:

- ✔ **Assets minus liabilities equals net worth.** In other words, take what you own (your assets), subtract what you owe (your liabilities), and the rest is yours (net worth)! Your own personal finances work the same way as Microsoft's (except with fewer zeros).

    A company's balance sheet shows you its net worth at a specific point of time (such as December 31). The net worth of a company is the bottom line of a company's asset and liability picture, and it tells you whether the company is solvent (*solvent* means the ability to pay your debts without going out of business). The net worth should be regularly growing; compare it from the same point a year earlier. A company that has a $4 million net worth on December 31, 2000, and a $5 million net worth on December 31, 2001, is doing well; its net worth has gone up 25 percent ($1 million) in one year.

- ✔ **Income less expenses equals net income.** In other words, take what you make (your income), subtract what you spend (your expenses), and the remainder is your net income (or net profit or net earnings — your gain).

    A company's net income is the whole point of investing in stock. As it profits, the company becomes more valuable, and in turn, its stock price will become more valuable. To discover a company's net income, look at its income statement. Try to determine whether the company uses its gains wisely, either reinvesting it for continued growth or paying down debt.

- ✔ **Do a comparative financial analysis.** That's a mouthful, but, it's just a fancy way of saying how a company is doing now compared with something else (like a prior period or a similar company).

    If you know that a company you're looking at had a net income of $50,000 for the year, you might ask, "Is that good or bad?" Obviously, making a net profit is good, but you also need to know whether it's good compared to something else. If last year the net profit was $40,000, then you know that the company's doing better than before. But if a similar company has a net profit of $100,000 for the same period, you might wonder what's wrong with the company you're looking at (and steer clear of its stock).

Accounting can be this simple. If you understand these three basic points, you'll be ahead of the curve (in stock investing as well as your personal finances). For more information on how to use a company's financial statements to pick good stocks, see Chapter 11.

Economics is dismal only if you don't understand it

Economics. Double ugh! No, no one is asking you to understand "the inelasticity of demand aggregates" (thank heavens!) or "marginal utility" (say what?). But a working knowledge of basic economics is crucial (and I mean crucial) to your success and proficiency as a stock investor. The stock market and the economy are joined at the hip. The good (or bad) things that happen to one have a direct effect on the other.

Alas, economics is lost on many investors (and some so-called experts on TV, too). I owe my personal investing success to my status as a student of economics. Understanding basic economics helped me (and will help you) filter the financial news to separate relevant information from the irrelevant in order to make better investment decisions. Here a few important economic concepts to be aware of:

- ✔ **Supply and demand:** How can anyone possibly think about economics without thinking of the ageless and timeless concept of supply and demand? Supply and demand can be simply stated as the relationship between what's available (the supply) and what people want and are willing to pay for (the demand). This equation is the main engine of economic activity and is extremely important for your stock investing analysis and decision-making process. I mean, would you really buy stock in a company that makes elephant-foot umbrella stands if you found out that there was an oversupply and nobody wants them anyway?

- ✔ **Cause and effect:** If you were to pick up a prominent news report and read, "Companies in the table industry are expecting plummeting sales," would you rush out and invest in companies that sell chairs or manufacture tablecloths? Considering cause and effect is an exercise in logical thinking, and believe you me, logic is a major component of sound economic thought.

  When you read business news, play it out in your mind. What good (or bad) can logically be expected given a certain event or situation? If you're looking for an effect ("I want a stock price that keeps increasing"), then you should understand the cause. Here are some typical events that could cause a stock's price to rise:

  - • **Positive news reports about a company:** The news may report that a company is enjoying success with increased sales or a new product.

  - • **Positive news reports about a company's industry:** The media may be highlighting that the industry is poised to do well.

- **Positive news reports about a company's customers:** Maybe your company is in industry A, but its customers are in industry B. If you see good news about industry B, that could be good news for your stock.

- **Negative news reports about a company's competitors:** If they are in trouble, their customers may seek alternatives to buy from, including your company.

✔ **Economic effects from government actions:** Political and governmental actions have economic consequences. As a matter of fact, nothing (and I mean nothing!) has a greater effect on investing and economics than government. Government actions usually manifest themselves as taxes, laws, or regulations. They also can take on a more ominous appearance, such as war or the threat of war. Government can willfully (or even accidentally) cause a company to go bankrupt, disrupt an entire industry, or even cause a depression. It controls the money supply, credit, and all public securities markets. A single government action can have a far-reaching and systemic effect that can have a direct (or indirect) economic impact on your stock investments.

What would happen to the elephant-foot umbrella stand industry if a 50 percent sales tax were passed for that industry? Such a sales tax would certainly make a product uneconomical and would encourage consumers to seek alternatives to elephant-foot umbrella stands. It may even boost sales for the wastepaper basket industry.

The opposite can be true as well. What if a tax credit is passed that encourages the use of solar power in homes and businesses? That would obviously have a positive impact on industries that manufacture or sell solar power devices. Just don't ask me what would happen to solar-powered elephant-foot umbrella stands.

Is the topic of government appropriate in a chapter about economics? Actually, I don't see how you can understand one without being aware of the other. It's like understanding boats without understanding the sea. It's that relevant.

Because most investors ignored some basic observations about economics in the late 1990s, they subsequently lost trillions in their stock portfolios. In the late 1990s, the United States experienced the greatest expansion of debt in history, coupled with a record expansion of the money supply. (Both are controlled by the Federal Reserve, the U.S. government central bank referred to as the Fed.) This growth of debt and money supply resulted in more consumer (and corporate) borrowing, spending, and investing. This activity hyperstimulated the stock market and caused stocks to rise 25 percent per year for five straight years.

Of course, you should always be happy to earn 25 percent per year with your investments, but such a return can't be sustained and encourages speculation. This artificial stimulation by the Fed resulted in the following:

- ✔ More and more people depleted their savings. After all, why settle for 3 percent in the bank if you can get 25 percent in the stock market?

- ✔ More and more people bought on credit. If the economy is booming, why not buy now and pay later? Consumer credit hit record highs.

- ✔ More and more people borrowed against their homes. Why not borrow and get rich now? I can pay off my debt later.

- ✔ More and more companies sold more goods as consumers took more vacations and bought SUVs, electronics, and so on. Companies then borrowed to finance expansion, open new stores, and so on.

- ✔ More and more companies went public and offered stock to take advantage of more money that was flowing to the markets from banks and other financial institutions.

In the end, spending started to slow down as consumers and businesses became too indebted. This slowdown in turn caused the sales of goods and services to taper off. However, companies had too much overhead, capacity, and debt as they expanded too eagerly. At this point, companies were caught in a financial bind. Too much debt and too many expenses in a slowing economy mean one thing: Profits shrink or disappear. Companies, to stay in business, had to do the logical thing — cut expenses. What is usually the biggest expense for companies? People! To stay in business, many companies started laying off employees. As a result, consumer spending dropped further as more people were either laid off or had second thoughts about their own job security.

As people had little in the way of savings and too much in the way of debt, they had to sell their stock to pay their bills. This was a major reason that stocks started to fall in 2000. Earnings started to drop because of shrinking sales from a sputtering economy. As earnings fell, stock prices also fell.

The lessons from the 1990s are important ones for investors today:

- ✔ Stocks are not a replacement for savings accounts. Always have some money in the bank.

- ✔ Stocks should never occupy 100 percent of your investment funds.

- ✔ When anyone (including experts) tells you that the economy will keep growing indefinitely, be skeptical and read diverse sources of information.

- ✔ If stocks do well in your portfolio, consider protecting your stocks (both your original investment and any gains) with stop-loss orders. (See Chapter 16 for more on these strategies.)

- ✔ Keep debt and expenses to a minimum.

- ✔ Remember that if the economy is booming, a decline is sure to follow as the ebb and flow of the economy's business cycle continues.

Know thyself

If you're reading this book, you're probably doing so because you want to become a successful investor. Granted, to be a successful investor, you have to select great stocks, but having a realistic understanding of your own financial situation and goals is equally important. I recall one investor who lost $10,000 in a speculative stock. The loss wasn't that bad because he had most of his money safely tucked away elsewhere. He also understood that his overall financial situation was secure and that the money he lost was "play" money whose loss wouldn't have a drastic effect on his life. But many investors often lose even more money, and the loss does have a major, negative effect on their lives. You may not be like the investor who could afford to lose $10,000. Take time to understand yourself, your own financial picture, and your personal investment goals before you decide to buy stocks.

Staying on Top of Financial News

Reading the financial news can help you decide where or where not to invest. Many newspapers, magazines, and Web sites offer great coverage of the financial world. Obviously, the more informed you are, the better, but you don't have to read everything that's written. The information explosion in recent years has gone beyond overload, and you could easily spend so much time reading that you have little time left for investing.

The most obvious publications of interest to stock investors are *The Wall Street Journal* and *Investor's Business Daily.* These excellent publications report the news and stock data as of the day before. Some of the more obvious Web sites are CBS's MarketWatch (`www.marketwatch.com`) and Bloomberg (`www.bloomberg.com`). These Web sites can actually give you news and stock data within 15 to 20 minutes of when an event occurs.

Appendix A at the back of this book provides more information on these resources along with a treasure trove of some of the best publications, resources, and Web sites to assist you.

The following sections suggest some topics that stock investors should be on the lookout for when considering the purchase of individual stocks.

Figuring out what a company's up to

Before you invest, you need to know what's going on with a company. When you read about a company, either from the company's literature (its annual report, for example) or from media sources, be sure to get answers to some pertinent questions:

- ✔ **Is the company making more net income than the prior year?** You want to invest in a company that is growing.

- ✔ **Are the company's sales greater than the year before?** Remember, you won't make money if the company isn't making money.

- ✔ **Is the company issuing press releases on new products, services, inventions, or business deals?** All of these achievements indicate a strong, vital company.

Knowing how the company is doing, no matter what is happening with the general economy, is obviously important. To better understand how companies tick, see Chapter 11.

Discovering what's new with an industry

As you consider investing in a stock, make it a point to know what's going on in that company's industry. If the industry is doing well, your stock will likely do well, too. But then again, the reverse is also true.

Yes, I have seen investors pick successful stocks in a failing industry, but those are exceptional cases. By and large, succeeding with a stock is easier when the entire industry is doing well. As you're watching the news, reading the financial pages, or viewing financial Web sites, check out the industry to see that it's strong and dynamic. See Chapter 12 for information on analyzing industries.

Knowing what's happening with the economy

No matter how well or how poorly the overall economy is performing, you should stay informed about its general progress. It's easier for the value of stock to keep going up when the economy is stable or growing. The reverse is also true; if the economy is contracting or declining, the stock will have a tougher time keeping its value. Some basic items you should keep tabs on include the following:

- ✔ **Gross domestic product (GDP):** This is roughly the total value of output for a particular nation measured in the dollar amount of goods and services. GDP is reported quarterly, and a rising GDP bodes well for your stock. When the GDP is rising 3 percent or more on an annual basis, that is solid growth. If it rises at faster than zero or less than 3 percent, that is generally considered less than stellar (or mediocre). GDP under zero (or negative) means that the economy is shrinking. As a general rule, two consecutive quarters of negative growth indicate a recession. Persistent shrinkage in the economy indicates a depression.

✔ **The index of leading economic indicators (LEI):** The LEI is a snapshot of a set of economic statistics covering activity that precedes what's happening in the economy. Each statistic helps you understand the economy in much the same way that barometers (and windows!) help you understand what's happening with the weather. Economists don't just look at an individual statistic; they look at a set of statistics to get a more complete picture of what's happening with the economy. Certain indicators lead the economy, some coincide with the economy, and others lag behind the economy.

Housing starts (the number of houses that have been contracted to be built), for example, is a leading economic indicator. If more houses are being built, other sectors, such as building supplies and home services, get more business. Because stock investors usually look to the future, any clues about the general direction of the economy are valuable as a guide to the public's investment decision-making process. Chapter 13 goes into greater detail on ways the economy affects stock prices.

Seeing what the politicians and government bureaucrats are doing

Being informed about what public officials are doing is vital to your success as a stock investor. Because literally thousands of laws are passed every year by federal, state, and local governments, monitoring the political landscape is critical to your success. The news media reports what the president and Congress are doing, so always ask yourself, " How will this new law or event affect my stock investment?"

When taxes are increased or decreased, some people and organizations benefit, and others don't. When laws and regulations get passed, usually someone wins, and someone loses. Ask yourself constantly, "In this particular situation, who will win, and who will lose? Will the company I bought stock in win or lose?" Be aware of ways that the political environment can affect the value of your stocks.

Rarely do changes in taxes, laws, and regulations affect merely one company. Usually, an entire industry or the entire economy feels the effects of change. So if a company that you're considering investing in appears to be affected by a new law or regulation, you can probably assume that the company's stock will also be affected.

Wassup! Checking for trends in society, culture, and entertainment

As odd as it sounds, trends in society, popular culture, and entertainment affect your investments, directly or indirectly. For example, headlines such as "The graying of America — more people than ever before will be senior citizens" give you some important information that can make or break your stock portfolio. With that particular headline, you know that as more and more people age, companies that are well positioned to cater to this growing market's wants and needs will mean a successful stock for you.

Keep your eyes open to emerging trends in society at large. What trends are evident now? What wants and needs can be anticipated for tomorrow's society? Being alert, staying a step ahead of the public, and choosing stock appropriately gives you a profitable edge over other investors. If you own stock in a solid company with growing sales and earnings, other investors will eventually notice. As more investors buy up your company's stocks, you will be rewarded as the stock price increases.

Reading (And Understanding) Stock Tables

The stock tables in major business publications, such as *The Wall Street Journal* and *Investor's Business Daily,* are loaded with information that can help you become a savvy investor — *if* you know how to interpret them. You need the information in the stock tables for more than selecting promising investment opportunities. You also need to consult the tables after you invest to monitor how your stocks are doing. If you bought HokySmoky common stock last year at $12 per share and you want to know what it's worth today, check out the stock tables.

If you look at the stock tables without knowing what or why you're looking, it's the equivalent of reading *War and Peace* backwards through a kaleidoscope. Nothing makes sense. But I can help you make sense of it all (well, at least the stock tables!). Table 6-1 shows a sample stock table for you to refer to as you read the sections that follow.

Table 6-1		Deciphering Stock Tables						
52-Wk High	52-Wk Low	Name (Symbol)	Div	Vol	Yld	P/E	Day Last	Net Chg
21.50	8.00	SkyHighCorp (SHC)	3143	76	21.25	+.25		

52-Wk High	52-Wk Low	Name (Symbol)	Div	Vol	Yld	P/E	Day Last	Net Chg
47.00	31/75	LowDownInc (LDI)	2.35	2735	5.7	18	41.00	-.50
25.00	21.00	ValueNow Inc (VNI)	1.00	1894	4.5	12	22.00	+.10
83.00	33.00	DoinBadlyCorp (DBC)		7601			33.50	-.75

Every newspaper's financial tables are a little different, but they give you basically the same information. Updated daily, this section is not the place to start your search for a good stock; this is usually where it ends. The stock tables are the place to look when you already know what you want to buy and you're just checking to see the most recent price or when you already own it and you want to check the latest stock price.

Each item gives you some clues about the current state of affairs for that particular company. The sections that follow describe each column to help you understand what you're looking at.

52-week high

The column labeled "52-Wk High" (refer to Table 6-1) gives you the highest price that particular stock has reached in the most recent 52-week period. The value in knowing this is so that you can gauge where the stock is now versus where it has been recently. SkyHighCorp's (SHC) stock has been as high as $21.50, while its last (most recent) price was $21.25, the number listed in the "Day Last" column. (Flip down to the "Day Last" section for more on understanding this information.) SkyHighCorp's stock is trading very high right now because it's hovering right near its overall 52-week-high figure.

Now, take a look at the DoinBadlyCorp's (DBC) stock price. It seems to have tumbled big time. Its stock price has had a high in the past 52 weeks of $83, but it's currently trading at $33.50. Something just doesn't seem right here. During the past 52 weeks, DBC's stock price fell dramatically. If you're thinking about investing in DBC, find out why the stock price fell. If the company is a strong company, it may be a good opportunity to buy it at a lower stock price. If the company is having tough times, avoid it. In any case, research the company and find out why its stock has declined.

52-week low

The column labeled "52-Wk Low" gives you what has been the lowest price that particular stock has reached in the most recent 52-week period. Again, this information is crucial to your ability to analyze stock over a period of time. Looking at DBC back in Table 6-1, you can see that its current trading price of $33.50 is right about where its 52-week low is. So far, DBC doesn't look like a real catch right now.

Keep in mind that the high and the low prices just give you a range for how far has that particular stock's price has moved within the past 52 weeks. They could alert you that a stock has problems, or they could tell you that a stock's price has fallen enough to make it a bargain. Simply reading the 52-wk high and 52-wk low columns isn't enough to determine which of those two things is happening. They basically tell you to get more information before you commit your money.

Name and symbol

This is the simplest column. It tells you the company name (usually abbreviated) and the stock symbol assigned to the company. Once you have your eye on a stock for potential purchase, get familiar with its symbol. Knowing the symbol makes it easier for you to find it in the financial tables, which list stocks in alphabetical order by symbol. Stock symbols are the language of stock investing, and you need to use them in all stock communications, from getting a stock quote at your broker's office to buying stock over the Internet.

Dividend

Dividends (shown under the "Div" column in Table 6-1) are basically payments to owners (stockholders). If a company pays a dividend, it's shown in the dividend column. The amount you see is the annual dividend quoted as if you owned one share of that stock. If you look at LowDownInc (LDI) in Table 6-1, you can see that you would get $2.35 as an annual dividend for each share of stock that you own. The dividend is usually paid in quarterly amounts. If I own 100 shares of LDI, the company would pay me a quarterly dividend of $58.75 ($235 total per year). A healthy company strives to maintain or upgrade the dividend for stockholders from year to year. In any case, the dividend is very important to investors seeking income from their stock investment. For more about investing for income, see Chapter 9. Companies that don't pay dividends are bought by investors primarily for growth. For more information on growth stocks, see Chapter 8.

Volume

Normally, when you hear the word *volume* on the news, it refers to how much stock is bought and sold for the entire market. ("Well, stocks were very active today. Trading volume at the New York Stock Exchange hit 2 billion shares.") Volume is certainly important to watch because the stocks that you're investing in are somewhere in that activity. For our purposes here, though, the volume (the "Vol" column in Table 6-1) refers to the individual stock.

Volume tells you how many shares of that particular stock were traded that day. If only 100 shares are traded in a day, then the trading volume is 100. SHC had 3,143 shares change hands on the trading day represented in Table 6-1. Is that good or bad? Neither, really. Usually volume for a particular stock is mentioned in the business news media when it is unusually large. If a stock normally has volume in the 5,000 to 10,000 range and all of a sudden has a trading volume of 87,000, then it's time to sit up and take notice.

Keep in mind that a low trading volume for one stock may be high trading volume for another stock. You can't necessarily compare one stock's volume against that of any other company. The large cap stocks like IBM or Microsoft typically have trading volumes in the millions of shares almost every day, while less active, smaller stocks may have average trading volumes in far, far smaller numbers.

The main point to remember is that trading volume that is far in excess of that stock's normal range is a sign that something is going on with that stock. It may be negative or positive, but something newsworthy is happening with that company. If the news is positive, the increased volume is a result of more people buying the stock. If the news is negative, the increased volume is probably a result of more people selling the stock. What are typical events that cause increased trading volume? Some positive reasons include the following:

- ✔ **Good earnings reports:** A company announces good (or better-than-expected) earnings.

- ✔ **A new business deal:** A company announces a favorable business deal, such as a joint venture, or lands a big client.

- ✔ **A new product or service:** A company's research and development department creates a potentially profitable new product.

- ✔ **Indirect benefits:** A company may benefit from a new development in the economy or from a new law passed by Congress.

Some negative reasons for an unusually large fluctuation in trading volume for a particular stock may include the following:

- ✔ **Bad earnings reports:** Profit is the lifeblood of a company. If a company's profits fall or disappear, you'll see more volume.

✔ **Governmental problems:** The stock is being targeted by government action (such as a lawsuit or SEC probe).

✔ **Liability issues:** The media report that a company has a defective product or similar problem.

✔ **Financial problems:** Independent analysts report that a company's financial health is deteriorating.

The bottom line is to check out what's happening when you hear about heavier than usual volume (especially if you already own the stock).

Yield

In general, yield is a return on the money you invest. However, in the stock tables, *yield* ("Yld" in Table 6-1) is a reference to what percentage that particular dividend is to the stock price. Yield is most important to income investors. It is calculated by dividing the annual dividend by the current stock price. In Table 6-1, you can see that the yield du jour of ValueNowInc. (VNI) is 4.5 percent (a dividend of $1 divided by the company's stock price of $22). Notice that many companies have no yield reported; because they have no dividends, yield cannot be calculated.

Keep in mind that the yield reported in the financial pages changes daily as the stock price changes. Yield is always reported as if you're buying the stock that day. If you bought VNI on the day represented in Table 6-1, your yield would be 4.5 percent. But what if VNI's stock price rose to $30 the following day? Investors who bought stock at $30 per share would obtain a yield of just 3.3 percent. (The dividend of $1 would then be divided by the new stock price, $30.) Of course, because you bought the stock at $22, you essentially locked in the prior yield of 4.5 percent. Lucky you. Pat yourself on the back.

P/E

The P/E ratio indicates the ratio between the price of the stock and the company's earnings. P/E ratios are widely followed and important barometers of value in the world of stock investing. The P/E ratio (also called the "earnings multiple" or just "multiple") is frequently used to determine whether a stock is expensive (a good value). Value investors (such as yours truly) find P/E ratios to be essential to analyzing a stock as a potential investment. As a general rule, the P/E should preferably be 10 to 20 for large cap or income stocks. For growth stocks, a P/E no greater than 30 to 40 is preferable.

In the P/E ratios reported in stock tables, *price* refers to the cost of a single share of stock. *Earnings* refers to the company's reported earnings as of the most recent four quarters. The P/E ratio is the price divided by the earnings.

In Table 6-1, VNI has a reported P/E of 12, which is considered a low P/E. Notice how SHC has a relatively high P/E (76). This stock is considered too pricey, as you're paying a price equivalent to 76 times earnings. Also notice that the stock DBC has no available P/E ratio. Usually this lack of a P/E ratio indicates that the company reported a loss in the most recent four quarters.

Day last

The "day last" column tells you how trading ended for a particular stock on the day represented by the table. In the stock table in Table 6-1 earlier in this chapter, the stock LDC ended the most recent day of trading at 41. Some newspapers report the high and low for that day in addition to the stock's ending price for the day.

Net change

The information in the net change column ("Net Chg" back in Table 6-1) answers the question "How did the stock price end today compared with its trading price at the end of the prior trading day?" Table 6-1 shows that SHC stock ended the trading day up 25 cents (at $21.25). This tells you that SHC ended the prior day at $21. On a day when VNI ends the day at $22 (up 10 cents), you can tell that the prior day it ended the trading day at $21.90. You get the picture.

Understanding Dividend News

Reading and understanding the news about dividends is essential if you're an *income investor* (someone who invests in stocks as a means of generating regular income).

Looking at important dates

In order to understand how buying stocks that pay dividends can benefit you as an investor, you need to know how dividends are reported and paid. Some important dates in the life of a dividend are as follows:

  ✔ **Date of declaration:** This is the date when a company reports a quarterly dividend and the subsequent payment dates. On January 15, for example, a company may report that it "is pleased to announce a quarterly dividend of 50 cents per share to shareholders of record as of February 10." That was easy. The date of declaration is really just the announcement. If you buy the stock before or after the date of declaration, it won't matter in regard to the stock. The date that matters is the date of record (see the relevant bullet later in this list).

✔ **Date of execution:** This is the day you actually initiate the stock transaction (buying or selling). If you call up a broker (or contact her online) today to buy a particular stock, then today is the date of execution, or the date on which you execute the trade. You don't own the stock on the date of execution; it is just the day you put in the order. For an example, skip down to the section "Why these dates matter," later in this chapter.

✔ **Closing date (settlement date):** The closing or settlement date is the date on which the trade is finalized, which usually happens three business days after the date of execution. The closing date for stock is similar in concept to a real estate closing. The closing date is the official date on which you are the proud new owner (or happy seller) of the stock.

✔ **Date of record:** The date of record is used to identify which stockholders will qualify to receive the dividend that was declared. Because stock is bought and sold every day, how does the company know which investors to pay? The company establishes a cut-off date by declaring a date of record. All investors who are official stockholders on the declared date of record will receive the dividend paid on the payment date regardless of whether or not they plan to sell the stock any time between the date of declaration and the date of record.

✔ **Ex-dividend date:** *Ex-dividend* means *without dividend.* Because it takes three days to process a stock purchase before you become an official owner of stock, you have to qualify (that is, you have to own or buy the stock) *before* the three-day period. That three-day period is referred to as the "ex-dividend period." If you buy stock during this short time frame, you won't be on the books of record, because the closing (or settlement) date falls after the date of record. See the next section, "Why these dates matter," to see the effect that the ex-dividend date can have on an investor.

✔ **Payment date:** The date on which a company issues and mails its dividend checks to shareholders. Finally!

For typical dividends, the events in Table 6-2 happen four times per year.

Table 6-2	The Life of the Quarterly Dividend	
Event	*Sample Date*	*Comments*
Date of declaration	January 15	The date that the quarterly dividend is declared by the company
Ex-dividend date	February 7	Starts the three-day period during which, if you buy the stock, you don't qualify for the dividend

Event	Sample Date	Comments
Record date	February 10	The date by which you must be on the books of record to qualify for the dividend
Payment date	February 27	The date that payment is made (a dividend check is issued and mailed to stockholders who were on the books of record as of February 10)

Why these dates matter

Remember that there are three business days between the date of execution and the closing date. There are also three business days between the ex-dividend date and the date of record. This information is important to know if you want to qualify to receive an upcoming dividend. Timing is important, and the following example is the best way to explain it.

Say that you want to buy Value Now, Inc. (VNI) in time to qualify for the quarterly dividend of 25 cents per share. Assume that the date of record (the date by which you have to be an official owner of the stock) is February 10. You have to execute the trade (buy the stock) no later than February 7 to be assured of the dividend. If you execute the trade right on February 7, the closing date would occur three days later, on February 10 — just in time for the date of record.

But what if you execute the trade on February 8, a day later? Well, the trade's closing date would be February 11, which would occur *after* the date of record. Because you wouldn't be on the books as an official stockholder on the date of record, you wouldn't get that quarterly dividend. In this example, the February 7–10 period is called the *ex-dividend period*.

Fortunately, for those people who buy the stock during this brief ex-dividend period, the stock actually trades at a slighter lower price to reflect the amount of the dividend. So the money you save by buying the stock during the ex-dividend period helps to make up for the money you miss out on by not buying the stock in time to qualify for the dividend payment. How's that for a silver lining?

Evaluating (Avoiding?) Investment Tips

Psssst. Have I got a stock tip for you! Come closer. You know what it is? Research! What I'm trying to tell you is that you should never automatically invest just because you get a hot tip from someone. Good investment selection means looking at several sources before you decide on a stock. There's no shortcut. That said, getting opinions from others never hurts — just be sure to carefully analyze the information you get. The following sections present some important points to bear in mind as you evaluate tips and advice from others.

Consider the source

Frequently, people buy stock based on the views of some market strategist or market analyst. People may see an analyst being interviewed on a television financial show and take that person's opinions and advice as valid and good. The danger here is that the analyst could easily be biased because of some relationship that isn't disclosed on the show.

It happens on TV all too often. The show's host interviews Analyst U.R. Kiddingme from the investment firm Foollum & Sellum. The analyst says, "Implosion Corp. is a good buy with solid, long-term, upside potential." You later find out that the analyst's employer gets investment banking fees from Implosion Corp. Do you really think that analyst would ever issue a negative report on a company that's helping to pay the bills? It's not likely. Being suspicious can keep you from being a sucker.

Get multiple views

One source isn't enough to base your investment decisions on unless you have the best reasons in the world for thinking that a particular, single source is outstanding and extremely accurate and prescient. A better approach is to scour current issues of independent financial publications, such as *Barron's, Money Magazine, SmartMoney,* and other publications listed in Appendix A. Search the Internet for information, too. Appendix A lists lots of informative Web sites for you to check out.

Gather data from the SEC

When you want to get objective information about a company, why not take a look at the reports that companies must file with the Securities and Exchange Commission (SEC)? These are the same reports that the pundits and financial reporters read. Arguably, the most valuable report you can look at is the 10K. The 10K is a report that all publicly traded companies must file with the SEC. It provides valuable information on the company's operations and financial data, and it's likely to be less biased than the information a company includes in other corporate reports, such as an annual report.

To access 10K reports, go to the SEC's Web site (www.sec.gov). From there, you can find the SEC's extensive database of public filings called EDGAR (Electronic Data Gathering, Analysis, and Retrieval system). By searching EDGAR, you can find companies' balance sheets, income statements, and other related information so that you can verify what others say and get a fuller picture of what a company is doing and its financial condition. All this information will help you make better investment decisions.

Chapter 7

Going for Brokers

*W*hen you're ready to dive in and start investing in stocks, you first have to choose a broker. It's kind of like buying a car: You can do all the research in the world and know exactly what kind of car you want to buy; still, you have to buy it through a car dealer. Similarly, when you want to buy stock, your task is to do all the research you can to select the company you want to invest in. Still, you need a broker to actually buy the stock, whether you buy in person or online. In this chapter, I set out to introduce you to the intricacies of the investor/broker relationship.

For information on various types of orders you can place with a broker, such as market orders, stop-loss orders, and so on, flip to Chapter 16.

Defining the Broker's Role

The broker is the intermediary between you and the world of stock investing. The broker's primary role is to serve as the vehicle through which you either buy or sell stock. When I talk about brokers, I'm referring to organizations such as Charles Schwab, Merrill Lynch, E*TRADE, and many other organizations that can buy stock on your behalf. Brokers can also be individuals who work for such firms. Although you can buy some stocks directly from the company that issues them (I discuss direct purchase plans in Chapter 17), to purchase most stocks, you still need a broker.

Although the primary task of brokers is the buying and selling of stocks, they can perform other tasks for you, including the following:

- ✔ **Providing advisory services:** Investors pay brokers a fee for investment advice.

- ✔ **Offering limited banking services:** Brokers can offer features such as interest-bearing accounts and check writing.

- ✔ **Brokering other securities:** Brokers can also buy bonds, mutual funds, and other investments on your behalf. Keep in mind that the word *securities* refers to the world of financial (or paper) investments and that stocks are only a small part of that world.

Personal stockbrokers make their money from individual investors like you and me through various fees, including the following:

- ✔ **Brokerage commissions:** This is a fee for buying and/or selling stocks and other securities.

- ✔ **Margin interest charges:** This is interest charged to investors for borrowing against their brokerage account for investment purposes.

- ✔ **Service charges:** These are charges for performing administrative tasks and other functions. Brokers charge fees to investors for Individual Retirement Accounts (IRA's) and for mailing stocks in certificate form.

Any broker you deal with should be registered with the National Association of Securities Dealers (NASD) and the Securities and Exchange Commission (SEC). In addition, to protect your money after you've deposited it into a brokerage account, that broker should be a member of Securities Investor Protection Corporation (SIPC). SIPC doesn't protect you from market losses; it protects your money in case the brokerage firm goes out of business. To find out whether the broker is registered with these organizations, contact the NASD, SEC, and SIPC. (See Appendix A for information on these three organizations.)

There is a distinction between personal stockbrokers and institutional stockbrokers. Institutional brokers make money from institutions and companies through investment banking and securities placement fees (such as initial public offerings and secondary offerings), advisory services, and other broker services. Personal stockbrokers generally offer the same services to individuals and small businesses.

Distinguishing between Full-Service and Discount Brokers

There are two basic categories of stockbrokers: full-service and discount. The type you choose really depends on what type of investor you are. In a nutshell, full-service brokers are suitable for investors who need some guidance, while discount brokers are better for those who are sufficiently confident and knowledgeable about stock investing to manage with minimal help.

Full-service brokers

Full-service brokers are just what the name indicates. They try to provide as many services as possible for investors who open accounts with them. When you open an account at a brokerage firm, a representative is assigned to your account. This representative is usually called an *account executive,* a *registered rep,* or a *financial consultant* by the brokerage firm. This person usually has a securities license and is knowledgeable about stocks in particular and investing in general.

What they can do for you

Your account executive is responsible for assisting you, answering questions about your account and the securities in your portfolio, and transacting your buy and sell orders. Here are some things that full-service brokers can do for you:

- ✔ **Offer guidance and advice.** The greatest distinction between full-service brokers and discount brokers is the personal attention you receive from your account rep. You get to be on a first-name basis, and you disclose much information about your finances and financial goals. The rep is there to make recommendations about stocks and funds that are hopefully suitable for you.

- ✔ **Provide access to research.** Full-service brokers can give you access to their investment research department, which can give you in-depth information and analysis on a particular company. This information can be very valuable, but be aware of the pitfalls. (See the section "Judging Brokers' Recommendations," later in this chapter.)

- ✔ **Help you achieve your investment objectives.** Beyond advice on specific investments, a good rep gets to know you and your investment goals and *then* offers advice and answers your questions about how specific investments and strategies can help you accomplish your wealth-building goals.

- ✔ **Make investment decisions on your behalf.** Many investors don't want to be bothered when it comes to investment decisions. Full-service brokers can actually make decisions for your account with your authorization. This service is fine, but be sure to require them to explain their choices to you.

What to watch out for

Although the full-service brokers, with their seemingly limitless assistance, can make life easy for an investor, you need to remember some important points to avoid problems:

- ✔ Brokers and account reps are still salespeople. No matter how well they treat you, they're still compensated based on their ability to produce revenue for the brokerage firm. They generate commissions and fees from you on behalf of the company. (In other words, they're paid to sell you things.)

✔ Whenever your rep makes a suggestion or recommendation, be sure to ask why and request a complete answer that includes the reasoning behind the recommendation. A good advisor should be able to clearly explain the reasoning behind every suggestion. If you don't fully understand and agree with the advice, don't take it.

✔ Know that working with a full-service broker costs a bit more than a discount broker. Discount brokers are paid simply for performing the act of buying or selling stocks for you. Full-service brokers do that and more. Additionally, they provide advice and guidance. Because of that, full-service brokers are more expensive (through higher brokerage commissions and advisory fees). Also, most full-service brokers expect you to invest at least $5,000 to $10,000 just to open an account.

✔ Handing over decision-making authority to your rep can be a possible negative because letting others make financial decisions for you is always dicey — especially when they're using *your* money. If they make poor investment choices that lose you money, you may not have any recourse, because you authorized them to act on your behalf.

✔ Some brokers engage in an activity called churning. *Churning* is basically buying and selling stocks for the sole purpose of generating commissions. Churning is great for brokers but bad for customers. Sometimes a broker may do a lot of trading in the account. The account may show little in terms of investment success but cost you dearly in commissions. Churning generates a lot of activity for the primary purpose of making more money for the broker (not for you!).

Before you deal with any broker, full-service or otherwise, get a free report on the broker from the National Association of Securities Dealers by calling 800-289-9999 or visiting the NASD Regulation Web site at www.nasdr.com. The report can indicate whether any complaints or penalties have been filed against that brokerage firm or the individual rep.

Examples of full-service brokers are Merrill Lynch and Morgan Stanley. Of course, all brokers now have full-featured Web sites to give you further information about their services. Get as informed as possible before you open your account. A full-service broker should be there to help you build wealth, not make you . . . uh . . . broker.

Discount brokers

Perhaps you don't need any hand-holding from a broker. You know what you want, and you can make your own investment decisions. All you want is someone to transact your buy/sell orders. In that case, go with a discount broker. Discount brokers, as the name implies, are cheaper to engage than full-service brokers. They don't offer advice or premium services, though — just the basics required to perform your stock transactions.

If you choose to work with a discount broker, you must know as much as possible about your personal goals and needs. You have a greater responsibility for conducting adequate research to make good stock selections, and you must be prepared to accept the outcome, whatever that may be. Because you're advising yourself, you can save on costs that you would have incurred had you paid for a full-service broker.

For the regular investor, there are two types of discount brokers: conventional discount brokers and Internet discount brokers. Conventional discount brokers (such as Charles Schwab and Waterhouse) have national offices that you walk into and speak to the customer service staff face-to-face. You can transact in person, over the phone, or through the Internet. Internet discount brokerage firms have essentially the same services except for the walk-in offices and face-to-face communication. Examples of Internet brokerage firms are E*TRADE.com and Ameritrade.com.

What they can do for you

Both conventional and Internet-based discount brokers share many of the same primary advantages over full-service brokers, including the following:

- **Lower cost:** This lower cost is usually the result of lower commissions.

- **Unbiased service:** Because discount brokers offer you the ability to transact your buys and sells only without advice, they have no vested interest in trying to sell you any particular stock.

- **Access to information:** Established discount brokers offer extensive educational materials at their offices or on their Web sites.

What to watch out for

Of course, doing business with discount brokers also has its downside:

- **No guidance:** Because you've chosen a discount broker, you *know* not to expect guidance, but the broker should make this clear to you anyway. If you're a knowledgeable investor, the lack of advice is considered a positive thing — no interference.

- **Hidden fees:** Discount brokers may shout about their lower commissions, but commissions aren't their only way of making money. Many discount brokers charge extra for services that you may think are included, such as issuing a stock certificate or mailing a statement. Ask whether they assess fees for maintaining IRA's or fees for transferring stocks and other securities (such as bonds) in or out of your account, and find out what interest rates they charge for borrowing through brokerage accounts.

> ✔ **Minimal customer service:** If you deal with an Internet brokerage firm, find out about its customer service capability. If you can't transact business at its Web site, find out where you can call for assistance with your order.

Choosing a Broker

Before you choose a broker, you need to analyze your personal investing style first. Once you know yourself and the way you invest, then you can proceed to finding the kind of broker that fits your needs. It's almost like choosing shoes; if you don't know your size, you can't get a proper fit. (And you can be in for a really uncomfortable future.)

Consider two knowledgeable, confident investors named Bob and Ed. Both men are competent investors, so they choose discount brokers — makes sense. Bob likes to trade stocks very frequently. Ed is a buy-and-hold type, but he likes to use margin. *Trading on margin* means using the stocks and other securities in your brokerage account as collateral to purchase more stock. (See Chapter 16 for more on margin.) Which discount brokers are suitable for which investors?

Say that you have two discount brokers named JumpCo and StayCo. JumpCo charges $9 per trade, while StayCo charges $25. However, when it comes to margin trading, JumpCo charges 10 percent, while StayCo usually charges a full percentage point lower.

In this example, JumpCo is better suited to Bob's style of investing, while StayCo is better for Ed. Because Bob likes to trade frequently, the commission charge makes it more economical. Ed will pay a higher commission, but he'll eventually make his money back through lower margin interest costs.

This example clearly illustrates how different investors can benefit by analyzing themselves and then choosing an appropriate broker. When it's time to choose a broker, keep the following points in mind:

> ✔ Match your investment style with a brokerage firm that charges the least amount of money for the services you're likely to use most frequently.

> ✔ Compare all the costs of buying, selling, and holding stocks and other securities through a broker. Don't compare only commissions. Compare other costs, too, such as margin interest and other service charges.

> ✔ Use broker comparison services such as Gomez Advisors at www.gomez.com and read articles that compare brokers in publications such as *SmartMoney* and *Barron's*. Check out Appendix A for a list of sources that compare brokers.

Finding brokers is easy. They're listed in the Yellow Pages as well as in many investment publications and on financial Web sites. Start your search by using the sources in Appendix A, which includes a list of the major brokerage firms.

Discovering Various Types of Brokerage Accounts

When you decide to start investing in the stock market, you have to somehow actually *pay* for the stocks you buy. Most brokerage firms offer investors several different types of accounts, each serving a different purpose. I present three of the most common types in the following sections. The basic difference boils down to how particular brokers view your "creditworthiness" when it comes to buying and selling securities. If your credit isn't great, your only choice is a cash account. If your credit is good, you can open either a cash account or a margin account.

To open an account, you'll have to fill out an application and submit a check or money order for the minimum amount required to establish an account.

Cash accounts

A *cash account* (also referred to as a *Type 1* account) is just what you think it means. You must deposit a sum of money with the new account application to begin trading. The amount of your initial deposit varies from broker to broker. Some brokers have a minimum of $10,000, while others will let you open an account for as little as $500. Use the resources in Appendix A to help you shop around.

With a cash account, your money has to be deposited in the account before the closing (or "settlement") date for any trade you make. The closing occurs three business days after the date you make the trade (date of execution).

In other words, if you call your broker on Monday, October 10, and order 50 shares of CashLess Corp. at $20 per share, then on Thursday, October 13, you better have $1,000 in cash sitting in your account (plus commission). Otherwise, the trade will not happen.

If you have cash in a brokerage account (remember, all accounts are brokerage accounts, and "cash" and "margin" are simply types of brokerage accounts), see whether the broker will pay you interest on it and how much. Some offer a service in which uninvested money earns money market rates.

Margin accounts

A *margin account* (also called a *Type 2* account) gives you the ability to borrow money against the securities in the account to buy more stock. Once you're approved, your brokerage firm gives you credit. A margin account has all the benefits of a cash account plus this ability of buying on margin (which you can read more about in Chapter 16). A margin account is also necessary if you plan on doing short selling. I cover short selling in Chapter 16, too.

For stock trading, the margin limit is 50 percent. In other words, if you plan to buy $10,000 worth of stock on margin, you need at least $5,000 in cash (or securities owned) sitting in your account. The interest rate that you pay varies depending on the broker, but most brokers generally charge a rate that is several points higher than their own borrowing rate.

Why use margin? Margin is to stocks what mortgage is to buying real estate. You can buy real estate with all cash, but many times, using borrowed funds makes sense.

Option accounts

An *option account* (also referred to as a *Type 3* account) gives you all the capabilities of a margin account (which in turn also gives you the capabilities of a cash account) plus the ability to trade stock and index options. To open an options account, the broker usually asks you to sign a statement that you are knowledgeable about options and are familiar with the risks associated with them.

Although options can be an effective addition to a stock investor's array of investing tools, the topic goes beyond the scope of this book. For more information, check out *Stock Options For Dummies* by Alan R. Simon (Hungry Minds, Inc.).

Judging Brokers' Recommendations

In recent years, Americans have become enamored with a new sport: the rating of stocks by brokers on the TV financial shows. Frequently these shows feature a dapper market strategist talking up a particular stock. Some stocks have been known to jump significantly right after an influential analyst issues a buy recommendation. Analysts' speculation and opinions make for great fun, and many people take their views very seriously. However, most investors should be very wary when analysts, especially the glib ones on TV, make a recommendation. It's often just showbiz.

Brokers issue their recommendations (advice) as a general idea of how much regard they have for a particular stock. The following list presents the basic recommendations (or ratings) and what they mean to you:

- ✔ *Strong buy* **and** *buy:* Hot diggity dog! This is the one to get. The analyst loves this pick, and you would be very wise to get a bunch of shares. The thing to keep in mind, however, is that *buy* recommendations are about as common as snow in Alaska.

- ✔ *Accumulate* **and** *market perform:* An analyst who issues these types of recommendations is positive, yet unexcited, about the pick. This is akin to asking a friend if he likes your new suit and getting the one-word response "nice" in a monotone voice. It's a polite reply, but you wish the opinion had been more enthusiastic.

- ✔ *Hold* **or** *neutral:* Analysts use this language when their back is to the wall but they still won't say, "Sell that loser!" This is like when your mother told you to be nice and either say something positive or keep your mouth shut. In this case, this is the analyst's way of keeping his mouth shut.

- ✔ *Sell:* Many analysts should have issued this recommendation during 2000 and 2001, but few actually uttered it. What a shame. So many investors lost money because some analysts were either too nice or just afraid to be honest and sound the alarm and urge people to sell.

- ✔ *Avoid like the plague:* I'm just kidding about this one, but I wish that this recommendation were available. I've seen plenty of stocks that I thought were dreadful investments — stocks of companies that made no money and were in terrible financial condition that should never have been considered at all. Yet investors gobbled up billions of dollars' worth of stocks that eventually became worthless.

Don't get me wrong. An analyst's recommendation is certainly a better tip than what you'd get from your barber or your sister-in-law's neighbor, but you should view them with a healthy dose of reality. Analysts have biases because their employment depends on the very companies that are being presented. What investors should listen to when a broker talks up a stock is the reasoning behind the recommendation. In other words, why is the broker making this recommendation?

Keep in mind that analysts' recommendations can play a useful role in your personal stock investing research. If you find a great stock and *then* you hear analysts give glowing reports on the same stock, you're on the right track! Here are some points to keep in mind:

- ✔ How does the analyst arrive at a rating? The analyst's approach to evaluating a stock can help you round out your research as you consult other sources such as newsletters and independent advisory services.

- ✔ What type of approach does this analyst use? Some use *fundamental analysis* (looking at the company's financial condition and factors related to its success, such as its standing within the industry and the overall market). Other analysts use *technical analysis* (looking at the company's stock price history and judging past stock price movements to derive some insight regarding the stock's future price movement). Many analysts may use a combination of the two. Is this analyst's approach similar to your approach or to those of sources that you respect or admire?

✔ What is the analyst's track record? Has the analyst had a consistently good record through both bull and bear markets? Major financial publications, such as *Barron's* and *Hulbert Financial Digest,* and Web sites, such as MarketWatch.com, regularly track recommendations from well-known analysts and stock pickers.

✔ How does the analyst treat important aspects of the company's performance, such as sales and earnings? How about the company's balance sheet? Industry? The essence of a healthy company is growing sales and earnings coupled with strong assets and low debt.

✔ Is the industry that the company is in doing well? Do the analysts give you insight on this important information? A strong company in a weak industry can't stay strong for long.

✔ What research sources does the analyst cite? Does the analyst quote the federal government or industry trade groups to support her thesis? These sources are important because they help to give a more complete picture regarding the company's prospects for success. Imagine that you decide on the stock of a strong company. But what if the federal government (through agencies such as the SEC) is penalizing the company for fraudulent activity? Or what if the company's industry is shrinking or has ceased to grow (making it tougher for the company to continue growing)? The astute investor looks at a variety of sources before buying stock.

✔ If the analyst cites a target price for the stock ("We think the stock will hit $100 per share within 12 months"), does she present a rational model, such as basing the share price on a projected price/earnings ratio? The analyst must be able to provide a logical scenario about why the stock has a good chance of achieving the cited target price within the time frame mentioned. You may not necessarily agree with the analyst's conclusion, but the explanation should help you decide whether the stock choice was well thought out.

✔ Does the company that is being recommended have any ties to the analyst or the analyst's firm? During 2000 and 2001, the financial industry got bad publicity because many analysts gave positive recommendations on stocks of companies that were doing business with the very firms that employed those analysts. This was probably the biggest reason that analysts were so wrong in their recommendations. Ask your broker to disclose any conflict of interest.

The bottom line with brokerage recommendations is that you shouldn't use them to buy or sell a stock. Instead, use them to confirm your own research. I know that if I buy a stock based on my own research and later discover the same stock being talked up on the financial shows, that will just be the icing on the cake. The experts may be great to listen to, and their recommendations can augment your own opinions; however, they're no substitute for your own careful research.

Chapter 8

Investing for Growth

Growth, actually watching your money grow, is the primary reason that investors choose stocks for their wealth-building portfolio. Keep in mind that growth stocks are a little riskier than average, but their potential for . . . um . . . growth is greater, too. If you're the type of investor who has enough time to let somewhat risky stocks trend upward or enough money so that a loss won't devastate you financially, then growth stocks are definitely for you. The challenge is to figure out which stocks will make you richer quicker.

Short of starting your own business, stock investing is the best way to profit from a business venture. I want to reemphasize that to make money in stocks consistently over the long haul, you must remember that you're investing in a company; buying the stock is just a means for you to participate in the company's success (or failure).

What does it matter that you think of stock investing as buying a *company* versus buying a *stock?* Invest in a stock only if you are just as excited about it as if you were the CEO and in charge of running the company. If you were the sole owner of the company, would you act differently than if you were one of a legion of obscure stockholders? Of course you would. As the owner of the company, you would have a greater interest in the company. You would have a strong desire to know how the enterprise is doing. As you invest in stocks, make believe that you're the owner and take an active interest in the company's products, services, sales, earnings, and so on. This attitude and discipline will enhance your goals as a stock investor. This approach is especially important if your investment goal is growth.

Understanding Growth Stocks

A stock is considered a *growth stock* when it's growing faster and higher than stocks of other companies with similar sales and earnings figures. I say *higher than other companies* because you have to measure growth against something. Usually, you compare the growth of a company with growth from other companies in the same industry or compare it with the stock market in general. In practical terms, when you measure the growth of a stock against the stock market, you're actually comparing it against a generally accepted benchmark, such as the Dow Jones Industrial Average (DJIA) or the Standard & Poor's 500 (S&P 500). For more on DJIA or S&P 500, see Chapter 5.

If a company has earnings growth of 15 percent per year over three years or more and the industry's average growth rate over the same time frame is 10 percent, then this stock qualifies as a growth stock. A growth stock is called that not only because the company is growing but also because the company is performing well with some consistency. Just because your earnings did great versus the S&P 500's average in a single year doesn't cut it. Growth must be consistently accomplished.

Although comparison is a valuable tool for evaluating a stock's potential, you don't want to pick growth stocks on the basis of comparison alone. You should also scrutinize the stock to make sure that it has other things going for it to improve your chance of success. (See the next section, "Tips for Choosing Growth Stocks," for examples.)

I have asked students in my investing classes, "What is Yahoo!?" Usually the answer I get is, "It's a search engine" or "It's a Web site directory." I tell them that Yahoo! is an advertising company. Yes, it does have a great search engine and offers great services for those who visit the Yahoo! Web site. But I label Yahoo! an advertising company because that's how it makes most of its money.

When choosing growth stocks, you should consider investing in a company only *if* it makes a profit and *if* you understand *how* it makes that profit. I know people who invested in Yahoo! because they were excited about the potential of the Internet. During 2000 and 2001, Internet companies were dropping like flies. As Internet companies failed, Yahoo!'s revenue fell, as well, because most of its money came from . . . Internet companies! So even though Yahoo! made money during that bad year, its sales and profits shrank in that time frame, and its stock fell 80 percent!

Unfortunately, many investors who bought Yahoo! stock didn't know *how* Yahoo! made money, so they couldn't have predicted that Yahoo!'s revenues would fall as sharply as they did. You need to know such information so that you can monitor the industry and more accurately predict whether the company you choose to invest in will continue to make money based on the likelihood that its customers, in turn, will be making money. For more on how industry success affects individual stocks, see Chapter 12.

Tips for Choosing Growth Stocks

Although the information in the previous section can help you shrink your stock choices from thousands of stocks to maybe a few dozen or a few hundred (depending on how well the general stock market is doing), the purpose of this section is to help you cull the so-so growth stocks to unearth the go-go ones. It's time to dig deeper for the biggest potential winners. Keep in mind that you probably won't find a stock to satisfy all the criteria presented here. Just make sure that your selection meets as many as realistically possible. But hey, if you do find a stock that meets all the criteria cited, *buy as much as you can!*

Checking out a company's fundamentals

When you hear the word *fundamentals* in the world of stock investing, that refers to the company's financial condition and related data. When investors do *fundamental analysis,* they look at the company's fundamentals — its balance sheet, income statement, cash flow, and other operational data, along with external factors such as the company's market position, industry, and economic prospects. Essentially, the fundamentals should indicate to you that the company is in strong financial condition. It has consistently solid earnings, low debt, and a commanding position in the marketplace. Chapter 10 goes into greater detail about analyzing a company's financial aspects. Here are several reasons to buy stock in companies that are in healthy financial condition:

- **Greater survivability during bad times:** Companies that have good earnings and sales and low debt are in stronger shape than companies that don't (duh!). When flash-in-the-pan growth stocks hit bad times, they wither and die. In 2001, many stocks that were once hot properties beloved by analysts and the talking heads on financial shows ended up filing for bankruptcy (the most obvious example being Enron).

- **Takeover money to build strength:** A strong financial position gives a company the ability to make purchases that can further the company's strength. A purchase can be something as simple as an equipment upgrade or as complex as the acquisition of another company.

- **Marketing opportunities to ensure continued success:** A company's strong finances can help launch new products or pay for new ways of selling existing goods and services.

Deciding whether a company is a good value

You already know that a *growth stock* is the stock of a company that is performing better than its peers in categories such as sales and earnings. *Value stocks* are stocks that are priced lower than the value of the company and its assets. You can identify a value stock by analyzing the company's fundamentals and looking at some key financial ratios, such as the price to earnings ratio. (For more on that topic, see Chapter 10.) If the stock's price is lower than the company's fundamentals indicate it should be (in other words, it's undervalued), then it's a good buy — a bargain — and the stock is considered a great value.

Comparing growth and value stocks

Over the years, a debate has quietly raged in the financial community about growth versus value investing. Some people believe that growth and value are mutually exclusive. They maintain that large numbers of people buying stock with growth as the expectation tend to drive up the stock price relative to the company's current value. Growth investors, for example, are not put off by price to earnings (P/E) ratios of 30 or 40 or higher. Value investors, meanwhile, would be too nervous buying a stock at those P/E ratio levels. Which is right?

Believe it or not, incorporating both when possible is the best approach. A value-oriented approach to growth investing will serve you best. Long-term growth stock investors spend time analyzing the company's fundamentals to make sure that the company's growth prospects lie on a solid foundation. But what if you had to choose between a growth stock and a value stock? Which would you choose? Growth stocks tend to have better prospects for growth for the immediate future (from one to four years), but value stocks tend to have less risk and more steady growth over a longer term.

The bottom line is that growth is much easier to achieve when you seek solid, value-oriented companies in growing industries. To better understand industries and how they affect stock value, see Chapter 12.

Learning from successful value-oriented growth investors

Being a value-oriented growth investor probably has the longest history of success versus most other stock investing philosophies. The track record for those who use value-oriented growth investing is enviable. Warren Buffett, Benjamin Graham, John Templeton, and Peter Lynch are a few of the more well-known practitioners. Each may have his own spin on the concepts, but all have successfully applied the basic principles of value-oriented growth investing over many years.

What also made them stand out from the crowd is that they were truly disciplined, long-term investors; they didn't speculate or constantly jump in and out. Investors, especially in recent years, have become impatient, short-term oriented, and lacking in discipline.

Looking for leaders and megatrends

A strong company in a growing industry is a common recipe for success. If you look at the history of stock investing, this point comes up constantly.

Investors should be on the alert for megatrends because they also help to ensure your success.

What is a megatrend? A *megatrend* is a major development that has huge implications for most (if not all) of society and for a long time to come. Good examples are the advent of the Internet and the aging of America. Both of these trends offer significant challenges and opportunities for our economy. Take the Internet for example. Its potential for economic application is still being developed. Millions are flocking to it for many reasons. And federal government studies tell us that senior citizens (over 65) will be the fastest growing segment of our population during the next 20 years. How does the stock investor take advantage of a megatrend?

Many people thought that the road to Internet riches was paved with dot-com businesses. Investors lost millions rushing into Internet stocks before they found out how these companies actually made money. The Internet is a fantastic technology, and its business and economic impact will become more and more evident in the months and years to come. However, investors should understand how people and businesses can actually profit from the Internet. For example, when people asked me what stocks would profit from the Internet, I said electric utilities, delivery services, and other companies that service Internet activity. They looked quizzically at me. "Huh? Why not invest in AMillionBucksRightNow.com?"

The serious investor says, "Hmmm. Where is the money *really* being made on the Internet?" As hundreds of the dot-coms spend tons of money to establish their businesses, who is getting *their* money? That's right . . . electric utilities, delivery services, and other companies that service Internet activity. A great example of a company that services the Internet is Cisco Systems. During the late 1990s, when the Internet megatrend was being established, Cisco was a phenomenal growth stock that turned patient, alert investors into millionaires. What industries and megatrends seem promising right now? Think about this question as you look for potential growth stocks.

Considering a company with a strong niche

Companies that have established a strong niche are consistently profitable. Look for a company with one or more of the following characteristics:

- ✔ **A strong brand:** Companies such as Coca-Cola and Microsoft come to mind. Yes, other companies out there can make soda or software, but a business needs a lot more to topple companies that have established an almost irrevocable identity with the public.

- ✔ **High barriers to entry:** United Parcel Service and Federal Express have set up tremendous distribution and delivery networks that competitors can't easily duplicate. High barriers to entry offer an important edge to companies that are already established.

✓ **Research & development (R&D):** Companies such as Pfizer and Merck spend a lot of money researching and developing new pharmaceutical products. This investment becomes a new product with millions of consumers who become loyal purchasers, so the company's going to grow.

Noticing who's buying and/or recommending the stock

You can invest in a great company and still see its stock go nowhere. Why? Because what makes the stock go up is demand — there need to be more buyers than sellers of the stock. If you pick a stock for all the right reasons and the market notices the stock as well, that attention will cause the stock price to climb. The things to watch for include the following:

✓ **Institutional buying:** Are mutual funds and pension plans buying up the stock you're looking at? If so, this type of buying power will exert tremendous upward pressure on the stock's price. Some resources and publications track institutional buying and how that will affect any particular stock. (You can find these in Appendix A.) Frequently, when a mutual fund buys a stock, others soon follow. In spite of all the talk about independent research, a herd mentality still exists.

✓ **Analysts' attention:** Are analysts talking about the stock on the financial shows? As much as you should be skeptical about an analyst's recommendation (given the stock market debacles of 2000–2001), it offers some positive reinforcement for your stock. Don't ever buy a stock solely on the basis of an analyst's recommendation. Just know that if you buy a stock based on your own research and analysts subsequently rave about it, it bodes well for the stock price. A single recommendation by an influential analyst can be enough to send a stock skyward.

✓ **Newsletter recommendations:** Newsletters are usually published by independent researchers (or so we hope). If influential newsletters are touting your choice, that praise is also good for your stock. Although some great newsletters are out there (find them in Appendix A) and they offer information that's as good or better than the research departments of some brokerage firms, don't use a single tip to base your investment decision on. But it should make you feel good if the newsletters tout a stock that you've already chosen.

✓ **Consumer publications:** No, you won't find investment advice here. This one seems to come out of left field, but it is a source that you should notice. Publications such as *Consumer Reports* regularly look at products and services and rate them for consumer satisfaction. If a company's offerings are well received by consumers, that's a strong positive for the company. This kind of attention will ultimately have a positive effect on that company's stock.

Learning investing lessons from history

A growth stock is not a creature like the Loch Ness monster — always talked about but rarely seen. Growth stocks have been part of the financial scene for nearly a century. Examples abound that offer rich information that you can apply to today's stock market environment. Look at past market winners, especially those of the 1970s and 1980s, and ask yourself, "What made them profitable stocks?" I mention these two decades because they offer a stark contrast to one another. The '70s were a tough, bearish decade for stocks, while the '80s were booming bull times. Being aware and acting logically is as vital to successful stock investing as it is to any other pursuit. Over and over again, history gives you the formula for successful stock investing:

✔ Pick a company that has strong fundamentals, including signs such as rising sales and earnings and low debt. (See Chapter 11.).

✔ Make sure that the company is in a growing industry. (See Chapter 12.)

✔ Be fully invested in stocks during a bull market, when prices are rising in the stock market and in the general economy. (See Chapter 14.)

✔ During a bear market, switch more of your money out of growth stocks (such as technology) and into defensive stocks (such as utilities).

✔ Monitor your stocks. Hold on to stocks that continue to grow, and sell those stocks that are declining. (See Chapter 23 for some warning signals to watch out for.)

Evaluating the management of a company

The management of a company is crucial to its success. Before you buy stock in a company, you want to know that the company's management is doing a great job. But how do you do that? If you call up a company and ask, it may not even return your phone call. How would you know whether management is running the company properly? The best way is to check the numbers. The following sections tell you the numbers you need to check. You will see that if the company's management is running the business well, the ultimate result is a rising stock price.

Return on equity

Although you can measure how well management is doing in several ways, you can take a quick snapshot of a management team's competence by checking the company's return on equity (ROE). ROE is a neat way to see

whether the company is using its equity (or net assets) efficiently and prof-
itably. The ROE is best expressed in the following table illustrating the balance sheet for Grobaby, Inc. (See Chapter 10 for more details on balance
sheets.) The balance sheet is a simple financial statement that illustrates
total assets minus total liabilities equals net assets (or "net equity"). For
public stock companies, the net assets are called "shareholders' equity"
or simply "equity."

Grobaby, Inc.	**Balance Sheet** December 1, 2000	**Balance Sheet** December 1, 2001
Total assets (TA)	$55,000	$65,000
Total liabilities (TL)	–$20,000	–$25,000
Equity (TA less TL)	$35,000	$40,000

As you can see, this table provides a simple summary of the company's balance sheet — the formula of assets minus liabilities. Look at the balance
sheet to discover the company's equity to help calculate the ROE.

Then there's the income statement. (Chapter 10 goes into detail about it.) The
income statement is a simple financial statement that expresses the equation
sales less expenses equals net earnings (or net income or net equity). You
want to look at a company's equity and relate it to the company's earnings.

Grobaby, Inc.	**Income Statement** Year 2000	**Income Statement** Year 2001
Sales	$82,000	$90,000
Expenses	–$75,000	–$78,000
Net earnings	$7,000	$12,000

In the first table, you can see that Grobaby, Inc., increased the equity from
$35,000 to $40,000 in one year. The second table shows that its earnings went
from $7,000 to $12,000. The ROE for the year 2000 is 20 percent ($7,000 in earn-
ings divided by $35,000 in equity), which is a solid number. The following year,
the ROE was 30 percent ($12,000 in earnings divided by $40,000 equity). For
ROE, the higher the number, the better. Any number higher than 10 percent is
great, and Grobaby, Inc.'s management is sprouting some great numbers.

Equity and earnings growth

Two additional barometers of success are a company's growth of equity and
growth in earnings. In the first table, Grobaby, Inc.'s equity grew by $5,000
(from $35,000 to $40,000), or 14 percent, which is very good. Also, look at the
growth in earnings (in the second table). The earnings grew from $7,000 to
$12,000, or a percentage increase of 71 percent ($12,000 less $7,000 equals
$5,000, and $5,000 divided by $7,000 is 71 percent), which is excellent —
management is doing good things here.

TECHNICAL STUFF

Protecting your downside

I become a Johnny-one-note on one topic: trailing stops. (See Chapter 16 for a full explanation of trailing stops.) *Trailing stops* are stop losses that you regularly manage with the stock you invest in. I always advocate using them, especially if you're new to the game of buying growth stocks. Trailing stops can help you, no matter how good or bad the economy is (or the stock in which you're investing).

Suppose that you had invested in Enron, a classic example of a phenomenal growth stock that went bad. In 1999 and 2000, when its stock soared, investors were as happy as chocoholics at Hershey. Along with many investors who forgot that sound investing takes discipline and research, Enron investors thought, "Downside risk? What downside risk?"

Here's an example of how a stop-loss order would have worked if you had invested in Enron. Suppose that you bought Enron in 2000 at $50 per share and put in a stop-loss order with your broker at $45. (Remember to make it a GTC or good-till-canceled order. This means that the stop-loss order will stay on indefinitely.) As a general rule, I like to place the stop-loss order at 10 percent below the market value. As the stock went up, you kept the stop-loss trailing upward like a tail. (Now you know why it's called a "trailing" stop; it trails the stock's price.) When Enron hit $70, your stop-loss went to, say, $63 and so on. At $84, your stop-loss was at $76. Then what?

When Enron started its perilous descent, you got out at $76. The stop-loss was triggered, and the stock was automatically sold — you stopped the loss! Actually, in this case, you could call it a "stop and cash in the gain" order. Because you bought the stock at $50 and sold at $76, you pocketed a nice capital gain of $26 (52 percent appreciation — a do-Enron-ron a do-en-ron!). Then you stepped aside and watched the stock implode.

But what if the market is doing well? Are trailing stops a good idea? Because these stops are placed below the stock price, you're not stopping the stock from rising upward indefinitely. All you're doing is protecting your investment from loss. That's discipline! Using trailing stops is a great example of how discipline helps you make money when others are watching their money vaporize.

Insider buying

Watching management as it manages the business is important, but another indicator of how well the company is doing is to see whether management is buying stock in the company as well. If a company is poised for growth, who better to know than management? And if it is buying up the company's stock en masse, then that's a great indicator of the stock's potential. See Chapter 18 for more details on insider trading.

Figuring out whether a company will continue to do well?

I met a senior credit officer at a bank who told me that he never made a bad business loan in the 30 years that he was at his position. Never! He has, however, made some loans that went bad later, but he has never made a bad loan. What's the secret of his success? He makes a loan by looking at the company applying for the loan. If it looks good, the loan is approved. But circumstances do change. The credit officer's experience is a very telling point that stock investors should be aware of.

The point of the preceding story is that a company's financial situation does change and that a diligent investor continues to look at the numbers for as long as the stock is in her portfolio. You may have chosen a great stock from a great company with great numbers in 2000, but chances are pretty good that the numbers have changed since then.

Great stocks don't always stay that way. A great selection that you're drawn to today may become tomorrow's pariah. Information, both good and bad, moves like lightning. In late 2000, Enron was considered a cream-of-the-crop stock. Analysts fell over themselves extolling its virtues. Even the celebrated market strategist Abby Joseph Cohen called Enron her number one choice in the energy sector as late as September 2001. Yet Enron shocked investors as it filed for bankruptcy in December 2001. Its stock price fell from $84 in December 2000 to a staggering 26 cents a share in October 2001! What's an investor to do?

Deciphering the key numbers of profitability

A great stock should continue to be great (or at least good) or why hold it? This is where you look at the underlying company's fundamentals. Are they holding up well? The main numbers you should look at include the following:

- **Sales:** Are the company's sales this year surpassing last year's? As a decent benchmark, sales should be at least 10 percent higher than last year.

- **Earnings:** Are earnings at least 10 percent higher than last year? Earnings should grow at the same rate than sales (or, hopefully, better).

- **Debt:** Is the company's total debt equal to or lower than the prior year? The death knell of many a company has been excessive debt.

There's more to a company's financial condition than what I mention here, but these are the most important numbers. I also realize that using the 10 percent figure may seem an oversimplification, but you don't need to complicate matters unnecessarily. I know someone's computerized financial model will come out to 9.675 or maybe 11.07, but keep it simple for now.

Exploring Small Caps and Speculative Stocks

Everyone wants to get in early on a hot new stock. Why not? You buy Shlobotky, Inc., at $1 per share and hope it zooms to $98 before lunchtime. Who wouldn't want to buy a stock that could become the next IBM or Microsoft? This is why investors are attracted to small cap stocks.

Small cap (or small capitalization) is a reference to the company's market size. *Small cap stocks* are stocks that have a market value under $1 billion. Investors may face more risk with small caps, but at least they also have the chance for greater gains.

Out of all the types of stocks, small cap stocks continue to exhibit the greatest amount of growth. In the same way that a tree planted last year will have more opportunity for growth than a mature 100-year-old redwood, small caps have greater growth potential than established large cap stocks. Of course, a small cap will not exhibit spectacular growth, just because it's small. It will grow when it does the right things, such as increasing sales and earnings by producing goods and services that customers want.

Keep in mind that for every small company that becomes a Fortune 500 firm, hundreds of companies don't grow at all or go out of business. When you try to guess the next great stock before any evidence of growth, you're not investing; you're speculating. Have you heard that one before? Of course you have, and you'll hear it again. Don't get me wrong — there's nothing wrong with speculating. The important point is that you should know it when you're doing it. If you're going to speculate in small stocks hoping for the next Cisco Systems, then use the guidelines I present in the following sections to increase your chances of success.

Avoid IPOs, unless . . .

Initial public offerings (IPOs) are the birthplace of public stocks. This is the proverbial ground floor. The *IPO* is the first offering to the public of a company's stock. The IPO is also referred to as "going public." Because a company's going public is frequently an unproven enterprise, investing in an IPO can be risky. Here are the two types of IPOs:

- ✔ **Start-up IPO:** This is a company that didn't exist before the IPO. In other words, the entrepreneurs get together and create a business plan. To get the financing they need for the company, they decide to go public immediately by approaching an investment banker. If the investment banker thinks that it's a good concept, the banker will fund it via the IPO.

✔ **A private company that decides to go public:** In many cases, the IPO is done for a company that already exists and is seeking expansion capital. The company may have been around a long time as a smaller private concern, but it decides to seek funding through an IPO to grow even larger (or to fund a new product, promotional expenses, and so on).

Which of the two IPOs do you think is less risky? That's right! The private company going public. Why? Because it's already a proven business, which is a safer bet than a brand-new start-up.

Every great stock started as a small company going public. We can all recount the stories of Federal Express, Dell, AOL, Home Depot, and hundreds of other great success stories. But do you remember an IPO by the company Lipschitz & Farquar? No? I didn't think so. It was among the majority of IPOs that did not succeed. For investors, the lesson is clear: Wait until a track record appears before you invest in a company. If you don't, you're simply rolling the dice.

If it's a small cap stock, make sure it's making money

You may recall that I emphasize two points when investing in stocks:

✔ Make sure that a company is established. (Being in business for at least three years is a good minimum.)

✔ Make sure that a company is profitable.

These points are especially important for investors in small stocks. Plenty of start-up ventures lose money but hope to make a fortune down the road. A good example is a company in the biotechnology industry. Biotech is an exciting area, but it's esoteric, and at this early stage, companies are finding it difficult to use the technology in profitable ways. You may say, "But shouldn't I jump in now in anticipation of future profits?" You may get lucky, but understand that when you invest in small cap stocks, you're speculating.

Investing in small cap stocks requires analysis

The only difference between a small cap stock and a large cap stock is a few zeros in their numbers and the fact that you need to do more research with small caps. By sheer dint of size, small caps are riskier than large caps, so you offset the risk by accruing more information on yourself and the stock in question. Plenty of information is available on large cap stocks because they're widely followed. Small cap stocks don't get as much press, and fewer analysts issue reports on them. Here are a few points to keep in mind:

- **Understand your investment style.** Small cap stocks may have more potential rewards, but they also carry more risk. No investor should devote a large portion of his capital to small cap stocks. If you're considering retirement money, you're better off investing in large cap stocks, bonds, bank accounts, and mutual funds. For example, retirement money should be in investments that are either very safe or have proven track records of steady growth over an extended period of time (five years or longer).

- **Check with the SEC.** Get the financial reports that the company must file with the SEC (such as its 10Ks and 10Qs). These reports offer more complete information on the company's activities and finances. Go to the SEC Web site at www.sec.gov and check its massive database of company filings at EDGAR (Electronic Data Gathering, Analysis, and Retrieval system). You can also check to see whether any complaints have been filed against the company.

- **Check other sources.** See whether the stock is followed by brokers and independent research services, such as Value Line. If two or more different sources like the stock, it's worth further investigation. Check the resources in Appendix A for further sources of information before you invest.

Don't rush to buy IPO stock

When a company goes public, it means that it undergoes an initial public offering (IPO). The *IPO* is the process by which a private firm seeks the assistance of an investment banking firm to gain financing by issuing stock that is purchased by the public. IPOs generate a lot of excitement, and many investors consider the IPO to be that proverbial ground-floor opportunity. After all, some people find it appealing to get a stock before its price skyrockets after investors subsequently flock to it. Why wouldn't people find IPOs appealing?

IPOs actually have a poor track record of success in their first year. A recent study revealed that IPOs actually declined in price during the first 12 months 60 percent of the time. In other words, it has a better than even chance of dropping in price. The lesson for investors is that they're better off waiting to see how the stock and the company perform. Don't worry about missing that great opportunity; if it's a bona fide opportunity, you'll still do well after the IPO.

Chapter 9

Investing for Income

· ·

In This Chapter

▶ Defining income stocks

▶ Selecting income stocks

▶ Looking at some typical income stocks

· ·

*I*nvesting for income means investing in stocks that will provide you with regular money payments (dividends). Income stocks may not offer stellar growth, but they're good for a steady infusion of money. What type of person is best suited to income stocks? Income stocks can be appropriate for many investors but they are especially well suited for the following individuals:

✔ **Conservative and novice investors:** These investors like to see a slow-but-steady approach to growing their money while getting regular dividend checks. Novice investors who want to start slowly also benefit from income stocks.

✔ **Retirees:** Growth investing is best suited for long-term needs, while income investing is best suited to current needs. Retirees may want some growth in their portfolios, but they're more concerned with regular income that can keep pace with inflation.

✔ **Dividend reinvestment plan (DRP) investors:** For those who like to compound their money with DRPs, income stocks are perfect. For more information on DRPs, see Chapter 17.

If you have a low tolerance for risk or if your investment goal is anything less than long term, income stocks are your best bet.

Understanding Income Stocks

When we talk about gaining income from stocks, we're usually talking about *dividends.* A dividend is nothing more than money paid out to the owner of stock. A good income stock is a stock that has a higher-than-average dividend (typically 4 percent or higher) and is purchased primarily for income — not for spectacular growth potential.

A dividend is quoted as an annual number but is usually paid on a quarterly, pro-rata basis. In other words, if the stock is paying a dividend of $4, you would probably be paid $1 every quarter. If, in this example, you had 200 shares, you would be paid $800 every year (if the dividend isn't changed during that period), or $200 per quarter. Getting that regular dividend check every three months (for as long as you hold the stock) can be a nice perk.

Dividend rates are not guaranteed — they can go up or down, or, in some extreme cases, the dividend can be discontinued. Fortunately, most companies that issue dividends continue them indefinitely and actually increase dividend payments from time to time. Historically, dividend increases have equaled (or exceeded) the rate of inflation.

Advantages of income stocks

Income stocks tend to be among the least volatile of all stocks, and many investors view them as defensive stocks. *Defensive stocks* are stocks of companies that sell goods and services that are generally needed no matter what shape the economy is in. (Don't confuse defensive stocks with *defense stocks,* which specialize in goods and equipment for the military.) Food, beverage, and utility companies are great examples of defensive stocks. Even if the economy is experiencing tough times, people still need to eat, drink, and turn the lights on. Companies that offer relatively high dividends are also typically very large, established firms in stable or highly regulated industries.

The share price of income stocks may not rise as high or as fast as growth stocks, but they do have the ability to rise, which increases your potential to grow your wealth, in addition to the dividend the stock pays you.

Some industries in particular are known for high-dividend stocks. Utilities (such as electric, gas, and water) and real estate investment trusts (REITs) are industries where you definitely find income stocks. Yes, you can find high-dividend stocks in other industries, but you will find a high concentration of them in these two industries. For more details, see the sections highlighting these industries later in this chapter.

Disadvantages of income stocks

Before you say, "Income stocks are great! I'll get my checkbook and buy a batch right now," take a look at some potential disadvantages (ugh!). Income stocks do come with some fine print.

What goes up . . .

Income stocks can go down as well as up, just as any stock does. Obviously, you won't mind your income stock going up in value, but it can go down just as easily. The factors that affect stocks in general — politics, economic trends, industry changes, and so on — affect income stocks, too. Fortunately, income stocks don't get hit as hard as other stocks when the market is declining. This is because high dividends tend to act as a support to the stock price. Therefore, income stocks' prices usually fall less dramatically than the prices of other stocks in a declining market.

Interest-rate sensitivity

Income stocks can be sensitive to rising interest rates. When interest rates go up, other investments (such as corporate bonds, U.S. treasury securities, and bank certificates of deposit) are more attractive. If your income stock is yielding 4 percent and interest rates are going to 5 percent, 6 percent, or higher, it can make you think, "Hmmm. Why settle for a 4 percent yield when I can get 5 percent or better elsewhere?" As more and more investors sell their low-yield stock, the prices for those stocks fall.

Another point to remember is that rising interest rates may hurt the company's financial strength. If the company has to pay more interest, that may affect the company's earnings, which in turn may affect the dividend.

Dividend-paying companies that are experiencing falling revenues tend to cut dividends.

Inflation eats into dividends

Although many companies raise their dividends on a regular basis, some don't. Or, if they do raise their dividends, the increases may be small. If income is your primary consideration, you want to be aware of this. If you're getting the same dividend year after year and this income is important to you, rising inflation will be a problem. Say that you have XYZ stock at $10 per share with an annual dividend of 30 cents (the yield is 30 cents divided by $10, or 3 percent). If the yield were 3 percent last year and again this year, how would you feel if inflation were 6 percent last year and 7 percent this year? Because inflation means that your costs are rising, inflation shrinks the value of the dividend income you receive.

As you can see, even conservative income investors can be confronted with different types of risk (Chapter 4 covers the topic of risk in greater detail). Fortunately, the rest of this chapter helps you carefully choose income stocks so that you can minimize these potential disadvantages.

Don't forget Uncle Sam

Another downside of income stocks is that the dividends paid by stocks are taxable as regular income, which means that you have to report the money you receive in dividends as income to the IRS. This dividend income is taxed at a much higher rate (especially for investors in the 28 percent bracket or higher) than that applied to long-term capital gains. For more information on capital gains, both short-term and long-term, see Chapter 19.

Playing it safe

If you're an investor seeking income and you're very nervous about potential risks with income stocks, here are some non-stock alternatives:

✔ **U.S. Treasury securities:** Issued by the federal government, these are considered the safest investments in the world. Examples of treasury securities are U.S. savings bonds and treasury bonds. They pay interest and are an ideal addition to any income investor's portfolio.

✔ **Bank certificates of deposit (CDs):** These investments are backed up by the FDIC (Federal Deposit Insurance Corporation) and are very safe.

✔ **Income mutual funds:** Many mutual funds, such as treasury bond mutual funds and corporate bond funds, are designed for income investors. They offer investors diversification and professional management, and investors can usually invest with as little as $1,000.

Analyzing Income Stocks

You should look at income stocks in the same way that you do growth stocks when assessing the financial strength of a company. Getting a nice dividend can come to a screeching halt if the company can't afford to pay them. If your budget depends on dividend income, then monitoring the company's financial strength is that much more important.

When comparing stocks that pay dividends, how do you know which one will give you the highest income? What if your hunt for income stocks boils down to two stocks and Stock A pays an annual dividend of $5 while Stock B pays $4? Do you take Stock A with the higher dividend? Well, if both companies are similar and their stock prices are the same, yes. But it's rarely that simple. Usually you have different stock prices to figure into the equation.

How do you decide which stocks will pay the most money? The main thing to look for in choosing income stocks is *yield* (the percentage rate of return paid on a stock in the form of dividends). Looking at a stock's dividend yield is the quickest way to find out how much money you'll earn from a particular income stock versus other dividend-paying stocks (or even other investments such as a bank account). Table 9-1 illustrates this point. Dividend yield is calculated in the following way:

Dividend yield = dividend income ÷ stock investment

Use the information in Table 9-1 to compare the yields from different investments and to see how evaluating yield can help you choose the stock that will earn you the most money.

Minding your dividends and interest

Dividends are sometimes confused with interest. However, *dividends* are payouts to owners, while *interest* is a payment to a creditor. A stock investor is considered a part owner and is entitled to dividends when they are issued. When you get interest at the bank, the bank is paying you this money because it borrowed the money from you and you're the creditor.

Table 9-1				**Comparing Yields**
Investment	**Type**	**Investment Amount**	**Annual Investment Income (Dividend)**	**Yield (Annual Investment Income ÷ Investment Amount)**
Smith Co.	Common stock	$20 per share	$1.00 per share	5%
Jones Co.	Common stock	$30 per share	$1.50 per share	5%
Wilson Bank	Savings account	$1,000 deposit	$40	4%

Most people have no problem understanding yield when it comes to bank accounts. If I tell you that my bank certificate of deposit (CD) has an annual yield of 3.5 percent, you can easily figure out that if I deposit $1,000 in that account, a year later I will have $1,035. The CD's market value in this example is the same as the deposit amount — $1,000. That makes it easy to calculate.

How about stocks? When you see a stock listed in the financial pages, the dividend yield is provided along with the stock's price and annual dividend. The dividend yield in the financial pages is always calculated as if you bought the stock on that given day. Just keep in mind that, based on supply and demand, stock prices change virtually every day (every minute!) that the market is open. Therefore, if the stock price changes every day, the yield will change as well.

What if you bought stock in Smith Co. a month ago at $20 per share? With an annual dividend of $1, you know that your yield is 5 percent. But what if today Smith Co. is selling for $40 per share? If you look in the financial pages, the yield quoted would be 2.5 percent. Gasp! Did the dividend get cut in half?! No, not really. You're still getting 5 percent because you bought the stock at

$20 instead of the current $40; the quoted yield is for investors who purchase Smith Co. today. Investors who buy Smith Co. stock today would pay $40 and get the $1 dividend, but the yield has changed to 2.5 percent, which is the yield that they lock into. So, while Smith Co. may have been a good income investment for you a month ago, it's not such a hot pick today because the price of the stock doubled, cutting the yield in half. Even though the dividend hasn't changed, the yield has changed dramatically because of the stock price change.

Another way to look at yield is by looking at the amount of investment using Smith Co. as the example. The investor who bought, say, 100 shares of Smith Co. when it was $20 per share, would have only paid $2,000 (100 shares times $20 — leave out commissions to make the example simple). If the same stock were purchased later at $40 per share, the total investment amount would be $4,000 (100 shares times $40). In either case, the investor would get a total dividend income of $100 (100 shares times $1 dividend per share). From a yield perspective, which investment is yielding more — the $2,000 investment or the $4,000 investment? Of course, it's better to get the income ($100 in this case) with the smaller investment (5 percent yield is better than a 2.5 percent yield).

A final point about income stocks in general is that you don't stop scrutinizing them after you acquire them. You may have made a great choice that gives you a great dividend, but that doesn't mean that it will be that way indefinitely. Monitor the company's progress for as long as it is in your portfolio. Use resources such as www.bloomberg.com and www.marketwatch.com (see Appendix A for more resources) to track your stock and to monitor how well that particular company is continuing to perform.

Introducing Tips for Selecting Income Stocks

Income stocks may be less volatile and less risky than growth stocks, but you still must do your homework when selecting them. The following sections introduce some important points to keep in mind before you choose an income stock.

Understanding your needs first

You choose income stocks primarily because you want or need income now. As a secondary point, income stocks have the potential for steady, long-term appreciation. So if you're investing for retirement needs that won't occur until 20 years from now, maybe income stocks aren't suitable for you — better to invest in growth stocks because they're more likely to grow your money faster over your stated lengthy investment term.

If you're certain that you want income stocks, do a rough calculation to figure out how big a portion of your portfolio income stocks should occupy. Suppose that you need $25,000 in investment income to satisfy your current financial needs. If you have bonds that give you $20,000 interest income and you want the rest to be dividends from income stocks, you need to choose stocks that will pay you $5,000 in annual dividends. To obtain that $5,000 income if the investment amount that you have remaining to allocate is $80,000, you know that you need a portfolio of income stocks that provide $5,000 in dividend income or a yield of 6.25 percent ($5,000 divided by $80,000 equals a yield of 6.25 percent).

Use the following table as a general guideline for understanding your need for income:

Item	Your amounts	Sample amounts
A. How much annual income do you need?		$10,000
B. The value of your portfolio (or money available for investment)		$150,000
C. Yield necessary to achieve income (divide item A by item B)		6.7%

With this simple table, you know that if you have $150,000 in income stocks yielding 6.7 percent, you would receive income of $10,000 to meet your financial needs. You may ask, "Why not just buy $150,000 of bonds (for instance) that yield at least 6.7 percent?" Well, if that $10,000 is sufficient for you and inflation for the foreseeable future is zero, then you would have a point. Unfortunately, inflation will probably be with us for a long time. This is where the feature of steady growth that income stocks provide will benefit you.

The most sensible portfolio for income investors is obviously a mix of both dividend-paying stocks as well as bonds, so that you can have diversification. Even something as simple as a mix of 50 percent dividend-paying stocks and 50 percent bonds provides a sufficient balance of both income and some growth potential (as well as reduced risk as a nice bonus).

If you do have income stocks and don't have any immediate need for the dividends, consider reinvesting the dividends in the company's stock. For more details on this kind of reinvesting, see Chapter 17.

Obviously, the points in this section merely serve as illustrations for the uses of income stocks. Every investor is different. If you're not sure about your current or future needs, your best choice is to consult with a financial planner.

Checking the stock's payout ratio

The payout ratio is simply a way to figure out what percentage of the company's earnings are being paid out in the form of dividends. Keep in mind that companies pay dividends from their net earnings. Therefore, the company's earnings should always be higher than the dividends the company pays out.

Say that the company Urn More Corp. (UMC) has annual earnings of $1 million dollars. (Remember that earnings are what you get when you subtract expenses from sales.) Total dividends are to be paid out of $500,000, and the company has 1 million outstanding shares. Using those numbers, you know that UMC has earnings per share (EPS) of $1.00 ($1 million in earnings divided by 1 million shares) and that it pays an annual dividend of 50 cents per share ($500,000 divided by 1 million shares). The dividend payout ratio is 50 percent (the 50 cents dividend is 50 percent of the $1.00 EPS). This is a healthy dividend payout ratio because even if the company's earnings were to fall by 10 percent or 20 percent, it would still have plenty of room to pay dividends. People concerned about the safety of their dividend income should regularly watch the payout ratio.

When a company suffers significant financial difficulties, its ability to pay dividends is compromised. So if you need dividend income to help you pay your bills, you better be aware of the dividend payout ratio. Generally, a dividend payout ratio of 60 percent or less is safe. Obviously, the lower the percentage is, the safer the dividend.

Diversifying your stocks

If most of your dividend income comes from stock in a single company or from a single industry, consider reallocating your investment to avoid having all your eggs in one basket. The same concerns for diversification you may have for a portfolio of growth stocks apply to income stocks as well. If all of your income stocks are in the electric utility industry, then any problems in the electric utility industry will be potential problems for your portfolio as well.

Before you choose an income stock, look at the other stocks you currently have to make sure that they're not exposed to similar risks, and select a new one from a different industry. For example, tobacco stocks usually have a nice dividend, but the tobacco industry has been experiencing legal and political challenges that offer special risks to the companies (and their dividends).

Examining the company's bond rating

Bond rating? Huh? What's that got to do with dividend-paying stocks? Actually, the company's bond rating is very important to income stock investors. The bond rating offers insight into the company's financial strength. Bonds get rated for quality for the same reasons that consumer agencies rate products such as cars or toasters. Standard & Poor's (S&P) is the major independent rating agency that looks into bond issuers. It looks at the issuer of a bond and asks the question "Does the bond issuer have the financial strength to pay back the bond and the interest as stipulated in the bond indenture?" To understand why this is important, consider the following:

- If the bond rating is good, that means the company is strong enough to pay its obligations. These obligations include expenses, payments on debts, and dividends. If a bond rating agency gives the company a high rating (or if it raises the rating), that's a great sign for anyone holding the company's debt or receiving dividends.

- If a bond rating agency lowers the rating of a bond, that means that the company's financial strength is deteriorating — a red flag for anyone who owns the company's bonds or its stock. A lower bond rating today may mean trouble for the dividend later on.

- If the bond rating is not good, that means that the company is having difficulty paying its obligations. If the company can't pay all of its obligations, then it will have to choose which ones to pay. More times than not, a financially troubled company chooses to cut dividends or (in a worst case scenario) not pay dividends at all.

The highest rating issued by S&P is AAA. The grades AAA, AA, and A are considered "investment grade" or of high quality. Bs and Cs indicate a poor grade, while anything lower than that is considered very risky (the bonds are referred to as "junk bonds"). So if you see a XXX rating, then . . . gee . . . you better stay away! (You might even get an infection.)

Exploring Some Typical Income Stocks

Although every industry has stocks that pay dividends, some industries have a greater number of stocks that pay dividends. You won't find too many dividend-paying income stocks in the computer or biotech industry; odds are that you won't even find one! The reason is that these types of companies need a lot of money to finance expensive research and development (R&D) projects to create new products. Without R&D, the company can't create new products to fuel sales, growth, and future earnings. Computer, biotech, and other innovative industries are better for growth investors.

Income stocks tend to be in established industries with established cash flows and less emphasis on financing or creating new products and services. When you're ready to start your search for a great income stock, start looking at utilities and real estate trusts — two established industries with proven track records — for high-dividend stocks.

Utilities

Utilities generate a large cash flow. (If you don't believe me, look at your gas and electric bills!) Cash flow includes money from income (sales of products and/or services) and other items (such as the selling of equipment, for example). This cash flow is needed to cover things such as expenses, including dividends. Utilities are considered the most common type of income stocks, and many investors have at least one in their portfolios. Investing in your own local utility isn't a bad idea. At least you know that when you pay your energy bill, you're helping out at least one investor. Before you invest in a utility company, consider the following:

- **The utility company's financial condition:** Is the company making money, and are its sales and earnings growing from year to year? Make sure that the utility's bonds are rated A or higher for further assurance regarding the company's financial strength. I cover bond ratings in the section, "Bond rating," earlier in this chapter.

- **The company's dividend payout ratio:** Because utilities tend to have a good cash flow, don't be too concerned if the ratio reaches 70 percent. Again, from a safety point of view, however, the lower the rate the better. See the "Checking the stock's payout ratio" section, earlier in this chapter, for more on payout ratios.

- **The company's geographic location:** If the utility covers an area that is doing well and offers an increasing population base and business expansion, that bodes well for your stock.

Real estate investment trusts (REITs)

Real estate investment trusts (REITs) are a special breed of stock. A *REIT* is an investment that has the elements of both a stock and a *mutual fund* (a pool of money received from investors that is managed by an investment company). It is like a stock in that it is a company whose stock is publicly traded on the major stock exchanges, and it has the usual features that you expect from a stock — it can be bought and sold easily through a broker, income is given to investors as dividends, and so on. A REIT resembles a mutual fund in that it doesn't make its money selling goods and services; it makes its money by buying, selling, and managing an investment portfolio — in the case of a REIT, the portfolio is full of real estate investments. It generates revenue from rents and property leases as any landlord would. In addition, some REITs own mortgages, and they gain income from the interest.

REITs are called trusts only because they meet the requirements of the Real Estate Investment Trust Act of 1960. This act exempts REITs from corporate income tax and capital gains taxes as long as they meet certain criteria, such as dispensing 95 percent of their net income to shareholders. There are other criteria, but this is the one that interests income investors. This provision is the reason why REITs generally issue generous dividends. Beyond this status, REITs are, in a practical sense, like any other publicly traded company.

The main advantages to investing in REITs include the following:

✔ Unlike other types of real estate investing, REITs are easy to buy and sell. Just as you would purchase any stock, you can buy a REIT by making a phone call to a broker or visiting the broker's Web site.

✔ REITs have higher-than-average yields. Because they must distribute at least 95 percent of their income to their shareholders, their dividends usually yield a return of 5 to 12 percent.

✔ REITs involve a lower risk than the direct purchase of real estate. Because you're investing in a company that buys the real estate, you don't have to worry about managing the properties — the company's management does that on a full-time basis. Usually, the REIT doesn't just manage one property; it's diversified in a portfolio of different properties.

✔ Investing in a REIT is affordable for small investors. REIT shares usually trade in the $10 to $40 range, meaning that you can invest with very little money. You can get started by buying as little as one share (because REITs are bought in the stock market, the usual broker commissions would apply when you buy or sell them). Why do that? So that you can

- Join the REIT's dividend reinvestment plan (DRP). You can have the dividends reinvested so that you can purchase more shares.

- Borrow money at low rates. If your REIT shares are in your brokerage account, you can borrow up to 50 percent of the market value and use those funds for other purposes.

Of course, REITs have disadvantages, too, including the following:

✔ **Real estate risks:** Owning shares in a REIT carries the same investment risks as any real estate investment. If the property owned by the REIT is in trouble, so is the REIT.

✔ **Less profit than direct real estate investing:** That's the trade-off. Because REITs offer less risk than buying real estate on your own, they also offer a lower return on your investment.

When you're looking for a REIT to invest in, analyze it the way you would analyze a property. Look at the location and type of the property. If shopping malls are booming in California and your REIT buys and sells shopping malls in California, then you'll do well. However, if your REIT invests in office buildings across the country and the office building market is overbuilt and having tough times, so will you.

Part III
Picking Winners

The 5th Wave   By Rich Tennant

"The first thing we do is get you two into a good small cap stock. Let me get out the 'Magic 8 Ball' and we'll run some options."

In this part . . .

Now that you have the basics down, it's time to become a pro at picking individual stocks. When you consider investing in a company, you need to know the key indications that a particular stock's price is going to rise. And because the stock market doesn't operate in a vacuum, I introduce general economic and political factors that can have a huge effect on the stock market. The chapters in this part steer you to key financial information and important company documents and show you how to interpret the information you find.

Chapter 10

Running the Numbers: Using Basic Accounting to Choose Winning Stocks

Stock picking can seem like a combination of art, luck, timing, and science. It may seem like there is no rhyme or reason to it. When you turn to the so-called experts, you get all sorts of opinions, which frequently are contradictory. You may hear about someone's "successful system" or see a book titled *Make a Fortune in the Stock Market*. Then you read the horror stories of people who lost a fortune on stock investing. Does any approach work with some consistency? What's an investor to do?

The most tried-and-true method for picking a good stock starts with picking a good company. Don't rely on luck to help you pick good stocks; good old-fashioned homework, research, and common sense are your best diagnostic tools. What constitutes a good company? And just what is a good price? Hey, that's what this chapter is all about!

Recognizing Value When You See It

If you pick a stock based on the value of the company that's issuing it, you're a *value investor* — an investor who looks at a company's value and judges whether he can purchase the stock at a good price. (Is the stock price a fair representation of the company's value?) Value investors analyze a company's fundamentals (earnings, assets, and so on) and give a "buy" signal if the stock price is low relative to these verifiable, quantifiable factors.

When you look at a company from a value-oriented perspective, here are some of the most important items to consider:

- ✔ The balance sheet to figure out the company's net worth
- ✔ The income statement to figure out the company's profitability
- ✔ Ratios that let you analyze just how well (or not so well) the company is doing

See the section, "Accounting for Taste," later in this chapter, for more on using balance sheets, income statements, and ratios to help you analyze stock values.

A value investor doesn't buy a company's stock because it's cheap; he buys it because it's *undervalued* (the company is worth more than the price of its stock reflects — its market value is less than its book value).

A company may be undervalued from a simple comparison of the book value and the market value, but that doesn't mean it's a screaming buy. For example, what if you find out that a company is in trouble and losing money this year? Would you buy it then? No, you wouldn't. Why invest in the stock of a losing company? (If you did, you wouldn't be investing — you would be gambling or speculating.) The heart of a company's value, besides its net worth, is its ability to generate profit.

Companies have values the same way many things have value, such as eggs or elephant-foot umbrella stands. And there is such a thing as a fair price to buy them at, too. Eggs, for example, have value. You can eat them and have a tasty treat while getting nutrition as well. But would you buy an egg for $1,000 (and, no, you're not a starving millionaire on a desert island)? No, of course not. But what if you could buy an egg for 5 cents? At that point it has value *and* a good price. This kind of deal is a value investor's dream.

Value investors can find thousands of companies that have value, but they can probably buy only a handful at a truly good price. The number of stocks that can be bought at a good price is relative to the market. In mature bull markets, a good price is hard to find because most stocks have probably seen significant price increases, but in bear markets, good companies at bargain prices are easier to come by.

Value investors basically look for a bargain. That being the case, they generally don't look at companies that everyone is talking about because by that point, the stock of those companies will have ceased to be a bargain. The value investor searches for a stock that will eventually be discovered by the market and then watch as the stock price goes up. But before you bother digging into the fundamentals to find that bargain stock, first make sure that the company is making money.

Value may seem like a murky or subjective term, but it is the essence of good stock picking. You can measure value in different ways, so it's important to know the difference and to understand the impact that value has on your investment decisions.

Market value

When you hear someone quoting a stock at $47 per share, that price reflects the stock's market value. The total market valuation of a company's stock is also referred to as its *market cap,* or *market capitalization.* How is a company's market cap determined? With the following simple formula:

Market capitalization = share price × number of shares outstanding

If Bolshevik Corp.'s stock is $35 per share and it has 1 million shares outstanding (or shares available for purchase), then its market cap is $35 million. Thirty-five million dollars may sound like a lot of money, but Bolshevik Corp would be considered a small cap stock. For more information about small cap stocks, dip into Chapter 8.

Who sets the market value of stock? The market — millions of investors directly and through intermediaries such as mutual funds — determines the market value of stock. If the market perceives that the company is desirable, investor demand for the company's stock will push up the share price.

The problem with market valuation is that it's not always a good indicator of a good investment. In recent years, plenty of companies have had astronomical market values, yet they proved to be terrible companies and subsequently terrible investments. For example, eToys.com was a billion-dollar stock, yet the company eventually went bankrupt, and the stock became worthless. Investors (and analysts) misunderstood the difference between the fleeting market value of the stock and the true value of the underlying company.

Book value

Book value (also referred to as *accounting value*) looks at a company from a balance sheet perspective (assets minus liabilities equals net worth or *stockholders' equity*). It's a way of judging a company by its net worth to see whether the stock's market value is reasonable compared to the company's intrinsic value.

Generally, market value usually tends to be higher than book value. If market value is substantially higher than book value, the value investor becomes more reluctant to buy that particular stock because it's overvalued. The closer the stock's market capitalization is to the book value, the safer the investment.

As a general rule, be very cautious with a stock whose market value is more than twice the company's book value. If the market value is $1 billion and the book value is $500 million or more, that is a good indicator that the company may be overvalued, or valued at a higher price than the company's book value and ability to generate a profit.

Keep in mind that you can't base your decision of whether or not to invest in a company on its book value alone. You still must look at other factors, such as earnings, economic conditions, and so on. As a matter of fact, you should never base a stock investing decision on just one criterion.

Earnings and sales value

A company's intrinsic value is directly tied to its ability to make money. In that case, many analysts like to value stocks from the perspective of the company's income statement. Two common barometers of value are expressed in ratios: the price to sale ratio and the price to earnings ratio. In both instances, the price is a reference to the company's market value (as reflected in its share price). Sales and earnings are references to the company's ability to make money. These two ratios will be covered more fully in the section "Tooling around with ratios," presented later in this chapter.

For investors, the general approach is clear. The closer the market value is to the company's intrinsic value, the better. And, of course, if the market value is lower than the company's intrinsic value, then you have a potential bargain worthy of a closer look. Part of looking closer means examining the company's income statement, also called the *profit and loss statement,* or simply the *P & L.* A low price to sales ratio (PSR) is 1, a medium PSR is between 1 and 2, and a high PSR is 3 or higher.

Accounting for Taste

Profit is for a company what oxygen is to you and me. That's neither good nor bad; it just is. Without profit, a company can't survive, much less thrive. Without profit, it can't provide jobs, pay taxes, and invest in new products, equipment, or innovation. Without profit, the company eventually goes bankrupt, and the value of its stock evaporates.

During the heady days of 1998–2001, many investors lost a lot of money simply because they invested in stocks of companies that weren't making a profit. The year 2001 saw a lot of companies with previous market values in the billions go belly up because they weren't making money. A good example is Global Crossing. It had a market value of nearly $40 billion. However, it lost a lot of money and subsequently filed for bankruptcy, and its market value vanished.

Preventing another Enron

In 2001, the seventh largest company in the United States filed for bankruptcy. The implosion of the once-invincible Enron Corporation sent shockwaves through the financial markets. Enron fell from its all-time high in 2000 of nearly $90 per share to 26 cents in early December 2001. It lost a mind-boggling 99 percent of its market value in only 12 months! Yet only a few months before its final descent, an army of analysts was crowing about the company's bright future. What went wrong?

Although the fingers of blame pointed to lack of oversight, funny accounting, and other skulduggery, the problem boiled down to a case of the company's management racking up huge losses in speculative ventures and hiding them from investors and analysts. Enron didn't make these ventures clear in its reporting, which is why so many were caught off guard by the staggering losses that surfaced.

In this case, even investors who performed diligent research could have easily missed the well-concealed losses. The SEC has cautioned the investing public that other Enron-type companies are out there. How can investors protect themselves so that they don't find themselves in the same situation as Enron investors? First of all, be on the alert for warning signs. Enron did have warning signs that should have been heeded. High debt and a high P/E ratio (90!) are red flags that any value investor must pay attention to. In addition, you can minimize any potential losses by using investment techniques such as trailing stops to prevent a free fall in the stock's price. (For more on P/E ratios, see Chapter 6, and for information on trailing stops, see Chapter 16.)

The list of once-mighty companies that went bankrupt between 2000 and 2002 is an eye-popping one. Stock investors as a group lost trillions of dollars investing in glitzy companies that sounded good but weren't making money. When their brokers were saying, "buy, buy, buy," their hard-earned money was saying, "bye, bye, bye!" What were they thinking?

Stock investors need to pick up some rudimentary knowledge of accounting to round out their stock-picking prowess and to be sure that they're getting a good value for their investment dollars. Accounting is the language of business. If you don't understand basic accounting, then you'll have difficulty being a successful investor. Investing without accounting knowledge is like traveling without a map. However, if you can run a household budget, using accounting analysis to evaluate stocks will be easier than you think.

Walking on a wire: The balance sheet

A company's balance sheet gives you a financial snapshot of what the company looks like in terms of the following equation:

Assets – liabilities = net worth

By looking at a company's balance sheet, you can address the following questions:

- What does the company own (assets)? The company can own assets, which can be financial, tangible, and/or intangible. *Assets* can be anything that has value or that can be converted to or sold for cash. Financial assets can be cash, investments, or accounts receivable. Assets can be tangible things such as inventory, equipment, and/or buildings. They can also be intangible things such as licenses, trademarks, or copyrights.

- What does the company owe (liabilities)? *Liabilities* are anything of value that the company must ultimately pay to someone else. Liabilities can be invoices (accounts payable) or short-term or long-term debt.

- What is the company's net equity (net worth)? After you subtract the liabilities from the assets, the remainder is called either *net worth, net equity,* or *net stockholders' equity.* This is also the critical number when calculating a company's book value.

As you can see, a balance sheet is not difficult to understand. It is an important document that you should look at carefully to make sure the company is in a strong financial position. Fortunately, we live in the age of information, so finding the relevant financial data on a company isn't difficult. Web sites such as www.nasdaq.com, for example, can give you the most recent balance sheets and income statements of most public companies.

The assets and liabilities relationship for a company has the same logic as the assets and liabilities in your own household. When you look at a snapshot of your own finances (your personal balance sheet), how can you tell if you're doing well? Odds are that you would start by comparing some numbers. If your net worth was $5,000, you might say, "That's great!" But a more appropriate remark would be something like, "That's great compared to, say, a year ago."

You need to compare the company's balance sheet at a recent point in time to a past time. You should do this comparative analysis with all the key items on the balance sheet. You do this to see the company's progress. Is it growing its assets and/or shrinking its debt? Most importantly, is the company's net worth growing? Is it growing by at least 10 percent from a year ago? All too often, investors stop doing their homework after they make an initial investment. You should continue to look at the company's numbers on a regular basis so that you can be ahead of the curve. If the company starts to have problems, you can get out before the rest of the market starts getting out, which will cause the stock price to fall.

To judge the financial strength of a company, ask yourself the following questions:

✔ Are the company's assets greater in value than they were three months ago, a year ago, or two years ago? Compare current asset size to the most recent two years to make sure that the company is growing in size and financial strength.

✔ How do the individual items compare with prior periods? Some particular assets that you should take note of are cash, inventory, and accounts receivable.

✔ Are liabilities such as accounts payable and debt about the same or lower or higher compared to prior periods? Are they growing at a similar, faster, or slower rate than the company's assets? Remember that debt that rises faster and higher than items on the other side of the balance sheet is a warning sign of pending financial problems.

✔ Is the company's net worth or equity greater than the previous year? And is that year greater than the year before? In a healthy company, the net worth should be constantly rising. As a general rule, net worth should be at least 10 percent higher than the previous year.

Looking at the income statement

Where do you look if you want to find out what a company's profit is? Check out the company's income statement. It reports in detail a simple accounting equation that you probably already know:

Sales – expenses = net profit (or net earnings or net income)

Looking at the income statement, an investor can try to answer the following questions:

✔ What sales did the company make? Companies sell products and services that generate revenue (known as *sales* or *gross sales*). Sales are also referred to as the *top line*.

✔ What expenses did the company incur? In generating sales, companies pay expenses such as payroll, utilities, advertising, administration, and so on.

✔ What is the net income? Also called earnings or net profit, net income is the *bottom line*. After paying for all expenses, what profit did the company make?

The information you glean should give you a strong idea about the company's current financial strength and whether or not it's successfully increasing sales, holding down expenses and ultimately maintaining profitability. You can find out more about sales, expenses, and profits in the sections that follow.

Sales

Sales refers to the money that a company receives as customers buy its goods and/or services. It is a simple item on the income statement and a useful number to look at. Analyzing a company by looking at its sales is called *top line analysis.*

As an investor, you should take into consideration the following points about sales:

- ✔ Sales should be increasing. A healthy, growing company has growing sales. They should grow at least 10 percent from the prior year, and you should look at the most recent three years.

- ✔ Core sales (sales of those products or services that the company specializes in) should be increasing. Frequently, the sales figure has a lot of stuff lumped into it. Maybe the company sells widgets (what the heck is one, anyway?), but the core sales number may also include other things, such as the sale of a building or other unusual item. Take a close look. Isolate the company's primary offerings and ask whether these sales are growing at a reasonable rate (such as 10 percent).

- ✔ Are there odd items or odd ways of calculating sales? In the late 1990s, many companies boosted their sales by aggressively offering affordable financing with easy repayment terms. Say you find out that Suspicious Sales Inc. (SSI) had annual sales of $50 million, reflecting a 25 percent increase from the year before. Looks great! But what if you find out that $20 million of that sales number comes from sales made on credit that the company extended to buyers? Some companies that use this approach later have to write off losses as uncollectible debt because often the customer ultimately can't pay for the goods.

If you want to get a good clue whether a company is artificially boosting sales, check the company's *accounts receivable* (listed in the asset section of the company's balance sheet). Accounts receivable refer to money that is owed to the company for goods that customers have purchased on credit. If you find out that sales went up by $10 million (great!) but accounts receivable went up by $20 million (uh-oh), then something is just not right. That might be a sign that the financing terms were too easy, and the company could have a problem collecting payment (especially in a recession).

Expenses

What a company spends has a direct relationship on its profitability. If spending isn't controlled or held at a sustainable level, it could spell trouble for a company.

When you look at a company's expense items, consider the following:

✔ Compare expense items to the prior period. Are expenses higher, lower, or about the same from the prior period? If there is a significant difference, you should see commensurate benefits elsewhere. In other words, if overall expenses are 10 percent higher compared to the prior period, are sales at least 10 percent more during the same period?

✔ Are some expenses too high? Look at the individual expense items. Are they significantly higher than the year before? If so, why?

✔ Have any unusual items been expensed? Sometimes an unusual expense isn't necessarily a negative. Expenses may be higher than usual if a company writes off uncollectible accounts receivable as bad debt expense. Doing so inflates the total expenses and subsequently results in lower earnings. Pay attention to nonrecurring charges that show up on the income statement and determine whether they make sense.

Profit

Earnings or profit is the single most important item on the income statement. It's also the one that receives the most attention in the financial media. When a company makes a profit, it's usually reported as earnings per share (EPS). So if you hear that the XYZ Corporation beat last quarter's earnings by a penny, here's how to translate that news. Suppose that the company made $1 per share this quarter and 99 cents per share last quarter. If that company had 100 million shares of stock outstanding, then its profit this quarter is $100 million (the EPS times the number of shares outstanding), which is $1 million more than it made in the prior quarter ($1 million is one cent per share times 100 million shares).

Don't simply look at current earnings as an isolated figure. Always compare current earnings to earnings in past periods (usually a year). For example, if you're looking at a retailer's fourth quarter results, you can't compare that with the retailer's third quarter. Doing so is like comparing apples to oranges. What if the company usually does well during the December holidays but poorly in the fall? In that case, you don't get a fair comparison.

A strong company should show consistent earnings growth from the period (such as the year or the same quarter from the prior year) before, and you should check the period before that, too, so that you can determine whether earnings are consistently rising over time. Earnings growth is an important barometer of the company's potential growth and bodes well for the stock price.

When you look at earnings, here are some things to consider:

✔ **Total earnings:** This is the most watched item. Total earnings should grow year to year by at least 10 percent.

✔ **Operational earnings:** Break down the total earnings and look at a key subset — that portion of earnings derived from the company's core activity. Is the company continuing to make money from its primary goods and services?

✔ **Nonrecurring items:** Are earnings higher (or lower) than usual or than expected and why? Frequently, the difference results from items such as the sale of an asset or a large depreciation write-off.

Tooling around with ratios

A ratio is a helpful numerical tool that you can use to find out the relationship between two or more figures found in the company's financial data. A ratio can add meaning to a number or put it in perspective. Ratios sound complicated, but they're easier to understand than you think.

Say that you're considering a stock investment and the company you're looking at has earnings of $1 million this year. You may think that's a nice profit, but in order for this amount to be meaningful, you have to compare it to something. What if you find out that the other companies in the industry (of similar size and scope) had earnings of $500 million? Would that change your thinking? Or what if you find out that the same company had earnings of $75 million in the prior period? Would that change your mind?

Two key ratios to be aware of include

✔ Price to earnings ratio (P/E)

✔ Price to sales ratio (PSR)

Every investor wants to find stocks that have a 20 percent average growth rate over the past five years and have a low P/E ratio (sounds like a dream). Use stock screening tools available free on the Internet to do your research. Many brokers have them at their Web sites (such as Charles Schwab at www.schwab.com and E*TRADE at www.etrade.com). The American Stock Exchange at www.amex.com provides an excellent one. A stock screening tool lets you plug in numbers such as sales or earnings and ratios such as the P/E ratio or the debt to equity ratio and then click! Up come stocks that fit your criteria. This is a good starting point for serious investors. Check out Appendix B for even more on ratios.

Running into the P/E ratio

The price to earnings (P/E) ratio is very important in analyzing a potential stock investment because it's one of the most widely regarded barometers of a company's value, and it's usually reported along with the company's stock price in the financial page listing. The major significance of the P/E ratio is that it establishes a direct relationship between the bottom line of a company's operations — the earnings — and the stock price.

The *P* in P/E stands for the stock's current price. The *E* is for earnings per share (typically the most recent 12 months of earnings). The P/E ratio is also referred to as the "earnings multiple" or just "multiple."

The P/E ratio is calculated by dividing the price of the stock by the earnings per share. If the price of a single share of stock is $10 and the earnings (on a per-share basis) is $1, then the P/E is 10. If the stock price goes to $35 per share and the earnings are unchanged, then the P/E is 35. Basically, the higher the P/E, the more you pay for the company's earnings.

Why would you buy stock in one company with a relatively high P/E ratio instead of investing in another company with a lower P/E? Keep in mind that investors buy stocks based on expectations. They may bid up the price of the stock (subsequently raising the stock's P/E ratio) because they feel that the company will have increased earnings in the near future. Perhaps they feel that the company has great potential (a pending new invention or lucrative business deal) that will eventually make the company more profitable. This in turn would have a beneficial impact on the company's stock price. The danger with a high P/E is that if the company doesn't achieve the hopeful results, the stock price could fall.

You should look at two types of P/E to get a balanced picture of the company's value.

- ✔ **Trailing P/E:** This is the most frequently quoted P/E because it deals with existing data. The trailing P/E uses the most recent 12 months of earnings in its calculation.

- ✔ **Forward P/E:** This is based on projections or expectations of earnings in the coming 12-month period. Although this may seem preferable because it does look into the near future, it's still considered an estimate that may or may not prove to be accurate.

The following example illustrates the importance of the P/E ratio. Say that you want to buy a business and I'm selling a business. If you come to me and say, "What do you have to offer?" I might say, "Have I got a deal for you! I operate a retail business downtown that sells spatulas. The business nets a cool $2,000 profit per year." You reluctantly say, "Uh, okay, what's the asking price for the business?" I reply, "You can have it for only $1 million! What do you say?"

If you're sane, odds are that you would politely turn down that offer. Even though the business is profitable (a cool $2,000 a year), you would be crazy to pay a million bucks for it. In other words, the business is way overvalued (too expensive for what you're getting in return for your investment dollars). The million dollars would generate a better rate of return elsewhere and probably with less risk. As for the business, the P/E ratio ($1 million divided by $2,000 = a P/E of 500) is outrageous. This is definitely a case of an over-valued company — and a lousy investment.

What if that business were offered for $12,000? Would that price make more sense? Yes. The P/E ratio would be a more reasonable 6 ($12,000 divided by $2,000). In other words, the business would pay for itself in about 6 years (versus 500 years in the prior example).

Looking at the P/E ratio offers a shortcut for investors asking the question, "Is this stock overvalued?" As a general rule, the lower the P/E, the safer (or more conservative) the stock is. The reverse is more noteworthy: The higher the P/E, the greater the risk.

Just remember that when a P/E is referred to as high or low, you have to ask the question, "Compared to what?" A P/E of 30 is considered very high for a large cap electric utility but quite reasonable for a small cap, high-technology firm. Keep in mind that phrases such as "large cap" and "small cap" are just a reference to the company's market value or size. "Cap" is short for capitalization (the total number of shares of stock outstanding times the share price).

The following basic points can help you evaluate P/E ratios:

- ✔ Compare a company's P/E ratio with its industry. Electric utility industry stocks generally have a P/E that hovers in the 9–14 range. Therefore, if you're considering an electric utility with a P/E of 45, then something is wrong with that utility.

- ✔ Compare a company's P/E with the general market. If you're looking at a small cap stock on the Nasdaq that has a P/E of 100 but the average P/E for established companies on the Nasdaq is 40, find out why. You should also compare the stock's P/E ratio with the P/E ratio for major indexes such as the Dow Jones Industrial Average (DJIA), the Standard & Poor's 500 (S&P 500), and the Nasdaq Composite (for more on market indexes, see Chapter 5).

- ✔ Compare a company's current P/E with recent periods (such as this year versus last year). If it currently has a P/E ratio of 20 and it previously had a P/E ratio of 30, it is showing that either the stock price has declined or that earnings have risen. In this case, there is less risk that the stock could fall. That bodes well for the stock.

- ✔ Low P/E ratios aren't necessarily a sign of a bargain, but if you're looking at a stock for many other reasons that seem positive (solid sales, strong industry, and so on) and it also has a low P/E, that's a good sign.

- ✔ High P/E ratios aren't necessarily bad, but they do mean that you should investigate further. If a company is weak and the industry is shaky, heed the high P/E as a warning sign. Frequently, a high P/E ratio means that investors have bid up a stock price, anticipating future income. The problem is that if the anticipated income doesn't materialize, the stock price could fall.

- ✔ Watch out for a stock that doesn't have a P/E ratio. In other words, it may have a price (the P), but it doesn't have earnings (the E). No earnings means no P/E, meaning that you're better off avoiding it.

Better safe than sorry

The stocks listed in the following table were among the high fliers in the late 1990s, but they came crashing back to earth within 24 months. As of January 2002, eBay's P/E fell to 190 (still too high), while Cisco and Yahoo! don't have P/E ratios because they had losses (!) for the years 2000 and 2001. Yikes! For all three, the chances that the stocks might go lower are too great for serious investors. You're better off to wait and see whether their earnings improve.

Stock	P/E Ratio in 1999	Stock Activity in 2000 and 2001	P/E Ratio in 2002
Cisco Systems	190	Stock price fell from $80 to $15	0
eBay	3,980	Stock price fell from $120 to $59	190
Yahoo!	896	Stock price fell from $240 to $18	0

Listening to a PSR about PSR

The price to sales ratio (PSR) is the company's stock price divided by its sales. Because the sales number is rarely expressed as a per-share figure, it's easier to divide a company's total market value (see the section "Market value," earlier in this chapter, to find out what this term means) by its total sales for the last 12 months.

As a general rule, stock trading at a PSR of 1 or less is a reasonably priced stock worthy of your attention. For example, say that a company has sales of $1 billion and the stock has a total market value of $950 million. In that case, the PSR is 0.95. In other words, you could buy $1 of the company's sales for only 95 cents. All things being equal, that stock may be a bargain.

The PSR is frequently used as an evaluation tool in the following circumstances:

- In tandem with other ratios to get a more well-rounded picture of the company and the stock

- When you want an alternate way to value a company that doesn't have earnings

- By analysts who want a true picture of the company's financial health, because sales are tougher for companies to manipulate than earnings, which are easier to manipulate

✔ When you're considering a company offering products (versus services). PSR is more suitable for companies that sell items that are easily counted (such as products). Companies that make their money through loans, such as banks, are not usually valued with a PSR because it's more difficult to derive a usable PSR for them.

Lastly, remember to compare the company's PSR with other companies in the same industry along with the industry average so that you get a better idea of the company's relative value.

Chapter 11

Decoding Company Documents

*J*ust the thought of wading through financial documents probably makes your eyes glaze over. I know you'd rather wait for the movie. But this task isn't as bad as you think, and you really need to get familiar with corporate financial documents because your financial success is on the line.

In this chapter, I discuss the basic documents that you will come across (or should come across) most often in your investing life. How else will you know how well (or how poorly) a company is doing? This is essential information that all investors need to know, not only at the time of the initial investment decision, but for as long as that stock remains in their portfolio.

Message from the Muckety-Muck: The Annual Report

Once you're a regular stockholder, the company will send you its annual report. If you're not already a stockholder, contact the company's shareholder service department for a hard copy. Also, more and more companies allow you to download their annual report from their Web sites. A company's annual report (also referred to as the "stockholders report") can help you keep track of the company's progress. This is a critical document although it also doubles as a public relations tool for management's purpose. It is your job, as the investor, to ooh and aah at the nice graphics and carefully crafted prose while seeking out the critical nuggets of information regarding your stock and its potential future.

Before I get to the components of the annual report, I want to give you some good reasons to carefully analyze an annual report:

- You want to know how well the company is doing. Are earnings higher, lower, or the same as the year before? How are sales doing? These numbers should be clearly presented in the financial section of the annual report.

- You want to find out whether the company is making more money than it's spending. How does the balance sheet look? Are assets higher or lower than the year before? Is debt growing, shrinking, or about the same as the year before? For more details on balance sheets, see Chapter 10.

- You want to get an idea of management's strategic plan for the coming year. How will management build on the company's success? This is usually covered in the beginning of the annual report — frequently in the letter from the chairman of the board.

Your task boils down to figuring out where the company has been, where it is now, and where it's going. As an investor, you don't need to read the annual report like a novel — from cover to cover. Instead, approach it like a newspaper and jump around to the relevant sections to get the answers you need to decide whether or not you should buy or hold on to the stock.

If you plan to hold the stock for the long haul, reading the annual report and other reports covered in this chapter will be very helpful to you. If you intend to get rid of the stock soon or plan to hold it only for the short term, then reading these reports diligently isn't that important.

Anatomy of an annual report

Not every annual report is put together in exactly the same way — the style of presentation varies. Some annual reports have gorgeous graphics or actual coupons for the company's products, while others are in a standard black-and-white typeface with no cosmetic frills at all. But every annual report does include common basic content such as the income statement and the balance sheet. The following sections present typical components of an average annual report. Keep in mind that every annual report may not have the sections in the same order.

Letter from the chairman of the board

The first thing you see is usually the letter from the chairman of the board. It is the "Dear Stockholder" letter that communicates views from the head muckety-muck. The chairman's letter is designed to put the best possible perspective on the company's operations during the past year. Be aware of this bias. If the company is doing well, the letter will certainly point it out. If the company is having hard times, the letter probably puts a positive spin on the company's difficulties. If the *Titanic* had an annual report, odds are that the letter would have reported, "Great news! A record number of our customers participated in our spontaneous moonlight swimming program. In addition, we confidently project no operating expenses whatsoever for the subsequent fiscal quarter." You get the point.

To get a good idea of what issues the company's management team feels is important and what goals they want to accomplish, keep the following questions in mind:

- ✔ What does the letter say about changing conditions in the company's business? How about in the industry?

- ✔ If there are difficulties, does the letter communicate a clear and logical action plan (cutting costs, closing money-losing plants, and so on) to get the company back on a positive track?

- ✔ What is being highlighted and why? For example, is the company focusing on research and development for new products or on a new deal with China?

- ✔ Does the letter offer apologies for anything the company did? If, for example, the company fell short of sales expectations, does it offer a reason for the shortcoming?

- ✔ Were there (or will there be) new acquisitions or major developments (selling stuff to China or a new marketing agreement with a Fortune 500 company)?

The company's offerings

This section of an annual report can have various titles (such as "Sales and Marketing"), but it covers what the company sells. Whatever the company sells — products or services or both — understand what they are and why customers purchase them. If you don't understand what the company offers, then understanding how the company earns money, which is the driving force behind the company's stock, will be more difficult. Are the company's core or primary offerings selling well? If McDonald's' earnings are holding steady but earnings strictly from burgers and fries are fizzling, that should be a cause for concern. If a company ceases making money from its specialty, then become cautious. Here are some other questions to ask yourself:

- ✔ How does the company distribute its offerings? Is it through a Web site, malls, representatives, or some other means? Does it sell only to the U.S. market, or is its distribution international? The greater the distribution, the greater the sales and, ultimately, the higher the stock price.

- ✔ Are most of the sales to a definable marketplace? If, for example, most of the company's sales are to Argentina, you should worry because Argentina got into horrible financial shape during 2001 and 2002. If the company's customers are not doing well, that will have a direct impact on the company and, eventually, its stock.

✔ How are sales doing versus market standards? In other words, is the company doing better than the industry average? Is the company a market leader in what it offers? The company should be doing better than (or as well as) its peers in the industry. If the company is falling behind its competitors, that doesn't bode well for the stock in the long run.

✔ Does the report include information on the company's competitors and related matters? You should know who the company's competitors are because they have a direct effect on the company's success. If customers are choosing the competitor over your company, the slumping sales and earnings will ultimately hurt the stock's price.

Financial statements

Look over the various financial statements and find the relevant numbers. Every annual report should have (at the very least) a balance sheet and an income statement. Catching the important numbers on a financial statement is not that difficult to do. However, it certainly helps when you pick up some basic accounting knowledge. Chapter 10 can give you more details on evaluating financial statements.

First, review the income statement (also known as the profit and loss statement, or simply P&L). The income statement gives you the company's sales, expenses, and the result (net income or net loss). Look at the following figures:

✔ **Sales:** Are they increasing? If not, why not? By what percentage are sales increasing? Are they at least 10 percent higher than the year before? Sales are, after all, where the money is coming from to pay for the company's activities and subsequent profit.

✔ **Expenses:** Are there unusual items? Are total expenses reported higher than the prior year and by how much? If the item is significantly higher, why? A company with large, rising expenses will see profits suffer, which is not good for the stock price.

✔ **Research and development (R&D):** How much is the company spending on R&D? Companies that rely on new product development (such as pharmaceuticals or biotech firms) should spend an adequate amount because new products mean future earnings and growth.

✔ **Earnings:** This figure reflects the bottom line. Are total earnings higher? How about earnings from operations (leaving out expenses such as taxes and interest)? This is the heart and soul of the income statement and of the company itself. Out of all the numbers in the financial statements, earnings have the greatest single impact on the company's stock price.

Look at the balance sheet. The balance sheet provides a snapshot of a point in time (annual reports usually provide a year-end balance sheet) that tells you what the company owns (assets), what it owes (liabilities), and the end result (net worth). For a healthy company, assets should always be greater than its liabilities. Analyze the following items:

✔ **Assets:** Have they increased from the prior year? If not, was it due to the sale of an asset or a write-off (uncollectible accounts receivable, for example)?

✔ **Inventory:** Is inventory higher or lower than last year? If sales are flat but inventory is growing, that could be a potential problem.

✔ **Debts:** These are the biggest weakness on the corporate balance sheet. Make sure that debts aren't a growing item and that they're under control.

✔ **Derivatives:** A *derivative* is a speculative and complex financial instrument that does not constitute ownership of an asset (such as a stock, bond, or commodity), but rather a promise to convey ownership. Frequently used to generate income, derivatives carry risks that could increase liabilities. Options and futures are examples of derivatives. Find out whether the company dabbles in these complicated, dicey, leveraged financial instruments. Find out (from the company's 10K report) whether it has derivatives and, if so, the total amount. If a company has derivatives that are valued higher than the company's net equity, this could cause tremendous problems. (Speculating in derivatives was a major reason behind Enron's bankruptcy.)

✔ **Equity:** Equity is the company's net worth (what is left in the event that all the assets are used to pay off all the company debts). The stockholders' equity should be increasing steadily by at least 10 percent per year. If not, find out why.

Carefully read the footnotes to the financial statements. Sometimes big changes are communicated in small print.

Summary of past financial figures

The summary of past financial figures gives you a snapshot of the company's overall long-term progress. How many years does the annual report summarize? Some reports summarize three years, and some reports go as far as ten years.

Management issues

The management issues section of an annual report includes a reporting of current trends and issues, such as new things happening in the industry, that affect the company. See whether you agree with management's assessment of economic and market conditions that affect the company's prospects. What significant developments in society does management perceive as affecting the company's operations? Does the report include information on current or pending lawsuits?

CPA opinion letter

Annual reports typically include comments from the company's independent accounting firm. It could be an opinion letter or a simple paragraph with the firm's views regarding the financial statements that were prepared.

The CPA opinion letter should offer an opinion about the accuracy of the financial data presented and how the statements were prepared. Check to see whether the letter includes any footnotes regarding changes in certain numbers or how they were reported. For example, a company that wants to report higher earnings may show depreciation done more conservatively versus a more aggressive method of depreciating. In any case, you should verify the numbers by looking at the company's 10K document filed with the SEC.

Company identity data

The company identity data section informs you about the company's subsidiaries (or lesser companies that it owns), brands, and addresses. It also contains standard data such as the headquarters location and names of directors and officers. Many reports also include data on the directors' and officers' positions in stock ownership at year-end.

Stock data

The stock data section may include a history of the stock price along with information such as what exchange the stock is listed on, the stock symbol, the company's dividend reinvestment plan (if any), and so on. It also includes information on stockholder services and whom to contact for further information.

Proxy materials

As a shareholder (or stockholder — same thing), you're entitled to vote at the annual shareholders meeting. If you ever get the opportunity to attend one, do so. You get to meet other shareholders and ask questions of management and other company representatives. Usually, the shareholder services department provides you with complete details. At the meetings, shareholders vote on company matters, such as approving the new accounting firm or deciding whether a proposed merger with another company will go forward.

If you can't attend (which is usually true for the majority of shareholders), you can vote by proxy. *Voting by proxy* means essentially that you vote by mail. You indicate your votes on the proxy statement (or card) and authorize a representative to vote at the meeting on your behalf. The proxy statement is usually sent to all shareholders with the annual report just before the meeting. Proxy materials or statements must be provided in accordance with SEC regulations governing their use.

Getting a Second Opinion

A wealth of valuable information is available for your investing pursuits. The resources in this section are just a representative few — a good representation, though. The information and research they provide can be expensive if you buy or subscribe on your own, but fortunately, most of the resources mentioned are usually available in the business reference section of a well-stocked public library. To get a more balanced view of the company and its prospects, take a look at several different sources of information for the stocks you're researching.

Company documents filed with the SEC

The serious investor doesn't overlook the wealth of information that you can cull from documents filed with the Securities and Exchange Commission (SEC). Take the time and effort to review these documents because they offer great insight regarding the company's activities. Here's how to obtain the main documents that investors should be aware of:

- ✔ Drop by the company itself. Stockholder service departments keep these publicly available documents on hand and usually give them at no cost to interested parties.

- ✔ Visit the SEC, either in person or online. These documents are available for public viewing at the SEC offices. You can find out more by contacting Securities and Exchange Commission, Publications Unit, 450 Fifth Street, N.W., Washington, DC 20549.

    At the SEC's Web site at www.sec.gov, you can check out EDGAR (Electronic Data Gathering, Analysis, and Retrieval system) to search public documents filed. It is a tremendous source of documents that date back to 1994. You can search, print, or download documents very easily. Documents can be located either by document number or keyword search.

- ✔ Check out Public Registers Annual Report Service (www.prars.com). This organization maintains an extensive collection of annual reports. Visit its Web site or call the service at 800-4ANNUAL.

- ✔ Use *The Wall Street Journal* free annual report service. If you read this newspaper's financial pages and see a company with the club symbol (like the one you see on a playing card), then you can order that company's annual report by calling 800-654-CLUB or visit the Web site www.wsj.com.

Form 10K

Gee, how intimidating. Just the report name alone makes you scratch your head. To some people, 10K refers to running a race of 10 kilometers. But if you're reading (not running) a 10K, you may be wishing you were running one instead.

Form 10K is a report that companies must file with the SEC annually. It works like the annual report that you get from the company except that it probably provides more detailed financial information. It can be a little intimidating because it can be dry, cumbersome text. It's not exactly Shakespeare (high P/E Internet stocks would have also driven Lady Macbeth insane); then again, the data aren't laden with as much spin as the annual report the company sends to shareholders. Without going crazy, go through each section of the 10K. Take some extra time to scrutinize the section on financial data. Ask the same questions that you do when you're looking at the annual report. The following Web sites can help you make sense of 10K reports:

- ✔ FreeEDGAR (www.freeedgar.com)
- ✔ 10K Wizard Technology (www.10Kwizard.com)
- ✔ Edgar Online, Inc. (www.edgar-online.com)

Form 10Q

This form is a quarterly report that gives you the same basic information as the 10K, but it details only three months' worth of activity. Because a long time can pass between 10Ks (after all, it is a year), don't wait 12 months to see how your company is progressing, especially if you own 37,000 shares of a company called Surprise Corp. To see how the company is doing, compare the 10Q with a 10Q that covers the same quarter last year. For example, if you have stock in a large retail company, compare the 10Q for the quarter covering October, November, and December to the same quarter of the previous year because major retailers have entirely different results for other quarterly periods.

Keep in mind that not every company has the same fiscal year. A company with a calendar year fiscal year (ending December 31) files a 10Q for each of the first three quarters and files a 10K for the final quarter. The fourth quarter data is reported in the 10K along with the statistics for the full year.

Insider reports

There are two types of insiders: those who work within the company and those outside the company who have a significant (10 percent or more) ownership of company stock. Tracking insider activity is very profitable for investors who want to follow in the footsteps of the people who are in the know. See Chapter 18 for information about monitoring and benefiting from insider activity.

Every time an insider (such as the CEO or controller) buys or sells stock, the transaction has to be reported to the SEC. These reports become publicly available documents that allow you and me to see what the insiders are actually doing. It's one thing to hear what they say in public, but it is more important to see what they're actually doing with their stock transactions. To get further details about insider trading and the reporting requirements for insiders, go to the SEC Web site at www.sec.gov. Here are the main documents to view:

✔ **Forms 3, 4, and 5:** Company directors, top management, and related insiders as described in the 1934 Securities Act must file statements of stock ownership. Once a person becomes a recognized insider by the SEC, he makes the initial filing on Form 3. Whenever a stock purchase or sale is made, the insider files Form 4. In addition, the insider annually files Form 5, which contains all the information on stock ownership covering the entire year.

✔ **Form 144:** This form is filed as a public notice of the proposed sale of restricted stock (stock obtained by insiders, which have a limited transferability) by an insider. Form 144 is filed when the ownership interest being proposed for sale is either 500 or more shares or in excess of $10,000, whichever is less (this covers the total transactions over a three-month period).

Value Line

The Value Line Investment Survey, one of many information products provided by Value Line Publishing, Inc., is considered a longtime favorite by many stock investing professionals. You can look it over at any library that has a good business reference department. In the *Survey,* Value Line covers the largest 1,700 public companies and ranks them according to financial strength and several other key factors. Over the course of a year, the publication provides constant, updated information on each firm.

A valuable feature of the *Survey* is its famous rating system. It places stocks into one of five classes of strength. A stock rated in class 1 is strongest, while class 5 is the lowest. Over many years of testing and refining, the class 1 stocks have generally outperformed the general market. To get more information about Value Line, either head to the library or visit www.valueline.com.

Standard & Poor's

Another ubiquitous and venerable publisher is Standard & Poor's (S&P). Although it has a number of quality information products and services for both individual and institutional investors, the three you should take a look at include the following:

✔ *The S&P Stock Guide:* Available at many libraries, this guide comes out monthly and reports on stocks on the New York Stock Exchange, American Stock Exchange, and the largest firms listed on Nasdaq. It gives a succinct, two-page summary on each stock. It offers a snapshot of the company's current finances along with a brief history and commentary on the company's activities. This guide also rates the company based on its financial strength.

- ✔ *The S&P Industry Survey:* S&P gives detailed reports on the top indus- tries, cramming a lot of information about a given industry in four to seven pages. This annual publication provides a nice summary of what's happened in the industry in the past 12 months, what the industry looks like today, and the prospects for the coming year. It also provides the important numbers (earnings, sales, and industry ranking) for the top 50 to 100 firms in the industry.

- ✔ *The S&P Bond Guide:* Yes, I know we're talking stocks. But a company's bond rating is invaluable for stock investors. S&P analyzes the strength of the bond issuer and ranks the bond for creditworthiness. If S&P looks at the company and gives them a high rating, this serves as added assurance that the company is financially strong. It's preferable for the company to have a bond rating of AAA, AA, or A because this tells you that the com- pany is "investment-grade." The highest rating is AAA, which tells you that the company has superior financial ability to pay back its debt. AA and A are slightly lower ratings but are still an indication of financial strength.

Moody's Investment Service

Another stalwart publisher, Moody's offers vital research on stocks and bonds. *Moody's Handbook of Common Stocks* is usually available in the refer- ence section of a well-stocked library. It offers stock and bond guides similar to S&P and also provides an independent bond rating service. A stock rated highly by both Moody's and S&P is a great place for investors hunting for value investments.

Brokerage reports: The good, the bad, and the ugly

Clint Eastwood, where are you? Traditionally, brokerage reports have been a good source of information for investors seeking informed opinions about stocks. And they still are, but some brokerage reports have gotten bad press in recent years and deservedly so.

The good

Research departments at brokerage firms provide stock reports and make them available for their clients and investment publications. The firms' ana- lysts and market strategists generally prepare these reports. Good research is critical, and brokerage reports can be very valuable. What better source of guidance than full-time experts backed up by million-dollar research depart- ments? Brokerage reports have some strong points:

✔ The analysts are professionals who should understand the value of a company and its stock. They analyze and compare company data every day.

✔ They have at their disposal tremendous information and historical data that they can sift through to make informed decisions.

✔ If you have an account with the firm, you can usually access the information free.

During the late 1990s, some of these analysts gained celebrity status as the public fervor over stock investing turned it into a national pastime. Analysts said "X is a great stock. Buy it." Millions bought. Stocks soared. Brokerage firms made tons of money. Analysts got million-dollar bonuses. Common investors became wealthier. And they lived happily ever after! (Don't stop here. Keep reading through the rest of this "Brokerage reports: The good, the bad, and the ugly" section.)

The bad

Well, brokerage reports may not be bad in every case, but at their worst, they're quite bad. Brokers make their money from commissions and investment banking fees (nothing bad here). However, they can find themselves in the awkward position of issuing brokerage reports on companies that are (or could be) customers for the brokerage firm that employs them (hmmm — could be bad). Frequently, this relationship can result in a brokerage report that paints an overly positive picture of a company that can be a bad investment (yup, that's bad).

Sometimes, good research can be compromised by conflicts of interest.

During 1998–2000, the overwhelming number of brokerage reports issued glowing praise of companies that were either mediocre or dubious. Investors bought up stocks such as tech stocks and Internet stocks. The sheer demand pushed up stock prices, which gave the appearance of genius to analysts' forecasts, yet they rose essentially as a self-fulfilling prophecy. The stocks were very overvalued and were cruisin' for a bruisin'. Analysts and investors were feeling lucky.

The ugly

Investors lost a ton of money (oooh, ugly). Money that was painstakingly accumulated over many years of work vanished in a matter of months as the bear market of 2000 hit (uglier). Retirees who had trusted the analysts saw nest eggs lose 40 to 70 percent in value (yikes, very ugly). In total, investors lost over $5 trillion during 2000 and 2001, much of it needlessly.

In 2001, a record number of lawsuits and complaints were filed against brokerage firms. For Wall Street and Main Street, some tough lessons were learned. Regarding research reports from brokerage firms, the following points can help you avoid getting a bad case of the uglies:

- ✔ Always ask yourself, "Is the provider of the report a biased source?" In other words, is the broker getting business in any way from the company that is being recommended?

- ✔ Never, never, NEVER rely on just one source of information, especially if it is the same source that is selling you the stock or other investment.

- ✔ Do your research first before you rely on a brokerage report.

- ✔ Do your due diligence before you buy stocks anyway. Look at the chapters in Part 1 and Part 2 to understand your need for diversification, risk tolerance, and so on.

- ✔ Verify the information provided with a trip to the library or Web sites (see Appendix A).

Clint would be proud.

Compiling Your Own Research Department

Don't spend an excessive amount of time or money, but you should maintain your own library of resources. You may only need one shelf (or a small amount of memory on your computer's hard drive). But why not have a few investment facts and resources at your fingertips? I maintain my own library loaded with books, magazines, newsletters, and tons of great stuff downloaded on my computer for easy search and reference. When you start your own collection, keep the following in mind:

- ✔ Keep some select newspapers. *Barron's, The Wall Street Journal,* and *Investor's Business Daily* regularly have some editions that are worth keeping. For example, *The Wall Street Journal* and *Investor's Business Daily* usually have a year-in-review issue that is done the first business week in January. *Barron's* has special issues reviewing brokers and financial Web sites.

- ✔ Subscribe to financial magazines. Publications such as *Forbes* magazine and *SmartMoney Magazine* offer great research and regularly review stocks, brokers, and resources for investors.

- ✔ Keep annual reports. Regarding the stocks that are the core holdings in your portfolio, keep all the annual reports (at the very least, the most recent three).

✔ Go to the library's business reference section periodically to stay updated (without spending a lot of money). If you pay taxes, then you may as well use the public library to sharpen your knowledge.

✔ The Internet (just bein' complete). There are plenty of great Web sites to peruse, and I list some of the best ones in Appendix A.

Financial reports are very important and easier to read than most people think. An investor can easily avoid a bad investment by simply noticing the data in what seems like a jumble of numbers. Learn to read them. For a great book to help you with reading financial reports (without needless technicality), check out *How to Read a Financial Report: Wringing Vital Signs Out of the Numbers,* 5th Edition, by John A Tracy (John Wiley & Sons, 1999).

Chapter 12

Analyzing Industries

. . . .

. . . .

Suppose that you have to bet your entire nest egg on a one-mile race. All you need to do is select a winning group. These are your choices:

  A group of thoroughbred race horses

  A group of overweight Elvis impersonators

  A group of lethargic snails

This isn't a trick question, and you have one minute to answer. Notice that I didn't ask you to pick a single winner out of a giant mush of horses, Elvii, and snails; I only asked you to pick the winning group in the race. The obvious answer is the thoroughbred race horses (and, no, they weren't ridden by the overweight Elvis impersonators because that would take away from the eloquent point being made). In this example, even the slowest member of group A would easily outdistance the fastest member of either group B or C.

Fortunately, this is where the comparison to stock investing ends. You don't have to choose the absolute winner because there are lots of winning stocks in second place, too. The basic point is that you increase your odds of winning when you choose a winning industry group as part of your strategy. In the race to build wealth, all you need to do is pick decent stocks (Chapters 8 and 9 give you that information based on your specific investment goals) in a decent industry (read on) and do so on a long-term basis in a disciplined manner.

A successful, long-term investor looks at the industry just as carefully as he looks at the individual stock. Luckily, choosing a winning industry to invest in is easier than choosing individual stocks. I know some investors who can pick a winning stock in a losing industry, and I also know investors who have chosen a losing stock in a winning industry (the former is far outnumbered by the latter). Just think how well you would do when you choose a great stock in a great industry! Of course, you would bang your head (or your broker's) against the wall if you chose a bad stock in a bad industry.

Badgering the Witness and Interrogating the Industries

Your common sense is an important tool in choosing industries with winning stocks. The following sections explore some of the most important questions to ask yourself when you're choosing an industry.

Is the industry growing?

The question may seem too obvious, but probably not. The saying "the trend is your friend" applies when choosing an industry in which to invest, as long as the trend is an upward one. If you look at three different stocks that are equal in every significant way but you find that stock A is in an industry growing 15 percent per year while the other two industries have either little growth or are shrinking, which stock would you choose?

Sometimes, the stock of a financially unsound or poorly run company goes up dramatically because the industry it's in is very exciting to the public. The most obvious example is Internet stocks from 1998–2000. Stocks such as Amazon.com shot up to incredible heights because investors thought the Internet was "it." Sooner or later, the measure of a successful company is its ability to be profitable. Serious investors look at the company's fundamentals (see Chapter 10 to find out how to do this) and the prospects for the industry's growth before settling on a particular stock.

To judge how well an industry is doing, various information sources monitor all the major industries and measure their progress. The more reliable sources include the following:

- ✔ CBS MarketWatch (www.marketwatch.com)
- ✔ Standard & Poor's Industry Survey (www.standardpoor.com)
- ✔ Hoover's Industry Snapshots (www.hoovers.com)
- ✔ Yahoo! Industry News (www.industry.yahoo.com)
- ✔ Dow Jones Business Directory (www.business.dowjones.com)

Ranking the industries

Standard and Poor's (S&P) Industry Survey is an excellent source of information on America's industries. Besides ranking and comparing them and informing you about their current prospects, the survey also lists the top companies by size, sales, earnings, and other key information. The survey and other S&P publications are available at the business reference sections of most libraries (or at the S&P Web site at `www.standardpoor.com`).

The preceding sources generally give you in-depth information about the major industries. Visit their Web sites to read their current research and articles along with links to relevant sites for more details. Dow Jones & Co., for example, publishes indexes for all the major sectors and industries so that you can get a useful snapshot of how well an industry is doing (including information about whether the stock is up or down and how it's performing year-to-date), and it updates its Web site daily.

Are the industry's products or services in demand?

Look at the products and services that an industry provides. Do they look like things that society will continue to want? Are products and services on the horizon that could replace them? Does the industry face a danger of potential obsolescence?

When evaluating future demand, look for a *sunrise industry*, which is one that is new or emerging or has promising appeal for the future. Good examples in recent years have been biotech and Internet companies. In contrast, a *sunset industry* is one that is either declining or has little potential for growth. For example, you probably shouldn't invest in the videocassette manufacturing industry as demand for the new DVD format increases. Owning stock in a strong, profitable company in a sunrise industry is obviously the most desirable choice.

Futurists, trend watchers, and other "seers into the future" predict the following megatrends:

- **The aging of America:** There will be more senior citizens than ever before. Because of this, financial and healthcare services will prosper.

- **Advances in high-technology:** Internet, telecom, medical, and biotechnology innovations will continue.

✔ **Increasing need for basic materials:** As society advances here and in the rest of the world, building blocks such as metals and other precious commodities will be in demand.

What does the industry's growth rely on?

An industry doesn't exist in a vacuum. External factors weigh heavily on its ability to survive and thrive. Does the industry rely on an established megatrend, in which case it will probably be strong for a while, or on factors that are losing relevance? Technological and demographic changes are other factors that may contribute to an industry's growth.

Perhaps the industry offers great new medical products for senior citizens. What are the prospects for growth? The graying of America is an established megatrend. As millions of Americans climb past age 50, great opportunities await companies that cater to them.

Is this industry dependent on another industry?

This twist on the prior question is a reminder that industries frequently are intertwined and can become codependent. When one industry suffers, you may find it helpful to understand which industries will subsequently suffer. The reverse can also be true — when one industry is doing well, other industries may also reap the benefits.

In either case, if the stock you choose is in an industry that is highly dependent on other industries, you should know about it. If you're considering stocks of resort companies and you see the headlines blaring "Airlines losing money as public stops flying," what would you do?

Who are the leading companies in the industry?

Once you've chosen the industry, what types of companies do you want to invest in? You can choose from two basic types of companies:

✔ **Established leaders:** These companies are considered industry leaders or have a large share of the market. This is the safer way to go; what better investment for novice investors than companies that have already proven themselves?

✔ **Innovators:** If the industry is hot and you want to be more aggressive in your approach, why not speculate in companies that offer new products, patents, or new technologies? These are probably smaller companies but have a greater potential for growth in a proven industry.

Is the industry a target of government action?

You need to know whether the government is targeting an industry because intervention by politicians and bureaucrats (rightly or wrongly) can have an impact on an industry's economic situation. For example, would you invest in a tobacco company now that the government has issued all of its regulations and warnings?

Investors need to take heed when political "noise" starts coming out about a particular industry. An industry can be hurt either by direct government intervention or by the threat of it. Intervention can take the form of lawsuits, investigations, taxes, regulations, or sometimes an outright ban. In any case, there is no greater external threat to a company's survival than being on the wrong end of government intervention.

Sometimes, government action can help an industry. Generally, beneficial action can take two forms:

✔ **Deregulation and/or tax decreases:** Government can sometimes reduce burdens on an industry. In 1979, the federal government deregulated the airlines, an action that in turn caused a boom in travel. The airline industry subsequently experienced tremendous growth as more people flew than ever before. This increase in the number of airline passengers, in turn, spurred growth for the lodging and resort industries.

✔ **Direct funding:** Government has the power to steer taxpayer money towards business as well. In the 1970s, when Chrysler was floundering, financing assistance helped the company get back on its feet, and Chrysler did well during the 1980s.

Which category does the industry fall into?

Most industries can neatly be placed in one of two categories: cyclical and defensive. In a rough way, these categories generally translate into what society wants and what it needs. Society buys what it *needs* in both good and bad times. It buys what it *wants* when times are good and holds off when times are bad.

Cyclical industries

Cyclical industries are industries whose fortunes rise and fall with the economy's rise and fall. In other words, if the economy is doing well and the stock market is doing well, cyclical industries tend to do well. When the economy is doing well, consumers and investors are confident and tend to spend and invest more money than usual. Real estate and automobiles are great examples of cyclical industries.

Your own situation offers you some common-sense insight into the concept of cyclical industries. Think about your behavior as a consumer, and you get a great clue into the thinking of millions of consumers. Think about the times you felt good about your career and your finances. When you (and millions of others) feel good about money and about the future, you have a greater tendency to buy more (and/or more expensive) stuff. When people feel financially strong, they're more apt to buy a new house or car or make some other large financial commitment. Also, people take on more debt because they feel confident that they can pay it back. In light of this, what industries do you think would do well?

The same point also holds for business spending. When businesses think that economic times are good and foresee continuing good times, they tend to spend more money on large purchases such as new equipment or technology. They think that when they're doing well and flush with financial success, it's a good idea to reinvest that money to increase future success.

Defensive industries

Defensive industries are industries that produce goods and services that are needed no matter what's happening in the economy. This is where your common sense kicks in. What will you still buy even if times are tough? Think about what millions of people buy no matter how bad the economy gets. A good example is food. People still need to eat regardless of good or bad times. Other examples of defensive industries are utilities and healthcare.

In bad economic times, defensive stocks tend to do better than cyclical stocks. However, when times are good, cyclical stocks tend to do better than defensive stocks. Defensive stocks don't do as well in good times because people don't eat twice as much or use up more electricity.

So how do defensive stocks grow? Their growth generally relies on two factors:

- **Population growth:** As more and more consumers are born, more people become available to buy.

- **New markets:** A company can grow by seeking out new groups of consumers who can buy their products and services. Coca-Cola, for example, found new markets in Asia during the 1990s. As Communist regimes fell from power and more societies embraced a free market and consumer goods, the company sold more beverages, and its stock soared.

It takes money to spend money

The economic boom of the late 1990s was in many respects due to an explosion of spending financed by debt. Consumers and businesses felt great about the economy's expansion and spent money accordingly. Among the winning industries were automobiles, real estate, and technology. Choosing strong stocks in these categories meant tremendous profits for investors who did their homework.

Please keep in mind that not every stock falls neatly into one of these categories. A good example of a stock that doesn't fall into either category is auto parts. Whether the economy is booming and people are buying more cars or the economy is struggling and people are buying fewer cars, auto parts get sold.

Also, both categories include a wide range of stocks — some stocks may be more defensive than others, for example. The bottom line is to understand the nature of the industry, what factors the industry is dependent on, and how it makes money.

Don't Shoot the Messenger: Key Industries

Not all industries go up and down in tandem. Indeed, at any given time, some industry is successful no matter what is happening with the general economy. In fact, investors have made a lot of money simply by choosing an industry that benefits from economic trends.

For example, the economy was in bad shape during the 1970s. It was a period of *stagflation* — low growth, high unemployment, and high inflation. This was the worst time for the economy since the Great Depression; most industries (and therefore most stocks) were having tough times. But some industries did well; in fact, some flourished. Real estate and precious metals, for example, performed well in this environment. Because the inflation rate soared into double digits, inflationary hedges such as gold and silver did very well. During the '70s, gold skyrocketed from $35 an ounce to $850 by the end of the decade. Silver went from under $2 to over $50 in the same period. What do you think happened to stocks of gold and silver mining companies? That's right. They skyrocketed as well. Gold stocks gave investors spectacular returns.

In the 1980s, the economy became rejuvenated when taxes were cut, regulations were decreased, and inflation fell. Most industries did well. But even in a growing economy, some industries struggle. Examples of industries that struggled during that time included precious metals and energy stocks.

For sale

I include real estate as a key industry because it is a cyclical *bellwether industry* (one that has a great effect on many other industries that may be dependent on it). It is looked at as a key component of economic health because so many other industries, including building materials, mortgages, household appliances, and contract labor services, are tied to it. When the real estate industry is booming, that bodes well for much of the economy.

Housing starts are one way to measure real estate activity. This data is an important leading indicator of health in the industry. Housing starts indicate new construction, which means more business for related industries.

Keep an eye on the real estate industry for negative news that could be bearish for the economy and the stock market. Because real estate is purchased with mortgage money, investors and analysts watch the mortgage market for trouble signs such as rising delinquencies and foreclosures. These statistics serve as a warning for general economic weakness.

Baby, you can drive my car

The auto industry is another business that that you should watch very carefully. When cars are selling well, you can generally interpret that as a positive indicator for the economy. People buy new cars when they're doing well. Autos are big-ticket items that are another barometer of people's economic well-being.

Conversely, trouble in the auto industry is a red flag for trouble. If auto repossessions and car loan delinquencies are rising, you should view that as a warning about general economic weakness.

Thanking Mr. Roboto

In recent years, technology became very popular with investors. Indeed, it is a great sector, and its impact on the economy's present and future success cannot be underestimated. The shares of technology companies can rise substantially because investors buy them based on expectations — today's untested, unproven companies may become the Microsofts and IBMs of tomorrow. In spite of the sector's potential, companies can still fail if customers don't embrace their products. Even in technology stocks, you still must apply the rules and guidelines that I discuss throughout this book about financially successful companies. Pick the best in a growing industry, and you'll succeed over the long haul.

Banking on it

Banking and financial services are an intrinsic part of any economy. Debt is the most telling sign of this industry for investors. If debt is growing faster than the economy, you need to watch to see how it will impact their stocks and mutual funds. If debt gets out of control, it can be disastrous for the economy.

Chapter 13

Money, Mayhem, and Votes

In This Chapter

▶ Looking at the effects of politics on the economy

▶ Taking a crash course in general economics

*P*olitics and economics set the environment for stock success (or failure) more than any other influence. Politics (especially manifested in taxes, regulations, and legislation) can make or break a company or industry quicker than any other external force. Economics — how people spend, save, and invest their money in society — also does its share to drive stock prices up and down. Understanding these effects on stock prices will either save you a lot or make you a lot of money.

What people must understand (especially government policy makers) is that a new tax, law, regulation, or government action has a *macro* effect on a stock, an industry, or even an entire economic system, whereas a company has a *micro* effect on an economy. The following gives you a simple snapshot of this:

> Politics → policy → economy → industry → the company → the stock → stock investor

If the world of politics produces negative policy, ultimately negative results will ensue. If it produces positive policy, then positive results ensue.

Now, this chapter doesn't moralize about politics or advocate a political point of view; after all, this book is about stock investing. In general, policies can be good or bad regardless of their effect on the economy — some policies are enacted to achieve greater social purposes even if they kick you in the wallet. However, in the context of this chapter, politics is covered from a cause-and-effect perspective: How does politics affect prosperity in general and stock investing in particular?

A proficient stock investor cannot — must not — look at stocks as though they existed in a vacuum. My favorite example of this is the idea of fish in a lake. You can have a great fish (your stock) among a whole school of fish (the stock market) in a wonderful lake (the economy). But what if the lake gets polluted (bad policy)? What will happen to the fish? Politics controls the lake and can make it hospitable — or dangerous — for the participants. You get the point. The example may sound too simple, yet it isn't. So many people — political committees, corporate managers, bureaucrats, and politicians — still get it so wrong time and time again, to the detriment of the economy and stock investors.

Although the two get inexorably intertwined, I try to treat politics and economics as separate issues.

Avoiding the Bull When Elephants and Donkeys Talk Turkey

The campaigns heat up. Democrats, Republicans, and smaller parties vie for your attention and subsequent votes. Conservatives, liberals, socialists, moderates, and libertarians joust in the battlefield of ideas. But, after all is said and done, voters make their decisions. Election day brings a new slate of politicians into power, and they, in turn, will joust and debate on new rules and programs in the legislative halls of power. Before and after election time, investors must keep a watchful eye.

For stock investors, politics manifests itself as a major factor in investment-making decisions in ways shown in Table 13-1.

Table 13-1	Politics and Investing
Possible Legislation	*Effect on Investing*
Taxes	Will a new tax affect a particular stock (industry or economy)? Generally, more or higher taxes ultimately have a negative impact on stock investing. Income taxes and capital gains taxes are good examples.
Laws	Will Congress (or, in some instances, state legislatures) pass a law that will have a negative impact on a stock, the industry, or the economy? Price controls — laws that set the price of a product, service, or commodity — are examples of negative laws.
Regulations	Will a new (or existing) regulation have a negative (or positive) effect on the stock of your choice? Generally, more or tougher regulations have a negative impact on stocks.

Possible Legislation	Effect on Investing
Government spending and debt	If government agencies spend too much or misallocate resources, they may create greater burdens on society, which in turn will be bearish for the economy and the stock market. (For information on investing in bear or bull markets, see Chapter 14.)
Money supply	The U.S. money supply — the dollars you use — is controlled by the Federal Reserve. It is basically a governmental agency that serves as America's central bank. How can it affect stocks? You can find more on this question in the "Money supply" section, later in the chapter.
Interest rates	The Federal Reserve has crucial influence here. It can raise key interest rates that in turn can have an effect on the entire economy and the stock market. I cover this in the "Interest rates" section, later in this chapter.

When many of the items in Table 13-1 work in tandem, they can have a magnified effect that can have tremendous consequences for your stock portfolio. Alert investors keep a constant vigil when the legislature is open for business, and they adjust their portfolio accordingly.

California energy crisis: Case in point

The California energy crisis is a great example for people concerned not only about investments but also about the general well-being of our economy. This example is evidence that if you don't understand the economics of a situation, you'll lose money.

During the 1990s, the state of California was an economic powerhouse. During this decade, one of the strongest public utility stocks was Pacific Gas & Electric (PG&E). Many analysts consider a good utility to be a safe component in the portfolio of a cautious investor. PG&E had strong cash flow and a solid financial foundation. It served a large, growing population in a flourishing state. What could possibly go wrong?

During the 1990s, California's population nearly doubled. Utilities were pressured to meet the burgeoning demand for energy by consumers and businesses. They needed to build more power plants, but the challenge was to do it while addressing concerns and opposition from activist environmental groups. These groups persuaded politicians to pass laws and regulations that effectively prevented the building of any new power plants. Additionally, politicians passed legislation that imposed price controls that froze the price that consumers paid for electricity while simultaneously deregulating the wholesale energy market where utilities bought their electricity. The situation became a classic example of how price controls can be a devastating reality for businesses and consumers.

Consumers cheered the new legislation because it kept their electricity prices low. Consumers are the ones who vote, and politicians responded to that incentive by passing this questionable legislation. Utilities succumbed because they don't have the same voting clout as millions of consumers, and because wholesale energy prices at that time were very low, the legislation didn't seem like a problem. The stage was set.

As oil and gas prices started to rise dramatically during late 1999 and early 2000, seeing the problem emerge became quite easy. PG&E and other California utilities were stuck between a rock and a hard place. By law, they couldn't build new power plants, and they couldn't raise prices for consumers. However, their wholesale costs were soaring. This regulatory situation caused an energy shortage. Electricity demand continued to increase, but existing supply couldn't meet this demand. Ultimately, PG&E had no choice but to file for bankruptcy. How were investors affected?

Alert investors who saw the situation as it initially developed sold their PG&E stock immediately. Just prior to the energy crisis, PG&E stock sold in the $30 to $35 range. By early 2001, PG&E stock fell to $6 per share! Economically astute investors got out before the stock fell over 80 percent. Investors who had a buy-and-hold strategy and ignored the effects of politics and economics lost a lot of money. However, the losses didn't stop there.

TIP

Doomed to repeat it?

History provides abundant lessons for stock investors because you can easily see how government policies have impacted our economy in general and the stock market specifically. The greatest financial calamities in history occurred either because politicians made mistakes or because they made purposeful policies that produced unintended negative effects.

During the 1920s and 1930s, Presidents Herbert Hoover and Franklin D. Roosevelt and Congress produced disastrous policies that turned what should have been a minor recession into the Great Depression. From 1928 to 1938, federal government spending ballooned out of control,

and stringent regulations were placed on the country's domestic economy and its international trade (including the Smoot-Hawley Tariff Act). These events, along with increasing income tax rates to 91 percent (yikes!), placed a drag on economic growth that lasted an entire decade.

How did successful stock investors react in those tough years? In the late 1920s, when the signs of pending trouble were clearly becoming evident, alert investors such as Bernard Baruch got out of the stock market before it crashed in 1929, when the Great Depression produced the "mother of all bear markets."

In 2000, California's economy was the sixth largest in the world (if it were considered a country). Its avoidable energy crisis caused much economic damage to both the state and the nation because California is about ⅓ of the national economy. Energy costs affect all businesses as well as consumers. Many investors felt the ripple effect in both good and bad ways. How did alert investors take advantage of a difficult situation? What would you do to avoid losses? The following sections provide some insight to help answer these questions.

Understanding price controls

Stock investors should be very wary of price controls (they're a great example of regulation). Price controls have been tried continuously throughout history, and they have continuously been removed because they ultimately did more harm than good. It's easy to see why. Imagine if you ran a business that sold chairs and a law were passed that stated, "From this point onward, chairs can be sold only for $10." If all your costs stayed constant at $9 or less, the regulation wouldn't be that bad. However, price controls put two dynamics in motion. First, the artificially lower price encourages consumption — more people will buy chairs. Secondly, production is discouraged. Who wants to make chairs if they can't sell them for a decent profit?

What happens to the company with a fixed sales price (in this example, $10) and rising costs? Profits will shrink, and depending on how long the price controls are in effect, the company will eventually experience losses. The chair producer will eventually be driven out of business. The chair-building industry will shrink, and a chair shortage will be the result. Profits (and jobs) will soon vanish. So what will happen if you own stock in a company that builds chairs? I'll just say that if I tell which way the stock price is going, you'd better be sitting down (if, of course, you have a chair).

Ascertaining the political climate

The bottom line is that you ignore political realities at your own (economic) risk. To be and stay aware, ask yourself the following questions about the stock of each company in which you invest:

- What laws will directly affect my stock investment adversely?
- Will any laws affect that company's industry?
- Will any current or prospective laws affect the company's sources of revenue?
- Will any current or prospective laws affect the company's expenses or supplies?

🖰 Am I staying informed about political and economic issues that may possibly have a negative impact on my investment?

🖰 Will such things as excessive regulations, price controls, or new taxes have a negative impact on my stock's industry?

Oil and gas service and exploration companies benefited from the U.S. need for more energy supplies. But investment opportunities didn't stop there. As oil and gas supplies became costly and problematic, alternative energy sources gained national attention. The debate was rekindled on solar power and exciting new technologies, such as fuel cells. Investors who anticipated the new interest in alternative energy sought companies that would logically benefit. A good example of this is Ballard Power Systems, Inc. It became recognized as a leader in fuel cell technology and quickly saw its stock price rise in early 2001 from $41 per share to $60 in a matter of weeks.

Politics and economics are a double-edged sword. Understand them, and you can profit; misunderstand and become a financial victim. To choose investments that will gain in value, flip back to Chapter 10, where I explain how to analyze potential stock value.

Systemic versus nonsystemic effects

Politics can affect our investment in two basic ways: systemic and nonsystemic.

Nonsystemic means that the system is not affected but a particular participant is affected. A *systemic effect* means that all the players in that system are affected. In this case, the "system" is the economy at large. Politics imposes itself (through taxes, laws, regulations, and so on) and has an undue influence on all the members of that system.

Nonsystemic

Say that you decide to buy stock in a company called Golf Carts Unlimited, Inc. (GCU). You believe that the market for golf carts has great potential and that GCU stands to grow substantially. How could politics affect GCU?

What if politicians believed that GCU was too big and that it controlled too much of the golf cart industry? Maybe they viewed GCU as a monopoly and wanted the federal government to step in to shrink GCU's reach and influence for the benefit of competition and consumers. Maybe the government believed that GCU engaged in unfair or predatory business practices and that it was in violation of antitrust (or antimonopoly) laws. If the government acts against GCU, the action is a nonsystemic issue: The action is directed toward the participant (in this case, GCU) and not the golf cart industry.

Playing monopoly

Government action against large companies for real (or alleged) monopolistic abuses has happened many times. Investors saw share prices drop dramatically when the government initiated lawsuits against companies such as IBM (during the 1970s) and Microsoft (during 1999 and 2000). The federal government is a massive entity, and it has trillions of taxpayer dollars at its disposal. When it targets a company, regardless of the merits of the case, avoid investing in that company (until the trouble has passed). Investors should be wary when the government starts making noise about any company and potential legal actions against it.

What would happen if you were an investor in GCU? Would your stock investment suffer as a result of government action directed against the company? Absolutely.

Systemic

Say that politicians want to target the golf industry for intervention because they maintain that golf should be free for all to participate in and that a law must be passed to make it accessible to all, especially those who can't afford to play. So to remedy the situation, the following law is enacted: "Law #67590305598002 declares that from this day forward, all golf courses that operate must charge only one dollar for any golfers who choose to participate."

That law would sound great to any golfer. But what would the unintended effects be should such a law become reality? Many people agree with the sentiment of the law, but what about the cause-and-effect aspects of it? Obviously, all things being equal, golf courses would be forced to close. Staying in business would be uneconomical if their costs were higher relative to their income. If they couldn't charge any more than a dollar, how could they possibly stay open? Ultimately (and ironically), no one could play golf.

What would happen to investors of Golf Carts Unlimited, Inc.? If the world of golf shrinks, then demand for golf carts would shrink as well. The value of GCU's stock would be certainly be "triple-bogeyed."

Examples of politics creating systemic problems are endless, but you get the point.

Poking into politics: Resources

To find out about new laws being passed or proposed, check out Congress and what's going on at its primary Web sites: the U.S. House of

Representatives (www.house.gov) and the U.S. Senate (www.senate.gov). For presidential information and proposals, check the White House's Web site at www.whitehouse.gov.

You also may want to check out THOMAS, the service performed by the Library of Congress, at http://thomas.loc.gov. THOMAS is a search engine that helps you find any piece of legislation either by bill number or keyword. This is an excellent way to find out whether an industry is being targeted for increased regulation or deregulation.

You can find more resources in Appendix A. The more knowledge you pick up about how politics and government actions can help (or harm) an investment, the better you'll be at growing your wealth.

Easing into Economics

Economics sounds like a deadly dull pursuit. Actually, the wrong book on the topic or the wrong instructor can make the topic so boring that you feel like you're crawling backward through Death Valley. Does economics really matter, and do you have to really understand phrases such as "inelasticity coefficient" and the "Index of Leading Economic Indicators"? No, not really. But do you need to be familiar with phrases such as "supply and demand" and "price controls don't work" to operate in today's modern stock market? The answer is a resounding yes. Of course, you can invest without knowing much about economics. However, your chances for success are tremendously enhanced when you have a basic understanding of how economics works. Actually, economics explained in the proper way is fascinating. Knowing how the world ticks can be fun and profitable.

By the way, I'm proud of you; you've made it past the halfway point in a difficult chapter. Don't be shy about taking a break and getting a refreshment or taking a nap. I'll wait. Okay? Are you back? Great! Let's get back to the fascinating world of economics!

When people comment about the economy, they make it sound like a giant, amorphous thing in the same way they talk about the stock market and the weather. To put it into perspective, the economy is you and me and millions of others — producers, consumers, entrepreneurs, and workers all trading money for goods and services, millions of people and organizations voluntarily transacting with each other day in and day out. People and organizations buy, spend, save, and invest billions every hour of every day.

Looking at the economy should be like seeing a huge picture and deciding where on the canvas are the greatest points of interest — investment opportunities. When you look at the economy, you look at the major numbers and trends and judge whether a particular company is well suited to profit from trends and opportunities. You simply rely on your common sense and apply it with the statistics that track the economy in general. If millions of consumers are buying product X and the market and demand for X are growing, then it stands to reason that the best company offering product X will prosper as well. The reverse can be true as well: If more and more people avoid, or just don't spend their money on, a particular product or industry, then the fortunes of those companies will decline as well.

Economic reports are important because sometimes just one report or statistic released is enough to move the stock market. The economic statistics and reports that are the most meaningful to you are the ones that have a direct bearing on your stock or industry. If you invest in real estate or construction stocks, reports that cover housing starts and interest rates are critical to you. If you invest in retail stocks, then information on consumer confidence and debt is important to you.

In the following table, I give some examples of key industries and a statistic that's a relevant indicator:

Industry	Statistic	Comments
Real estate	Housing starts	This indicator tracks permits given for new housing to be built. Rising housing starts are desirable.
Auto	Auto sales	The industry's annual sales figure is a closely watched indicator. Rising sales are desirable.
Retail	Retail sales	The overall sales are watched, and they should be rising (especially in the fourth quarter of the year).

Note: Industry trade publications and general financial publications, such as *The Wall Street Journal* and *Investor's Business Daily*, regularly report this data. You can also find it (along with a tremendous database of economic data and statistics) at www.freelunch.com.

What are some important things in economic data that you should be aware of? Keep reading. The following sections make this information clear.

Grossing you out with GDP

Gross domestic product (GDP), which measures the nation's total output of goods and services for the quarter, is considered the broadest measure of economic activity. Although it's measured in dollars (the U.S. GDP is currently valued at about $11 trillion), it is usually quoted as a percentage. You typically hear a news report that says something like, "The economy grew by 2.5 percent last quarter." Because the GDP is an important overall barometer for the economy, it should be a positive number.

The GDP is released quarterly by the Commerce Department (www.doc.gov).

To give you a rough idea about how the GDP measures economic activity, I give you a very simplified example of GDP. First, look at the following table regarding hula hoops and pogo sticks.

Year	Number of Hula Hoops Produced	Price per Hoop	Number of Pogo Sticks Produced	Price per Stick	Total GDP Value
2000	10	$3	20	$5	$130
2001	11	$4	21	$6	$170

In 2000, the value of hula hoops and pogo stocks produced is $130 (10 hula hoops times $3 plus 20 pogo sticks times $5 equals $130). In 2001, the number of units increased as well as the price per unit. Because the value of this production was $170, GDP increased from 2000 by $40. (The percentage is 23.5 percent, but remember, this isn't a real-world example! However, you get the point.)

You should regularly monitor this macro snapshot along with economic data that relate directly to your stock portfolio. The following list gives some general guidelines for evaluating GDP:

- **Over 3 percent:** This number indicates strong growth and bodes well for stocks. At 5 percent or higher, the economy is sizzling!

- **1 to 3 percent:** This figure indicates moderate growth and can occur either as the economy is rebounding from a recession or as it is slowing down from a previously strong period.

- **0 percent or negative (as low as –3 percent):** This number isn't good and indicates that the economy is either not growing or is actually shrinking a bit. A negative GDP is considered *recessionary* (meaning that the economy's growth is receding).

- **Under –3 percent:** A GDP this low indicates a very difficult period for the economy. A GDP under –3 percent, especially for two or more quarters, indicates a serious recession or possibly a depression.

Looking at a single quarter isn't that useful. Track GDP over many quarters to see which way the general economy is trending. When you look at GDP for a particular quarter of a year, ask yourself whether it is better (or worse) than the quarter before. If it's better (or worse), then ask yourself to what extent it has changed. Is it dramatically better (or worse) than the quarter before? Is the economy showing steady growth, or is it slowing? If several or more quarters show solid growth, the overall economy is generally bullish.

Traditionally, if two or more consecutive quarters show negative growth (economic output is shrinking), the economy is considered to be in a recession. A recession can be a painful necessity; it usually occurs when there is too much excess production and the economy can't absorb the total amount of goods being produced. A bear market in stocks usually accompanies a recession.

GDP is just a rough estimate at best. It can't possibly calculate all the factors that go into economic growth. For example, crime has a negative effect on economic growth, but it's not reflected in GDP. Still, most economists agree that GDP provides a ballpark snapshot of the overall economy's progress.

Showing interest in the Fed

The Federal Reserve System (often called simply the Fed) is the nation's independent central bank. It plays a pivotal role in the U.S. economy and — because the United States is the most powerful economy — in the global economy as well.

Although it performs a number of functions, the Fed's most fundamental role is controlling the money supply (controlling or managing the money supply is also referred to as *monetary policy*) and influencing interest rates. As a result, the Fed is one of the most closely watched institutions in the world because it has such an impact on financial markets as well as the growth of the U.S. economy.

Money supply

Because the Fed controls the actual quantity of dollars that is circulated, it has the responsibility of fighting or controlling inflation. People think that inflation is the cost of goods and services going up, when actually *inflation* refers to the value of money going down because there is too much money (the currency being "inflated"). In other words, too many dollars are chasing too few goods and services.

The Fed tries to manage the very difficult task of having just the right amount of money in the economy. Having too much money can create inflation, meaning that consumers will see the purchasing power of their dollars shrink. Too little money means that not enough money is circulating in the economy. (In these financial conditions, some people use the terminology "tight money," and others say that "the economy lacks liquidity.") Inflation, if not held in check, can have very negative consequences. After all, how would you feel if the money in your pocket was rapidly shrinking in value? (The odds are that you would feel like a parent with too many teenagers in the house!)

Inflation is reported as the consumer price index (CPI). The CPI (also known as the cost-of-living index) is calculated by the Bureau of Labor Statistics (www.dol.gov) and measures changes in the price of a typical basket of consumer goods that reflect what the average consumer buys on a regular basis. The CPI is considered a warning of pending inflation.

Interest rates

Financial markets, such as the stock market and the bond market, closely monitor the Fed's influence on interest rates. Because the Fed can raise or lower some key interest rates at will, its actions become a powerful lever that can raise or lower many rates that literally millions of individuals and businesses pay primarily on their short-term debt.

You need to watch interest rates for several reasons:

✔ Interest rates affect corporate earnings. If companies pay more interest, that additional cost directly affects their profits. If profits shrink, then that puts downward pressure on stock prices. Conversely, if interest rates are cut, companies will see a positive impact on profits.

✔ Interest rates influence income investors. (See Chapter 9 for more on income investing.) Investors looking for a higher return on their investments will make decisions to pull their money out of stocks and into other vehicles such as bonds or bank accounts. When interest rates continue to climb, more and more investors sell their stocks, sending stock prices down.

✔ Interest rates figure prominently in fighting inflation. Generally, interest rates have been a key weapon in the past 20 years in fighting inflation. Because inflation means that the value of a dollar shrinks, higher interest rates are used to offset this. In the late 1970s, when inflation hovered near double-digit rates, interest rates went through the roof (surpassing 15 percent). Conversely, lower interest rates coupled with an expanding money supply can ignite higher inflation.

For more information about the Fed's money supply and interest rate policies, go to its Web site at www.federalreserve.gov. Also, the American Institute for Economic Research (www.aier.org) offers useful, readable research on the relationships between money growth, interest rates, and the stock market.

Debting your sweet bippy

Debt can be very burdensome and have a negative impact on economic growth. As an investor, you need to know how much debt is in the economy and whether the debt is growing or shrinking. Whether the debt is consumer (credit cards, mortgages, and so on) or corporate (short-term borrowing, bonds, and so on), it will harm the economy if not kept under control.

A major reason for the economy's downturn in 2000 and 2001 was the economy's overexposure to debt. In fact, during the 1990s, virtually every major category of debt hit record levels. The only ways to remove debt are to pay it off or go bankrupt. Because so many individuals and businesses became overextended in debt during that time period, bankruptcies hit record levels as well.

Stock investors must monitor debt levels for bear market potential. Too much debt slows the economy, which in turn can adversely affect the stock market. Overly indebted individuals don't have money to spend or invest. Overly indebted companies may face employee layoffs, cuts in spending, declining profits, and other negative actions. Watch also for corporate problems. If you have stock in a company that has too much debt or that sells to customers who are overburdened with debt, then that company will suffer. The Fed and other sources, including such publications as *The Wall Street Journal,* report consumer and corporate debt levels.

Raising confident consumers

As you often hear on TV, consumer spending accounts for two-thirds of the economy. Therefore, the consumer's behavior is something that investors watch carefully. You can break down consumer activity into two categories:

- **Consumer income:** If consumers' income meets or exceeds the CPI rate (see "Money supply," earlier in this chapter), that bodes well for the economy.

- **Consumer confidence:** This index is measured by prominent surveys that essentially track how the consumer feels about the economy in general and their personal situations in particular. The University of Michigan and the Conference Board (which presents its survey in the Consumer Confidence Index) do the most widely followed surveys. If consumers feel good about the economy and their immediate futures, that bodes well for consumer spending.

Lumping together the data with economic indexes

Because so much economic data is available, many investors prefer to look at indexes that put the data in a nutshell. Indexes try to summarize many economic indicators and put them into a neat, digestible format.

Predicting the economic weather

The American Institute for Economic Research (AIER) is a nonprofit organization that offers excellent information for beginners on economics and markets. AIER offers a booklet called *Forecasting Business Trends* that gives investors some clear yet detailed explanations and insights on the business cycle. To find out more, write to American Institute for Economic Research, P.O. Box 1000, Great Barrington, MA 01230, or visit its Web site at www.aier.org.

Economic indicators are grouped into categories that try to give a rough idea about the economy's upward and downward cycle. These cyclical indicators are put in three categories that try to time the various phases of the economy's movement:

✔ **Leading:** The leading indicators try to be predictive of the economy's path. Stock investors are particularly interested in leading economic indicators because stock investors usually do not invest because of past or present conditions — investors buy stocks because of expectations for the future.

✔ **Coincident:** The coincident indicators essentially tell you where the economy is right now. (For stock investors, most coincident indicators are like the indicator on your car's dashboard blinking "hot" when you see steam rising from your hood.) The most valuable coincident indicator is the GDP. (See the section "Grossing you out with GDP," earlier in this chapter.)

✔ **Lagging:** This type of indicator tells you what just passed in the economy's path (which can be significant because some lagging indicators do precede leading indicators). The unemployment rate is a good example of a lagging indicator.

Of the three categories, the most widely followed is the Index of Leading Economic Indicators (LEI). A good example of an indicator that is included in the LEI is the statistic on new construction. If more new construction is being started, that is a positive harbinger of economic growth. The LEI is compiled monthly by the Conference Board (www.conferenceboard.org).

Inquiring about economics: Resources

Keep in mind that, because of the scope of the topic and the finite number of pages in this book, this chapter can't do justice to the burgeoning world of economics. I encourage you to continue learning about economics by doing some easy and interesting research with the resources listed here and in Appendix A.

Turn to the following sources for economic data:

- ✔ Conference Board, www.conferenceboard.org
- ✔ Department of Commerce, www.doc.gov
- ✔ The Federal Reserve, www.federalreserve.gov

Here are some sources to help you understand economics:

- ✔ American Institute for Economic Research, www.aier.org
- ✔ Dismal.com, www.dismal.com
- ✔ FinancialSense.com, www.financialsense.com
- ✔ Foundation for Economic Education, www.fee.org
- ✔ The Mises Institute, www.mises.org

Part IV
Investment Strategies and Tactics

The 5th Wave   By Rich Tennant

"SELL."

In this part . . .

Successful stock investing is more than choosing a particular stock. It's also understanding the environment in which the market operates. Just as goldfish can thrive in good water (or die in bad water), the stock market reacts to the general economic climate. Successful investors go beyond merely picking good stocks and watching the financial news. They implement techniques and strategies that help them either minimize losses or maximize gains (hopefully both). The chapters in this part introduce some of the most effective investing techniques to help you profit from stocks in a bull or a bear market and describe some smart ways to hold on to more of your profits when tax time rolls around.

Chapter 14

Taking the Bull (Or Bear) by the Horns

*U*nderstanding the investment environment may even be more important to your wealth-building success than choosing the right stock. Recent years — and a century of stock market history — bear (no pun intended) witness to this point.

Bull and bear markets have a tremendous effect on your stock choices. Generally, bull markets tend to precede economic uptrends (also called economic rebound, economic recovery, or economic growth), while bear markets tend to precede economic downtrends (also called recession, depression, or economic contraction).

The stock market's movement is based on the fact that stock prices go up (or down) based on people's buying or selling behavior. If more people are buying stock (versus selling), then stock prices will rise. If more people are selling stocks, then stock prices will fall. Why do people buy or sell a stock? It can be explained in one word: expectations. People generally buy (or sell) stock in expectation of economic events. If they feel that times are getting bad and the economic stats bear this out (in the form of rising unemployment, shrinking corporate profits, cutbacks in consumer spending, and so on), then they will become more cautious, which can have a couple results:

✔ They sell stock that they currently own.

✔ They won't buy stock because they feel that stocks will not do well.

Of course, when the economy is doing well, the reverse is true.

Bulling Up

In the beginning, a bull market doesn't look like a bull market at all. It looks like anything but. Maybe that's why so few catch on early. Bull markets are marked by great optimism as the economy roars forward and stocks go skyward. Everyone knows what a bull market should look like, and everyone can recognize it when it has become a mature trend. The saying "I don't know what it is, but I'll know it when I see it" is one that applies to a bull market. But if you can foresee it coming, you may be able to make a fortune by getting in just before the crowd sees it.

Because bull markets usually start in the depths of a bear market, do some research regarding bear markets; see the section "Identifying the beast," later in this chapter.

Recognizing the beast

Although in this book I concentrate on the modern era, starting in the early part of the twentieth century, bull markets in stocks have shown themselves many times throughout the past few hundred years — plenty of time to have established some recognizable traits:

✔ Bull markets tend to start at the depths of pessimism — the same way that dawn starts at the edge of darkness. People have probably just been beaten up by a bear market. The phrase "I'm into stock investing" is about as welcome in polite conversation as "I have a contagious disease." If investors are avoiding stocks like the plague (or selling stocks they already have), share prices drop to the point that much of the risk is wrung out of them. Value-oriented investors then can pick up some solid companies at great prices. (See Chapter 10 for information on recognizing a good stock value.)

✔ The major media mirror this pessimism and amplify it. Usually, the mainstream media have greater value as a *counterindicator* because by the time the major publications find out about the economic trend and report it, the trend has already changed course.

For example, *Time* magazine featured Amazon.com CEO Jeff Bezos as its Man of the Year in 2000, but immediately thereafter, Amazon.com's stock price continued a long and painful descent, ultimately dropping over 90 percent from its high in late 1999. Another example is the famous issue of *Business Week* with the pessimistic cover story titled "The Death of Equities" that came out at the tail end of the bear market of the 1970s. What timing — an issue warning investors about the dangers of stock investing just before the greatest bull market in history started.

✔ Economic statistics have stabilized. After the economy has hit rock bottom, the economic statistics start to improve. The most-watched set of economic indicators is called the Index of Leading Economic Indicators (described in Chapters 6 and 13). Investors want to make sure that the economy is getting back on its feet before it starts its next move upward. In 1982, the economy was just starting to recover from the 1981 recession. The economic expansion (and accompanying bull market) became the longest in history.

✔ Economic conditions for individuals and companies are stable and strong. You'll know that's true if profits are stable or growing for companies in general and if consumers are seeing strong and growing income growth. The logic holds up well: More money being made means more money to eventually spend and invest.

✔ Industries producing large-ticket items have hit rock bottom and begin their climb. After consumers and companies have been pummeled by a tough economy, they're not apt to make major financial commitments to items such as new cars, houses, equipment, and so on. Industries that produce these large, expensive items will see sales fall to a low and slowly start to rebound as the economy picks up. In a growing economy, consumers and companies experience greater confidence (both psychologically and financially).

✔ Demographics appear favorable. Take a look at the census and government statistics on trends for population growth, as well as the growth in the number of business enterprises. The 1980s and 1990s, for example, saw the rise of the baby boomers, those born during the post-World War II period of 1946 to 1964. Baby boomers wielded much financial clout, much of it in the stock market. Their investment money played a major role in propelling the stock market to new highs.

✔ General peace and stability prevail. A major war or international conflict may have just ended. War is not good for many reasons, and it usually doesn't bode well for the stock market.

Believe it or not, a mature bull market poses problems for investors and stock market experts. In a mature bull market, just about any stock — good, bad, or indifferent — tends to go up. You could be a blind monkey throwing darts and pick a rising stock. When everything goes up and everybody seems to be making a winning pick, human nature kicks in. Both beginning and serious investors believe that their good fortune can be chalked up to superior stock-picking prowess and not simple luck or circumstance. Such overconfidence is a dangerous characteristic for stock investors.

Once investors become convinced of their newfound ability, they grow more daring in their investment approach; they make riskier choices, using less discipline and relying on less diligence and research. Then . . . whammo! They get socked by the market. Overconfidence lures the unsuspecting investor to more dangerous territory, invariably resulting in a very expensive lesson. Overconfidence and money don't mix.

In the 1999–2001 period, this tendency to be foolishly bullish long after the bull was gone was a common phenomenon that I refer to as the Wile E. Coyote effect. Do you remember Wile E. Coyote from those great Road Runner cartoons? Of course you do! You know the plot: Mr. Coyote is chasing the Road Runner and seems to be gaining on him. He is confidently ready to pounce on the seemingly unsuspecting bird, but the Road Runner makes a quick turn and watches as Mr. Coyote continues running over the cliff and ultimately plummets down the ravine. A mature bull market does that to investors. Scores of true stories tell of investors lured to a game of easy riches (the dot-com fiasco, for example) only to watch their investment get pulverized. This phenomenon happened not only to beginners but also to experienced investors and many stock investing experts who were familiar faces on your TV screen.

No matter how good or bad the economy or stock market is, true financial success comes from work, diligence, and discipline. This advice is especially true when times seem extraordinarily good or resoundingly bad.

Toro! Approaching a bull market

Being fully invested in stocks at the beginning of a bull market makes for spectacular success. But doing so takes some courage. Billionaire business executive J. Paul Getty said that buying low and selling high was the very essence of successful investing. Although most people agree with that advice psychologically, they're very hesitant when it's time to actually take action.

When the bull market is in its infancy, start investing by using the following approach:

✔ Be a bargain hunter. Frequently, at the tail end of a bear market, stock prices have been sufficiently battered after going through an extended period of low demand and/or disproportionately more selling of the shares by nervous investors. When share prices are lower in value than the book value of companies they represent, there is less risk in acquiring the shares that are generating positive growth in sales and earnings. Chapter 10 can help you better understand concepts such as book value.

✔ Look for strong fundamentals. Is the company you're choosing exhibiting solid sales and earnings? Are sales and earnings rising compared to the prior quarter or year? Conduct top line and bottom line analyses (which I discuss in Chapter 10) to determine a company's fundamentals. Do the company's products and services make sense to you? In other words, is it selling stuff that the public is starting to demand more of?

✔ Consider the stock's class. Remember that some stocks are more aggressive choices than other ones. This choice reflects your risk tolerance as well. Figure out whether you want to invest in a small cap stock with phenomenal growth prospects (and commensurate risk) or a large cap stock that is a tried-and-true market leader.

All things being equal, small cap stocks exhibit the best growth performance in an emerging bull market. Small cap stocks are more appropriate for investors who have a higher risk tolerance. Of course, most stocks do well in an emerging bull market (actually, that's what makes it a bull market!), so even risk-adverse investors who put their money into larger companies will gain. (For more information on growth stocks such as small caps, see Chapter 8.)

✔ Choose appropriate industries. Look at industries that are poised to rebound as the economy picks up and individuals and organizations begin to spend again. In a rising market, cyclical stocks such as those in the automobile, housing, industrial equipment, and technology industries resume growth. When the economy is doing well, individuals and organizations begin to spend more on items that will meet their needs in an expanding economy. Companies upgrade their technology. Families get a new car or move to a bigger house. Construction firms need more and better equipment as residential and commercial building increases.

✔ Take stock of your portfolio. As you start to add stocks to your portfolio, have you first analyzed your situation to make sure that you have diversification not only in different stocks and/or stock mutual funds but also in nonstock investments, such as savings bonds and bank accounts? Just because it's a bull market doesn't mean that you should have 100 percent of your investments in stocks; it means that you should consider putting as much as 100 percent of the growth component of your investment money in stocks.

Say that you're investing for the long term. You're not that concerned with risk, and you want maximum growth from your investments. After setting aside money in an emergency fund, you decide that you want to devote your remaining funds of $50,000 to growth stocks. In this case, 100 percent of that sum becomes the *growth component* of your investment portfolio. If you decide to play it safer and split it 50/50 between bonds and stocks, then $25,000 (or 50 percent of your portfolio) would be your growth component. The bonds would then be your *income component*.

✔ Evaluate your personal goals. No matter how good the market and the foreseeable prospects for growth, stock investing is a personal matter that should serve your unique needs. For example, how old are you, and how many years away is your retirement? All things being equal, a 35-year-old should have predominately growth stocks, while a 65-year-old requires more proven, stable performance with large cap market leaders. The information in Chapter 2 can help you identify appropriate investment goals.

Some investors in a bull market may have very little money in stocks. Why? Maybe they have already reached their financial goals, so wealth preservation is more appropriate than growth. Perhaps they have a million-dollar portfolio and are 70 years old and no longer working. In that case, having, say, 80 percent of their investments in stable, income-producing investments and 20 percent in proven (yet modestly) growing stocks may make more sense for them.

The bottom line is that you choose the type of stocks as well as the mix to fit into your unique situation and needs.

Bearing Down

Alas, stocks go down as well as up. Some ferocious bear markets have hit stocks on several occasions since the Great Depression. The worst one was during the period 1973–1975, but a few brief, minor ones occurred during the 1980s and 1990s. You don't need to worry about the occasional dips and short-term bear markets; however, be wary about *secular* (long-term) bear markets, which can last years. Discipline and a watchful eye can keep you and your money out of trouble.

History in the making

The greatest bear market since the Great Depression started in 1973. The stock market was pummeled as the Dow Jones Industrial Average (DJIA) fell 45 percent during an 18-month period ending in 1975. The DJIA did not recover to its 1973 high until (you guessed it) 1982. The period from 1973 to 1982 had the hallmarks of tough times, high inflation, high unemployment, war (the Middle East conflict in 1973 and expansive Soviet aggression in Africa and Afghanistan), the energy crisis, and high taxes. The 1970s were a tough decade for most stocks. The 1980s and '90s were great decades for stock investors. Alas, 2000 and 2001 were rough years for stocks as investors cumulatively lost trillions.

Identifying the beast

Bear markets can be foreseen. When the bear market of 2000 started that spring, observers and advisors had predicted it. However, most advisors and commentators told people to "hang tight," "buy on the dips," and "stay long-term focused." These tips are great when the market is zigzagging upward but dangerous when it is zigzagging downward. The following sections present some telltale signs of an emerging bear market.

Optimism abounds

Everyone from Main Street to Wall Street feels great. Financial reports declare that the business cycle has been conquered and a new economy or new paradigm has arrived. Good times are here for the foreseeable future! You start to see books with titles such as *The Dow at 100,000* and *Easy Riches in the Stock Market* hit the bestseller lists. The *business cycle* refers to the economy's roller-coaster-like behavior when it expands (growth) and contracts (recession).

Sometimes, the financial experts believe that an economy is doing so well that it can continue to grow indefinitely. Examples of misguided exuberance abound in stock market history. In 1929, Irving Fisher, the best-known financial expert and stock millionaire of his day, made the ill-fated declaration "Stocks have reached a permanent plateau" as he predicted the bull market would continue for the foreseeable future. A few weeks later, the infamous stock market crash occurred. Everyone who had listened to Fisher got clobbered in the greatest bear market of the twentieth century. Even Irving Fisher himself filed for bankruptcy. Gee, not even Irving Fisher should have listened to Irving Fisher. In 1999, an economist boldly stated that the economy will continue growing forever and that "recessions are a thing of the past." Today, that economist is probably in a new job saying, "Would you like some fries with that?"

Debt levels hit new highs

When optimism is high, people buy things. In 1999, debt levels hit a record high in almost every category; corporate, consumer, mortgage, and margin debt ballooned during the late 1990s. This massive debt was mostly ignored by the financial press, yet it was one of the major reasons for the subsequent bear market and recession. When too much debt is accrued, it can be removed in only one of two ways: through repayment or by bankruptcy. The year 2001 became the fourth year in a row that more than 1 million bankruptcies were filed in the United States.

Excessive speculation, credit, and money supply expand

Whenever a country's money supply grows beyond the economy's needs, massive problems can result. When the money supply expands, more money is circulated into the banking system. (Go to www.federalreserve.gov to find out more about the money supply.) The banks then lend or invest this excess money. The oversupply of money flows into investment projects, such as initial public offerings and bond offerings. When too much money is available for too few worthy projects, invariably a lot of money is invested unwisely. This situation causes massive imbalances in the economic system, ultimately resulting in economic downturns that can take years to rectify.

History proves the truth of this economic situation. It happened to the U.S. economy in the late 1920s and to Japan in the late 1980s. Fortunately, statistics on credit and the money supply are easy to come by and readily available on the Internet. (See Appendix A for resources.)

Government intervention increases

Government has the power to do much good, but when it uses its power improperly, it can do a great deal of harm. Every economy throughout history that collapsed ultimately did so because of excessive government intervention. In progressive, free market economies, this intervention usually occurs in the form of taxes, laws, and regulations. Keep a watchful eye on the president and Congress to monitor government intervention. Are they proposing policies that add burdens to the private economy? Are they advocating stringent new laws and regulations? I explain more about this in Chapter 13.

National and/or international conflict arises

Nothing can have a more negative impact on the economy than war or political or civil unrest. Keep your eye on the news. Ask yourself what effect a particular conflict may have on the economy and the stock market.

Heading into the woods: Approaching a bear market

Sticking to a buy-and-hold strategy (where you buy stock and hold onto it for better or worse) at the onset of a bear market is financial suicide. People have a tough time selling, and financial advisors have an even tougher time telling them to cut their losses because that's tantamount to saying, "Sorry, I was wrong." Admitting failure is hard for most people to do.

Understand that investing should be a logical, practical, and unemotional pursuit. You can't be married to stocks — until death do you part — especially because bear markets can divorce you from your money.

Looking for Titanic tickets

In early 2000, I was infuriated when the dapper pundits on TV told viewers to hang tight and hold on for the long haul. Stocks then took a beating, prompting the pundits to say, " It's a buying opportunity. Add to your portfolio." Then what happened? The bear market took stocks down again.

The trillions that were lost during 2000 and 2001 would have been avoidable if investors had been more disciplined and if the pundits had been more careful in their pronouncements. When the economy is heading into treacherous waters, stocks get the worst of it, yet experts continue to advise people to buy stocks because they're good for the long term. Hold on! No matter how much you like stocks, that doesn't mean that you should always be in them. I mean, just because you like boating doesn't mean that you should take advantage of a free ticket on the *Titanic*.

In an emerging bear market, keep the following points in mind to maximize your gains (or just to minimize your losses):

- **Review your situation.** Before you consider any move in or out of the market, review your overall financial situation to make sure that your money and financial condition are as secure as possible. Make sure that you have an emergency fund of four to six months' worth of gross living expenses. Keep your debt at a comfortably low level. Review your career, insurance, and so on. Schedule a financial checkup with your financial planner.

- **Remember that cash is king.** When the bear market is coming and economic storm clouds are rolling in, keep the bulk of your money in safe, interest-bearing vehicles such as bank investments, U.S. treasury securities, and money market funds. Doing so keeps your money safe. If stocks are falling by 10 to 20 percent or more, you're better off earning a low-percentage interest in a secure, stable investment. In addition, you can do some research while your money is earning interest. Start looking for undervalued stocks with strong fundamentals.

- **Stick to necessities.** In an economic downturn, defensive stocks generally outperform the market. *Defensive stocks* are stocks of companies that sell goods and services that people need no matter how good or bad the economy is doing. Good examples are food and beverage, energy, utilities, and certain healthcare stocks.

- **Use trailing stops.** Trailing stops are my favorite disciplined approach. Just tighten the trail. Say, for example, that you once bought a stock for $50 per share and it's now at $110. Presume that you usually kept a trailing stop at 10 percent below the current market price. If the bear market is becoming more evident to you, then change that 10 percent to 5 percent. Before, that trailing stop on the $110 stock was $99 ($110 less 10 percent, or $11), but now it will be at $104.50 ($110 less 5 percent, or $5.50). See Chapter 16 for the scoop on trailing stops.

Straddling Bear and Bull: Uncertain Markets

Uncertain markets are . . . well . . . uncertain. Markets aren't always up or down. The end of a bear market doesn't automatically mean the beginning of a bull market and vice versa. Sometimes markets move sideways or very little either way until investors and participants in the economy figure out what's what.

Pinpointing uncertainty is tough

Clashing points of view in the media tell you that even the experts are not sure which way the market and the economy will go in the coming months. In uncertain markets, compelling evidence and loads of opinions will evenly line up on both the pro and con side of the economic debate. Bullish and bearish advisors and commentators may both seem persuasive, so you may be left scratching your head, wondering what to do. This is where your patience and diligence pay off.

Sure you want to approach an uncertain market?

The approach to take in uncertain markets is almost simplistic. If you think that a bull market is starting, you want to be 100 percent invested in stocks, and if a bear market is starting, you want the percentage to be 0. Therefore, in an uncertain market, 50 percent in stocks and 50 percent in other investments is just right. Of course, these three scenarios should be balanced by many nonstock factors, such as your individual financial situation, age, debt level, career concerns, and so on. However, all things being equal, those allocations aren't far off the mark.

Treat uncertain markets as bear markets until the data prove otherwise. No matter how adventurous you are, the first rule of stock investing is to minimize or avoid losses. If no one can agree on the direction of the market, then you stand a 50 percent chance of being wrong should you take the bullish stance. However, if you take a bearish stance and the market becomes decidedly bullish, no real harm is done except that you may miss a stock investing opportunity during a brief period of time. Just keep in mind that stock investing is indeed a long-term pursuit. Jumping into a bullish market is easy, but recovering losses isn't always easy.

Chapter 15

Choosing a Strategy That's Just Right for You

In This Chapter

▶ Basing your strategy on your needs

▶ Deciding where to allocate your assets

▶ Recognizing when to unload your stocks

Stocks are a means to an end. What end are you seeking? You should look at stocks as tools for wealth building. Sometimes they're great tools, and sometimes they're awful. It depends on your approach. Some stocks are appropriate for a conservative approach, while others are more suitable for an aggressive approach. Sometimes stocks aren't necessary at all. Golly! A stock investing book that suggests that stocks aren't always the answer! That's like a teenager saying, "Dad, I respectfully decline your generous offer of money for my weekend trip."

Laying Out Your Plans

An older student in one of my investment seminars in 2000 wanted to be aggressive with his portfolio; his broker was more than happy to cater to his desire for growth stocks. Of course, stocks got clobbered in the volatile stock market of 2000 and 2001, and yes, he did lose money. However, I soon discovered that even after the losses, he still had a substantial stock portfolio valued at over $1 million. He had more than enough to ensure a comfortable retirement. He had sought aggressive growth even though it was really unnecessary for his situation. If anything, the aggressive strategy could have put his portfolio (and hence his retirement) in jeopardy.

Don't get me wrong. Growth is desirable even in your twilight years because inflation can eat away at a fixed-income portfolio. But there are different rates of growth, and the type you choose should be commensurate with your unique situation and financial needs. Notice that I say "needs," not "wants." These are entirely different perspectives. You may *want* to invest in aggressive stocks regardless of their suitability (after all, it's your money), but your financial situation may dictate that you *need* to take another approach. Just understand the difference.

Stocks can play a role in all sorts of investment strategies, but in this chapter, I discuss only a few well-known approaches. Keep in mind that a stock investing strategy can change based on the major changes in your life and the lifestyle that you lead, such as the ones I present in the following sections.

Living the bachelor life: Young single with no dependents

If you're young (age 20–40) and single, with no children or other dependents, being more aggressive with your stock selection is fine (as long as you don't use your rent money for investments). The reasoning is that if you do make riskier choices and they backfire, individuals dependent on you won't get hurt. In addition, if you're in this category, you can usually bounce back a lot easier over the long term even if you have financial challenges or a bear market hits your stocks. Chapter 14 can tell you more about bear and bull markets.

Consider a mix of small cap, mid cap, and large cap (see Chapter 1 for an explanation of each of these) growth stocks in growth industries. Invest some of your money in five to ten stocks and the remainder in growth-stock mutual funds. You can revise your investment allocations along the way as the general economy changes and/or your personal situation (like when you finally say "I do" to the love of your life) changes.

Going together like a horse and carriage: Married with children

Married couples with children must follow a more conservative investing strategy, regardless of whether one spouse works or both spouses work. Children change the picture drastically — just try sleeping at night. You need more stable growth in your portfolio.

Consider a mix of large cap growth stocks and dividend-paying defensive stocks. (See Chapter 12 for more details on defensive stocks.) Invest some of your money in five to ten stocks and the remainder in growth and income mutual funds. Of course, you can tweak your allocations along the way according to changes in the general economic conditions or to your personal situation. Consider setting aside money for college in a growth fund and in treasury zero-coupon bonds (as early as possible).

When zeros can really add up

Treasury zero-coupon bonds are ultra-safe (backed up by the federal government) and ideal for long-term planning, such as a child's college tuition. A treasury zero-coupon bond is similar to a U.S. savings bond (EE series) in that you buy it at a deep discount and can cash it in at face value at maturity. Say that you're going to buy a treasury zero-coupon bond with a face value of $1,000 at 7 percent interest maturing in 18 years. You can buy that bond for as little as $285. If you need to have $100,000 in 18 years, you can invest $28,500 now and be certain that you have the full $100,000 at maturity. You can buy treasury zero-coupon bonds that mature 18, 19, 20, and 21 years into the future to coincide with each of the four years that your child will be in college. (Let's hope that the kid appreciates it!) For more details on treasury zero-coupon bonds, go to the Web site for the U.S. Treasury at www.ustreas.gov.

Getting ready for retirement: Over 40 and either single or married

Whether you're over 40 and single, or you're over 40 and married and you and your spouse both work, you should start to slowly convert your portfolio from aggressive growth to conservative growth. Shift more of your money out of stocks and into less-volatile investments, such as balanced funds, bonds, and bank certificates of deposit.

Devote some time and effort (with a financial planner if necessary) to calculating what your potential financial needs will be at retirement time. This step is critical in helping you decide what age to target for financial independence.

Consider a mix of large cap stocks dominated by dividend-paying defensive stocks (which I discuss in Chapter 12) in stable industries. Invest some of your money in three to six stocks and the remainder in balanced mutual funds and short-term bond funds. Have a large portion of your money in savings bonds and bank investments. Remember that you can revise your allocations in the future as necessary.

Kicking back in the hammock: Already retired

If you're retired, you're probably in your 60s or older. Income production and wealth preservation form the crux of your investment strategy. Some growth-oriented investments are okay as long as they're conservative and don't jeopardize your need for income. At one time, financial planners told their retired clients to replace growth-oriented investments with safe income-oriented investments. However, times have changed as senior citizens live longer than ever before.

Because inflation can significantly increase the cost of living, retirees will need growth in their portfolios to make sure that their portfolios will continue meeting their financial needs as the years pass.

Consider a mix of large cap stocks dominated by dividend-paying defensive stocks in stable industries. Spread your money over three to six stocks and the remainder in balanced mutual funds and short-term bond funds. Have a large portion of your money in savings bonds and bank investments. You need to monitor and tweak your investment portfolio along the way to account for changes in either the general economic environment or your lifestyle needs.

Allocating Your Assets

Asset allocation became a hot topic during the 1980s. To this day, most financial advisors seek to divine the proper mix of investments to fit the client's profile. Many portfolio models are created to perfect the right balance of growth, income, and safety. Because stocks are tools for a wealth-building program, they have to fit you and your needs, not the other way around. I don't discuss your total investment plan here, only the stock portion.

Asset allocation is really an attempt to properly implement the concept of diversification — the key to stability. *Diversification* is the inclusion in your portfolio of different (and frequently offsetting) investments to shield your wealth from most types of current risk while planning for future growth. To achieve proper diversification, you need to analyze your entire portfolio to look for glaring weaknesses or vulnerable areas.

Investors frequently believe that having different stocks in different industries constitutes proper diversification. Well . . . not quite. Stocks in closely related industries tend to be affected (in differing degrees) by the same economic events, government policies, and so on. It's best to invest in stocks across different sectors. "What's a sector?" you may ask. A *sector* is basically a mega-industry, for lack of a better description. For example, water, gas, and electric services are each separate industries, but together they (along with a few other industries) comprise the utilities sector. Pharmaceuticals and HMOs are each an industry, but both are part of the healthcare sector. For more on analyzing industries in order to pick winning stocks, see Chapter 12.

So far in this chapter, I talk about some basics for investing, depending on your lifestyle, but how do you know how much you need to invest in order to meet your financial goals? In the following sections, I present some typical amounts most typical investors can (and should) devote to stock investing.

Investors with less than $10,000

If you have $10,000 or less to allocate to stocks, you may want to consider a mutual fund rather than individual stocks because that sum of money may not be enough to properly diversify. But if you're going to invest a sum that small, consider allocating it equally into two to four stocks in two different sectors that look strong for the foreseeable future. For small investors, consider sectors that are defensive in nature (such as food and utilities).

Because any amount of $10,000 or less is a small sum in the world of stock investing, you may have to purchase in odd lots. (*Odd lots* mean 99 shares or less. Shares of 100 or more are considered *round lots*.) Say that you're buying four stocks and all of them are priced at $50 per share. An investment of $10,000 won't buy you 100 shares of each. You may have to consider investing $2,500 in each stock, which means that you would end up buying only 50 shares of each stock (not including commissions). If you do buy odd lots, find out whether the company has a dividend reinvestment plan (DRP) and use the dividend money you earn to buy more shares of stock. (I discuss DRPs more fully in Chapter 17.)

In that case, get into a company's dividend reinvestment plan (DRP) if it's available. The DRP is also useful in keeping transaction costs down because the typical DRP usually doesn't charge commissions for participants purchasing stock through the plan. For long-term investors, the DRP offers a great way to compound your investment because dividends are reinvested.

Try to avoid the temptation of getting into initial public offerings, penny stocks, and other speculative issues. Participation in them may cost little (stock prices are often under $10 per share), but the risk exposure is too high for inexperienced investors. (See Chapter 8 for more on IPOs.)

Investors with $10,000–$50,000

If you have between $10,000 and $50,000 to invest, you have more breathing space for diversification. Consider buying four to six stocks in two or three different sectors. If you're the cautious type, defensive stocks will do. For growth investors, seek the industries in those sectors that have proven growth. (See Chapter 12 for more on industries.) This approach will get you off to a good start, and the section "Knowing When to Sell," later in this chapter, can help you maintain your portfolio with changing strategy (if necessary).

Does this mean that you shouldn't in any circumstance have all your stocks in one sector? It depends on you. For example, if you've worked all your life in a particular field and you're knowledgeable and comfortable with the sector, having a greater exposure is okay, because the risk is offset by your greater personal expertise. If you worked in retail for 20 years and know the industry inside and out, you probably know more about the good, the bad, and the ugly of the retail sector than most Wall Street analysts. Use your insight for more profitability. You should still not invest all your money in that single sector, however, because diversification is still vital.

Investors with $50,000 or more

If you have $50,000 or more to invest, have no more than five to ten stocks in two or three different sectors. It's difficult to thoroughly track more than two or three sectors and do it successfully — best to keep it simple. For example, Warren Buffett, considered the greatest stock market investor of all time, never invested in Web site businesses because he didn't understand them. He invests only in businesses that he understands. If that strategy works for billionaire investors then, by golly, it can't be that bad for smaller investors.

I suggest investing in no more than ten stocks, because there is such a thing as overdiversification. The more stocks you have, the tougher it is to keep track of them. Owning more stocks means that you need to do more research, read more annual reports and news articles, and follow the business news of more companies. Even in the best of times, you need to regularly monitor your stocks because successful investing requires diligent effort.

A last point to consider is whether to hire a personal money manager. If you have $50,000 or $100,000 or more, doing so may make sense. Get a referral from a financial planner and carefully weigh the benefits against the costs. Here are some points to consider:

✔ **Make sure that the money manager has a philosophy and an approach that you agree with.**

Ask the money manager to give you a copy of her written investment philosophy. How does she feel about small cap stocks versus large caps? Income versus growth?

✔ **Find out whether you're comfortable with how the money manager selects stocks.**

Is she a value investor or a growth investor? Is she aggressive or conservative? Does she analyze a stock because of its fundamentals (sales, earnings, book value, and so on), or does she use stock price charts?

✔ **Ask the money manager to explain her strategy.**

A good way to evaluate the success (or failure) of the strategy is to ask the money manager for her past recommendations. Did she pick more winners than losers?

Knowing When to Sell

The act of buying stock is relatively easy. However, the act of selling stock can be an agonizing decision for investors. But it is agonizing only in two instances: when you have made money with your stock and when you have lost it. That about covers it. It sounds like a bad joke, but it's not that far from the truth.

The idea of selling stock when it has appreciated (the stock price has increased in value) comes with the following concerns:

✔ **Tax implications:** This is a good reason to consider selling. See Chapter 19 for information about how selling stocks under given circumstances can affect your taxes.

✔ **Greed factors:** "I could have squeezed more gain out of the stock." This means that you may want to hold onto the stock.

✔ **Emotional baggage:** "That stock was in our family for years." Believe it or not, investors cite this personal reason (or one of a dozen other personal reasons) for agonizing over the sale of an appreciated stock.

The following is a list of issues that investors should be aware of when they're selling a stock that has lost money:

- **Tax benefits:** This is a good reason to consider selling a stock. See Chapter 19 for more on timing your stock sales to minimize your tax burden.

- **Pride:** "If I sell, I'll have to admit I was wrong" (followed by silent sobbing). So what? The best investors in history have made bad investments (some that have been quite embarrassing, in fact). This is not a good reason to hold on to a loser.

- **Doubt:** "If I sell my stock now, it may rebound later." Frequently, when an investor buys a stock at $50 and it goes to $40, the investor believes that if he sells, the stock will make an immediate rebound and go to $60, and then he'll be kicking himself. That may happen, but usually the stock price goes lower.

- **Separation anxiety:** "But I've had this stock so long that it's become a part of me." People hang on to a losing stock for all sorts of illogical reasons. Being married to a person is great; being married to a stock is ludicrous. If a stock isn't helping your goals, then it's hurting your goals.

People have plenty more reasons to agonize over the sale of a bad stock. But you can learn to handle the stock sale in a disciplined manner.

There are only two reasons to consider selling a stock regardless of whether the stock price has gone up or down:

- You need the money. Obviously, if you need the money for a bona fide reason — such as paying off debt, wiping out a tax bill, or buying a home — then you need the money. This reason is easy to see. After all, regardless of investment or tax considerations, stocks are there to serve you. I hope that you do some financial planning so that you don't need to sell your stocks for these types of expenses, but you can't avoid unexpected expenditures.

- The stock ceased to perform as you desired. If the stock isn't serving your wealth-building goals or fulfilling your investment objectives, it's time to get rid of it and move on to the next stock. Just as soon as you get a stiff upper lip and resolve to unload this losing stock, a little voice saying, "If I sell my stock now, it may rebound later," starts to haunt you. So you hang on to the stock, but then — bam! — before you know it, you lose more money.

Selling a stock shouldn't require a psychologist. This is where discipline steps in. This is why I'm a big proponent of trailing stops. (See Chapter 16 for more on stops.) Trailing stops take the agony out of selling the stock. All else being equal, you shouldn't sell a winning stock. If it's doing well, why sell it? Keep it as long as possible. But if it stops being a winning stock, sell it. If you don't know how or when to sell it, then apply a stop-loss order at 5 or 10 percent below the market value and let the market action take its course.

Chapter 16

Stop! In the Name of Money

• •

In This Chapter

▶ Looking at different types of brokerage orders

▶ Using trailing stops to protect your profits

▶ Trading on margin to maximize profits

▶ Making sense of going short

• •

Investment success isn't just about picking rising stocks; it's also about how you go about doing it. Frequently, investors think that good stock picking means doing your homework and then making that buy (or sell). However, you can take it a step further to maximize profits (or minimize losses). As a stock investor, you can do so by taking advantage of techniques and services available through your standard brokerage account. (See Chapter 7 for more on brokerage accounts.) This chapter presents some of the best ways you can use these powerful techniques — useful whether you're buying or selling stock. In fact, if you retain nothing more from this chapter than the concept of *trailing stops* (see the section "Trailing stops"), you'll have gotten your money's worth.

In 1999 and 2000, I warned my students and readers that a bear market was on the way. All the data warned me about it, and undoubtedly, it seemed like a time for caution. (See Chapter 14 for information about bull and bear markets.) Investors didn't have to necessarily believe me, but they could have (at the very least) used trailing stops and other techniques to ensure greater investing success. Imagine how much of the trillions of dollars in stock losses could have been avoided if investors had understood and implemented stop orders, for example.

Orders you place with your stockbroker neatly fit into two categories:

> ✔ **Time-related orders:** Time-related orders mean just that; the order has a time limit. Typically, these are used in conjunction with conditional orders. (For an example, see the "Limit Orders" section, later in this chapter.) The two most common time-related orders are day orders and good-till-canceled (or GTC) orders, which I explain in their own sections later in this chapter.

✔ **Condition-related orders:** A condition-related order means that the order should be executed only when a certain condition is met. Conditional orders enhance your ability to buy stocks at a lower price, to sell at a better price, or to minimize potential losses. When stock markets become bearish or uncertain, conditional orders are highly recommended. A good example of a conditional order is a *limit order*. A limit order may say, "Buy Mojeski Corp. at $45." But if Mojeski Corp. is not at $45 (this is the condition), then the order isn't executed.

Get familiar with both orders because they're easy to implement and invaluable tools for wealth building and (more importantly) wealth saving!

Using a combination of orders helps you fine-tune your strategy so that you can maintain greater control over your investments. Speak with your broker about the different types of orders you can use to maximize the gains (or minimize the losses) from your stock investing activities. You also can read the broker's policies on stock orders at the brokerage Web site.

Call It a Day Order

A *day order* (a time-related order) is an order to buy a stock that expires at the end of that particular trading day. If you tell your broker, "Buy BYOB Inc. at $37.50 and make it a day order," you mean that you want to purchase the stock at $37.50. But if the stock doesn't hit that price, your order expires at the end of the trading day unfilled. Why would you place such an order? Maybe BYOB is trading at $39, but you don't want to buy it at that price because you don't believe the stock is worth it. Consequently, you have no problem not getting the stock that day.

When would you use day orders? It depends on your preferences and personal circumstances. I rarely use day orders because there are few events that cause me to say, "Gee, I'll just try to buy or sell between now and the end of today's trading action." However, you may feel that you don't want a specified order to linger beyond today's market action. Perhaps you want to test a price. ("I would like to get rid of stock A at $39 to make a quick profit, but it's currently trading at $37.50. However, I may change my mind tomorrow.") A day order is the perfect strategy to use in this case.

By the way, if you make any trade and don't specify time with the order, most (if not all) brokers automatically treat it as a day order.

Good-till-Canceled (GTC)

A good-till-canceled (GTC) order is the most commonly requested order by investors. Although GTC orders are time-related, they are always tied to a condition, such as when the stock achieves a certain price. The GTC order means just what it says: The order stays in effect until it is transacted or until the investor cancels it. Although the order implies that it could run indefinitely, most brokers do have a time limit to it. The time limit could be 30 days, 60 days, 90 days, or longer. Ask your broker about his particular policy on GTC orders.

A GTC order is usually coupled with conditional or condition-related orders. For example, say that you want to buy ASAP Corp. stock but you don't want to buy it at the current price of $48 per share. You've done your homework on the stock, including looking at the stock's price to earnings ratio, price to book ratio, and so on (see Appendix B for more on ratios), and you say, "Hey, this stock isn't worth $48 a share. I would only buy it at $36 per share." You think the stock would make a good addition to your portfolio but not at the current market price. (It is overpriced or overvalued according to your analysis.) How should you proceed?

Well, you wouldn't put in a day order to get the stock at $36. To go from $48 to $36 in a day means that the stock would need to fall by 25 percent. The odds are against that happening (unless you know something that I don't). However, the odds that such a decline could happen over a period of a few weeks or a few months are much better. If you want that stock at your price and you are patient, ask your broker do a "GTC order at $36." This means that your broker will buy the shares if and when they hit the $36 mark (or until you cancel the order). Just make sure that your account has the funds available to complete the transaction.

The bottom line is that GTC orders are very useful, so you should become familiar with your broker's policy on them. While you're at it, ask whether any fees apply. Many brokers don't charge for GTC orders because, if they happen to result in a buy (or sell) order, they generate a normal commission just as any stock transaction would. Other brokers may charge a small fee. In many cases, if a fee is charged, it's credited against the commission should the transaction occur. Fee or no fee, the GTC order is meant to protect you from further losses or to help you lock in a profit.

When you want to buy

In recent years, people have had a tendency to rush into buying a stock without giving some thought to what they could do to get more for their money. It doesn't occur to some investors that the stock market can be a place for bargain-hunting consumers. If you're ready to buy a quality pair of socks for $16 in a department store but the sales clerk says that those same socks are going on sale tomorrow for only $8, what would you do — assuming that you're a cost-conscious consumer? Unless you're barefoot, you're probably better off waiting. The same point holds true with stocks.

Say that you want to buy SOX Inc. at $26 but it's currently trading at $30. You think that $30 is too expensive, but you're happy to buy the stock at $26 or lower. However, you have no idea whether the stock will move to your desired price today, tomorrow, next week, or even next month. In this case, a GTC order is appropriate.

When you want to sell

Remember the socks you bought? Well, what if you have a hole in your sock (darn it!)? Wouldn't you want to get rid of it? Of course you would. If a stock's price starts to unravel, you want to be able to get rid of it as well.

Perhaps you already own SOX (at $25, for instance) but are concerned that market conditions may drive the price lower. You're not certain which way the stock will move in the coming days and weeks. In this case, a GTC order to sell the stock at a specified price is a suitable strategy. Because the stock price is $25, you may want to place a GTC order to sell it if it falls to $22.50, to prevent further losses. Again, in this example, GTC is the time frame, and it accompanies a condition (sell when the stock hits $22.50).

Market Orders

When you buy stock, the simplest type of order is a *market order* — an order to buy or sell a stock at the market's current best available price. It doesn't get any more basic than that.

Here's an example: Kowalski, Inc., is available at the market price of $10. When you call up your broker and instruct him to buy 100 shares "at the market," the broker will implement the order for your account, and you pay $1,000 plus commission.

I say "current best available price" because the stock's price is constantly moving, and catching the best price can be a function of the broker's ability to process the stock purchase. For very active stocks, the price change can happen within seconds. It's not unheard of to have three brokers simultaneously place orders for the same stocks and get three different prices because of differences in the broker's capability. (Some computers are faster than others.) The price difference within these seconds usually isn't worth getting concerned about because the difference amounts to pennies. It would matter to day traders and those who buy huge amounts of stock, but it's not a consequential difference to the everyday stock investor.

The advantage of a market order is that the transaction is processed immediately, and you get your stock without worrying about whether it hits a particular price. For example, if you buy Kowalski, Inc., with a market order, you know that by the end of that phone call (or Web site visit), you're assured of getting the stock. The disadvantage of a market order is that you can't control the price that you pay for the stock. Suppose that you learn that Kowalski, Inc., is currently trading at $10 per share. You call your broker to place an order. If the stock jumps to $11 per share before you finish ordering, you end up buying it for $1 more than you figured. Then again, you could get it for $9 if the price moves downward. With a fast-moving stock, you may get it at a significantly higher price than you planned. Conversely, if you're selling a particularly volatile stock, you might lock in a sale price lower (or higher) than you expected if the price changes before you finish your sale.

Market orders get finalized in the chronological order in which they're placed. Your price may change because the orders ahead of you in line caused the stock price to rise or fall based on the latest news.

Stop! 1 Order You!

A *stop order* (or *stop-loss order* if you own the stock) is a condition-related order that instructs the broker to sell a particular stock only when the stock reaches a particular price. It acts like a trigger, and the stop order converts to a market order to sell the stock immediately.

The stop-loss order isn't designed to take advantage of small, short-term moves in the stock's price. It's meant to help you protect the bulk of your money when the market turns against your stock investment in a sudden manner.

Say that your Kowalski, Inc., stock rises to $20 per share and you seek to protect your investment against a possible future market decline. A stop-loss order at $18 will trigger your broker to sell the stock immediately if it falls to the $18 mark. In this example, if the stock suddenly drops to $17, it will still trigger the stop-loss order, but the finalized sale price will be $17. In a volatile market, you may not be able to sell at your precise stop-loss price. However, because the order automatically gets converted into a market order, the sale will be done, and you prevent further declines in the stock.

The main benefit of a stop-loss order is that it prevents a major decline in a stock that you own. It's a form of discipline that is important in investing in order to minimize potential losses. Investors can find it agonizing to sell a stock that has fallen. If they don't sell, however, the stock often continues to plummet as investors continue to hold on while hoping for a rebound in the price.

A stop-loss amount is usually set at about 10 percent below the market value of a stock. This percentage gives the stock some room to fluctuate, which most stocks tend to do on a day-to-day basis.

Practice discipline

I have a stack of several years' worth of investment newsletters in which investment experts made all sorts of calls regarding the prospects of a company, industry, or the economy in general. Some made forecasts that were spectacularly on target, but you should see the ones that were spectacularly wrong — ouch! However, even some of the winners suffered because of a lack of discipline. Those spectacular gains disappeared like football fans at a chess match.

Stock	Original Recommended Price
Amazon.com	15.00

Yikes! I give him credit for being honest (in presenting the performance), but how would you feel if you had taken his recommendation from day one? You would have seen an exciting jump in your stock value and then watched, nauseated, as the stock plummeted. This example shows that there's something worse than investing in a stock and watching it become a

My favorite example is the newsletter expert who actually recommended Amazon.com at $15 in 1997. That stock immediately began an incredible ascent past $100. He looked like a genius! He continued to tell his newsletter subscribers to buy Amazon.com during the late 1990s. He told those who already owned Amazon.com to hold onto the stock and buy more "on the dips" (when the price falls). I saw a copy of his newsletter in 2001. Amazon.com was still in his portfolio. The line in the table read:

Current Price	Action to Take
9.00	Hold

loser. What's worse? Seeing it gain first, losing that gain, and then losing money! Hmmm . . . where's the antacid?

Investing can be an emotional roller coaster. Keep your sanity and your profits by being disciplined. Use your stop-loss orders and fasten those seat belts.

Trailing stops

Trailing stops are an important technique in wealth preservation for seasoned stock investors and can be one of your key strategies in using stop loss orders. A *trailing stop* is a stop-loss order that the investor actively manages by moving it up along with the stock's market price. The stop-loss order "trails" the stock price upward. As the stop-loss goes upward, it protects more and more of the stock's value from declining.

A real-life example may be the best way to help you understand trailing stops. Say that in 1999 you bought Lucent Technologies (LU) at $25 per share. As soon as you finished buying it, you immediately told your broker to put a stop-loss order at $22 and make it a good-till-canceled (GTC) order. Think of what you did. In effect, you placed an ongoing (GTC) safety net under your stock. The stock can go as high as the sky, but if it should fall, the stock's price will trigger a sell order at $22, at which point your stock will automatically be sold, minimizing your loss.

If Lucent goes to $50 per share in a few months, you can call your broker and cancel the former stop-loss order at $22 and replace it with a new (higher) stop-loss order. You simply say, "Please put a new stop-loss order at $45 and make it a GTC order." This higher stop-loss price protects not only your original investment of $20 but also a big chunk of your profit as well. As time goes by, and the stock price climbs, you can continue to raise the stop-loss price and add a GTC provision. Now you know why it is called a trailing stop: It trails the stock price upward like a giant tail. All along the way, it protects more and more of your growing investment without limiting its upward movement.

William O'Neill, publisher and founder of *Investor's Business Daily,* advocates setting a trailing stop of 8 percent below your purchase price. That's his preference. Some investors who invest in very volatile stocks may put in trailing stops of 20 or 25 percent. Is a stop-loss order desirable or advisable in every situation? No. It depends on your level of experience, your investment goals, and the market environment. Still, stop-loss orders are appropriate in most cases, especially if the market seems uncertain (or you do!).

A trailing stop is a stop-loss order that you actively manage. The stop-loss order is good-till-canceled (GTC), and it constantly trails the stock's price as it moves up. To successfully implement trailing stops, keep the following points in mind:

✔ **Brokers usually don't place trailing stops for you automatically.** In fact, they won't (or shouldn't) place any type of order without your consent. Deciding on the type of order to place is your responsibility. You can raise, lower, or cancel a trailing stop order at will, but you need to monitor your investment when substantial moves do occur and to respond to the movement appropriately.

✔ **Change the stop-loss order when the stock price moves significantly.** Hopefully, you won't call your broker every time the stock moves 50 cents. Change the stop-loss order when the stock price moves around 10 percent. When you initially purchase the stock (say at $90 per share), request the broker to place the stop-loss order at $81. When the stock moves to $100, cancel the $81 stop-loss order and replace it at $90. When the stock's price moves to $110, change the stop-loss order to $100, and so on.

✔ **Understand your broker's policy on GTC orders.** If your broker usually has a GTC order expire after 30 or 60 days, you should be aware of it. You don't want to risk a sudden drop in your stock's price with the stop-loss order protection. If your broker's time limit is 60 days, note it so that you can renew the order for additional time.

✔ **Monitor your stock.** Trailing stops is not a "set it and forget it" technique. Monitoring your investment is critical. Of course, if it falls, the stop-loss order you have will prevent further loss. Should the stock price rise substantially, remember to adjust your trailing stop accordingly. Keep raising the safety net as the stock continues to rise. Part of monitoring the stock is knowing the beta, which you can read more about in the next section.

1 beta you didn't know this

To be a successful investor, you need to understand the volatility of the particular stock you invest in. In stock market parlance, this is also called the beta of a stock. *Beta* is a quantitative measure of the volatility of a given stock (mutual funds and portfolios, too) relative to the overall market, usually the S&P 500 index. Beta specifically measures the performance movement of the stock as the S&P moves 1 percent up or down. A beta measurement above 1 is more volatile than the overall market, while a beta below 1 is less volatile. Some stocks are relatively stable in the price movements; others jump around.

Because beta measures how volatile or unstable the stock's price is, it tends to be uttered in the same breath as "risk" — more volatility indicates more risk. Similarly, less volatility tends to mean less risk.

Table 16-1 shows some sample betas of well-known companies (as of March 2002):

Table 16-1	Looking at Well-Known Betas	
Company	*Beta*	*Comments*
Exxon Mobil	.27	Is less volatile than the market. If the S&P moves $10, Exxon Mobil would only move $2.70.
Yahoo!	2.63	Is almost three times more volatile than the market.
Public Service Enterprise Group	.07	Statistically considered much less volatile than the market.

You can find a company's beta at Web sites that usually provide a lot of financial information about the company, such as Nasdaq's Web site (www. nasdaq.com).

The beta is useful to know because it gives you a general idea of the stock's trading range. If a stock is currently priced at $50 and it typically trades in the $48–$52 range, then a trailing stop at $49 doesn't make sense. Your stock would probably be sold the same day you initiated the stop-loss order. If your stock is a volatile growth stock that could swing up and down by 10 percent, you should more logically set your stop-loss at 15 percent below that day's price.

The stock of a large cap stock in a mature industry tends to have a low beta — one close to the overall market. Small and mid cap stocks in new or emerging industries tend to have greater volatility in their day-to-day price fluctuations; hence, they tend to have a high beta. (You can find an explanation of capitalization in Chapter 1.)

Limit Orders

A *limit order* is a very precise condition-related order, implying that there is a limit either on the buy or the sell side of the transaction. You want to buy (or sell) only at a specified price. Period. Limit orders work better for you if you're buying the stock, but they may not be good for you if you're selling the stock.

Usually there are no special fees for limit orders. Brokers make their money when the order is triggered. At that point, the transaction (buy or sell) would generate a regular commission. However, policies and fees can vary depending on the brokerage. Some Internet brokerages actually charge a small fee for limit orders because they charge low commissions. They may credit the fee against the sell or buy commission if the order is triggered. (This is also true of stop orders, which I discuss earlier in this chapter.)

When you're buying

Just because you like a particular company and you want its stock doesn't mean that you're willing to pay the current market price. Maybe you want to buy Kowalski, Inc., but the current market price of $20 per share isn't acceptable to you. You prefer to buy it at $16 because you think that price reflects its true market value. What do you do? You tell your broker, "Buy Kowalski with a limit order at $16."

Of course, you don't know exactly when the stock will hit your price of choice. In this example, stock in Kowalski, Inc., may hit $16 by the end of the day or sometime next month or possibly never. A limit order must have a specified time period in which it can transact. You have to specify whether it is a day order (good for the day) or a GTC order, which I discuss in its own section earlier in this chapter. Unless you know some bad news about the company that the rest of the market doesn't (in which case a day order is advisable), the better option is to make it a GTC limit order. If and when the stock goes to $16 during the time your GTC order is in effect, the order to buy will automatically be performed, and you receive a trade confirmation notice.

What happens if the stock experiences great volatility? What if it drops to $16.01 and then suddenly drops to $15.95 on the next move? Actually, nothing, you may be dismayed to hear. Because your order was limited to $16, it can be transacted only at $16, no more or less. The only way for this particular trade to occur is if the stock rises back to $16. However, if the price keeps dropping, then your limit order won't be transacted and may expire or be canceled.

When you're buying a stock, many brokers interpret the limit order as "buy at this specific price or better." Presumably, if your limit order is to buy the stock at $10, you'll be just as happy if your broker buys that stock for you at $9.95. This way, if you don't get exactly $10, because the stock's price was volatile, you'll still get the stock at a lower price. Speak to your particular broker to be clear on the meaning of the limit order.

When you're selling

Limit orders are activated only when a stock hits a specific price. If you buy Kowalski, Inc., at $20 and you worry about a decline in the share price, you may decide to put in a limit order at $18. If you watch the news and hear that Kowalski's price is dropping, you may sigh and say, "I sure am glad that I put in that limit order at $18!" However, in a volatile market, the share price may leapfrog over your specified price. It could go from $18.01 to $17.99 and then continue its descent. Because the stock price never hit $18 on the mark, it isn't sold. You may be sitting at home satisfied (mistakenly) that you played it smart, while your stock plummets to $15 or $10 or worse! It's best to have a stop-loss order in place.

Pass the Margin, Please

Margin means buying securities, such as stocks, by using funds you borrow from your broker. Buying stock on margin is similar to buying a house with a mortgage. If you buy a house at a purchase price of $100,000 and put 10 percent down, your equity (the part you own) is $10,000, and you borrow the remaining $90,000 with a mortgage. If the value of the house rises to $120,000 and you sell (for the sake of simplicity, I don't include closing costs in this example), you will make a profit of 100 percent. How is that? The $20,000 gain on the property represents a gain of 20 percent on the purchase price of $100,000, but because your real investment is $10,000 (the down payment), your gain works out to 200 percent (a gain of $20,000 on your initial investment of $10,000).

Buying on margin is an example of using leverage to maximize your gain when prices rise. *Leverage* is simply using borrowed money to increase your profit. This type of leverage is great in a favorable (bull) market, but it works against you in an unfavorable (bear) market. Say that a $100,000 house you purchase with a $90,000 mortgage falls in value to $80,000 (and property values can decrease during economic hard times). Your outstanding debt of $90,000 exceeds the value of the property. Because you owe more than you own, it is negative net worth. Leverage is a double-edged sword.

Marginal outcomes

Suppose that you think that the stock for the company Mergatroid, Inc., currently at $40 per share, will go up in value. You want to buy 100 shares, but you have only $2,000. What can you do? If you're intent on buying 100 shares (versus simply buying the 50 shares that you have cash for), you can borrow the additional $2,000 from your broker on margin. If you do that, what are the potential outcomes?

If the stock price goes up

This is the best outcome for you. If Mergatroid goes to $50 per share, your investment will be worth $5,000, and your outstanding margin loan will be $2,000. If you sell, the total proceeds will pay off the loan and leave you with $3,000. Because your initial investment was $2,000, your profit is a solid 50 percent because ultimately your $2,000 principal amount generated a $1,000 profit. (For the sake of this example, I leave out any charges, such as commissions and interest paid on the margin loan.) However, if you pay the entire $4,000 upfront — without the margin loan — your $4,000 investment will generate a profit of $1,000, or 25 percent. Using margin, you will double the return on your money.

Leverage, when used properly, is very profitable. However, it is still debt, so understand that you must pay it off eventually.

If the stock price fails to rise

If the stock goes nowhere, you still have to pay interest on that margin loan. If the stock pays dividends, this money can defray some of the cost of the margin loan. In other words, dividends can help you pay off what you borrow from the broker.

Having the stock neither rise nor fall may seem like a neutral situation, but you pay interest on your margin loan with each passing day. For this reason, margin trading can be a good consideration for conservative investors if the stock pays a high dividend. Many times, a high dividend from $5,000 worth of stock can exceed the margin interest you have to pay from the $2,500 (50 percent) you borrow from the broker to buy that stock.

If the stock price goes down, buying on margin can work against you. What if Mergatroid goes to $38 per share? The market value of 100 shares will be $3,800, but your equity will shrink to only $1,800 because you have to pay your $2,000 margin loan. You're not exactly looking at a disaster at this point, but you'd better be careful, because the margin loan exceeds 50 percent of your stock investment. If it goes any lower, you may get the dreaded *margin call,* when the broker actually contacts you to ask you to restore the ratio between the margin loan and the value of the securities. See the following section for information about appropriate debt to equity ratios.

Maintaining your balance

When you purchase stock on margin, you must maintain a balanced ratio of margin debt to equity of at least 50 percent. If the debt portion exceeds this limit, then you'll be required to restore that ratio by depositing either more stock or more cash into your brokerage account. The additional stock you deposit can be stock that's transferred from another account.

If, for example, Mergatroid goes to $28 per share, the margin loan portion exceeds 50 percent of the equity value in that stock — in this case, because the market value of your stock is $2,800 but the margin loan is still at $2,000. The margin loan is a worrisome 71 percent of the market value ($2,000 divided by $2,800 = 71 percent). Expect to get a call from your broker to put more securities or cash into the account to restore the 50 percent balance.

If you can't come up with more stock, other securities, or cash, then the next step is to sell stock from the account and use the proceeds to pay off the margin loan. For you, it means realizing a capital loss — you lost money on your investment.

The Federal Reserve Board governs margin requirements for brokers with Regulation T. Discuss this rule with your broker to understand fully your (and the broker's) risks and obligations. Regulation T dictates the minimum percentage that margin should be set at. For most listed stocks, it is 50 percent.

Margin, as you can see, can escalate your profits on the up side but magnify your losses on the down side. If your stock plummets drastically, you can end up with a margin loan that exceeds the market value of the stock you used the loan to purchase. In the emerging bear market of 2000, many people were hurt by stock losses, and a large number of these losses were made worse because people didn't manage the responsibilities involved with margin trading.

If you buy stock on margin, use a disciplined approach. Be extra careful when using leverage, such as a margin loan, because it can backfire. Keep the following points in mind:

- **Have ample reserves of cash or marginable securities in your account.** Try to keep the margin ratio at 40 percent or less to minimize the chance of a margin call.

- **If you're a beginner, consider using margin to buy stock in large companies that have a relatively stable price and pay a good dividend.** Some people buy income stocks that have dividend yields that exceed the margin interest rate, meaning that the stock ends up paying for its own margin loan. Just remember those stop orders.

✔ **Constantly monitor your stocks.** If the market turns against you, the result will be especially painful if you use margin.

✔ **Have a payback plan for your margin debt.** Margin loans against your investments mean that you're paying interest. Your ultimate goal is to make money, and paying interest eats into your profits.

Going Short and Coming Out Ahead

The vast majority of stock investors are familiar with buying stock, holding on to it for a while, and hoping its value goes up. This kind of thinking is called *going long,* and investors who go long are considered to be *long on stocks.* Going long essentially means that you're bullish and seeking your profits from rising prices. However, astute investors also profit in the market when stock prices fall. *Going short* (also called *shorting a stock, selling short,* or *doing a short sale*) on a stock is a common technique for profiting from a stock price decline. Investors have made big profits during bear markets by going short. A short sale is a bet that a particular stock is going down.

To go short, you have to be deemed (by your broker) creditworthy — your account needs to be approved for short selling. When you're approved for margin trading, you're probably set to sell short, too. Speak to your broker (or check for this information on the broker's Web site) about limitations in your account regarding going short.

Because going short on stocks has greater risks than going long, I strongly advise beginning investors to avoid shorting stocks until they become more seasoned.

Most people easily understand making money by going long. It boils down to "buy low and sell high." Piece of cake. Going short means making money by selling high and then buying low. Huh? Thinking in reverse is not a piece of cake. Although thinking of this stock adage in reverse may be challenging, the mechanics of going short are really simple. Consider an example that uses a fictitious company called DOA, Inc. As a stock, DOA ($50 per share) is looking pretty sickly. It has lots of debt and plummeting sales and earnings, and the news is out that DOA's industry will face hard times for the foreseeable future. This situation describes a stock that is an ideal candidate for shorting. The future may be bleak for DOA, but promising for savvy investors.

You must understand brokerage rules before you conduct short selling. The broker must approve you for it (see Chapter 7 for information on working with brokers), and you must meet the minimum collateral requirement, which is typically $2,000 or 50 percent of the shorted stock's market value.

If the stock generates dividends, those are paid to the owner of the stock, not to the person who is borrowing it to go short. (See the next section, "Setting up a short sale," to see how this technique works.) Check with your broker for complete details and review the resources in Appendix A.

Setting up a short sale

This section explains how to go short. Say that you believe that DOA is the right stock to short — you're pretty sure its price is going to fall. With DOA at $50, you instruct your broker to "go short 100 shares on DOA." (It doesn't have to be 100 shares. I'm just using that as an example.) Now, here's what happens next:

1. **Your broker borrows 100 shares of DOA stock, either from his own inventory or from another client or broker.**

    That's right. The stock can be borrowed from a client, no permission necessary. The broker guarantees the transaction, and the client/owner of the stock never has to be informed about it, because he never loses legal and beneficial right to the stock. You borrow 100 shares, and you'll return 100 shares when it's time to complete the transaction.

2. **Your broker then sells the stock and gives you the money.**

    Your account is credited with $5,000 (100 shares × $50) in cash — the money gained from selling the borrowed stock. This cash acts like a loan on which you're going to have to pay interest.

3. **You use the $5,000 for a little while.**

    Your broker has deposited the $5,000 in your account. You can use this money to buy other investments.

4. **You buy the stock back and return it to its rightful owner.**

    When it's time to close the transaction (either you want to close it, or the owner of the shares wants to sell them, so you have to give them back), you must return the number of shares you borrowed (in this case, it was 100 shares). If you buy back the 100 shares at $40 per share (remember that you shorted this particular stock because you were sure its price was going to fall) and these 100 shares are returned to their owner, you make a $1,000 profit. (To keep the example tidy, I don't include brokerage commissions.) By selling short, you made money when the stock price fell!

Oops! Going short when prices grow taller

I bet you guessed that there was a flip side to the wonderful profitability of selling short. Presume that you were wrong about DOA and that the stock price rises from the ashes as it goes from $50 to $87. Now what? You still have to return the 100 shares you borrowed. With the stock's price at $87, that means that you have to buy the stock for $8,700 (100 shares at the new, higher price of $87). Ouch! How do you pay for it? Well, you have that original $5,000 in your account from when you initially went short on the stock. But where do you get the other $3,700 ($8,700 less the original $5,000)? You guessed it — your pocket! You have to cough up the difference. If the stock continues to rise, that's a lot of coughing.

How much money do you lose if the stock goes to $100 or more? A heck of a lot. As a matter of fact, there's no limit to how much you can lose. That's why going short can be riskier than going long. With going long, the most you can lose is 100 percent of your money. However, with going short, you can lose more than 100 percent of the money you invest. Yikes!

Because the potential for loss is unlimited when you short a stock, I suggest that you use a stop order (also called a *buy-stop order*) to minimize the damage. Better yet, make it a good-till-canceled order, which I discuss earlier in this chapter. You can set the stop order at a given price, and if the stock hits that price, you buy the stock back so that you can return it to its owner before the price rises even higher. You still lose money, but you limit your losses.

Watching out for ticks

Short sellers should be aware of the *uptick rule,* which states that you can enter into a short sale only when the stock has just completed an uptick. "Tick" in this case means the actual incremental price movement of the stock you're shorting. For a $10 stock that was just $9.95 a moment ago, the 5-cent difference represents an uptick. If the $10 stock was just $10.10 a moment before, the 10-cent difference is a downtick. The amount of the tick doesn't matter. So, if you short a stock at the price of $40, the immediate prior price must have been $39.99 or lower. The reason for this rule (a Federal Reserve regulation) is that short selling can aggravate declining stock prices in a rapidly falling market. In practice, going short on a stock whose price is already declining can make the stock price fall even more so. Excessive short selling can make the stock more volatile than it would be otherwise.

Feeling the squeeze

If you go short on a stock, remember that, sooner or later, you have to buy that stock back so that you can return it to its owner. What happens when a lot of people are short on a particular stock and its price starts to rise? All those short sellers will be scrambling to buy the stock back so that they can close their transactions before they lose too much money. This mass selling quickens the pace of the stock's ascent and puts a squeeze (called a *short squeeze*) on the investors who had been shorting the stock.

Earlier in the chapter, I explain that your broker can borrow stock from another client so that you can go short on it. What happens when that client wants to sell the stock in her account — the stock that you borrowed and so is no longer in her account? When that happens, your broker asks you to return the borrowed stock. That's when you feel the squeeze — you have to buy the stock back at the current price.

Going short can be a great maneuver in a declining (bear) market, but it can be brutal if the stock price goes up. If you're a beginner, stay away from short selling until you have enough experience (and money) to risk it.

Chapter 17

Getting a Handle on DPPs, DRPs, and DCA . . . PDQ

You're investing the big bucks as a top-flight investor; you should be smart about it. Not only do you stand to make money on your investments, but you're paying to make money on your money. This chapter looks at *transaction costs,* or the cost of doing stock investing. For most investors, using a broker makes the most sense. Sometimes, however, you can avoid some of these costs. For example, you may be able to buy stock without using a broker and save big by not paying commissions or other sales charges.

Direct purchase programs (DPPs) and dividend reinvestment plans (DRPs) make a lot of sense for long-term stock investors, and you can do them on your own — no broker necessary. These types of programs aren't suitable for those who like to quickly jump in and out of a stock. They're meant for those who like to invest small sums of money and plan on doing so over a long period of time.

Being Direct with DPPs

If you're going to buy a stock anyway, why not buy it directly from the company and bypass the broker (and commissions) altogether? Several hundred companies now offer *direct purchase programs* (DPPs), also called DIPs (or direct investment programs), which give investors an opportunity to buy stock directly from these companies.

Pre-DPP

Long before DPPs became readily available, investors had to make their initial stock investment through stockbrokers. That wasn't a problem, because technically all you needed to buy was one share of stock. To get the best price, you had to buy a round lot (100 shares or more), which could be very expensive for small investors. Buying 100 shares of a $50 stock requires at least $5,000 plus commissions. How could small investors get involved if they had only a few hundred dollars?

If you bought 99 shares or less (called an *odd lot*), your transaction cost was relatively high. If you only bought one share, the commission ate up a large chunk of the investment. What's an investor to do?

Fortunately, many large companies had given investors the ability to invest directly as long as they had enough money to make an initial investment of at least one share of stock. But what's the point of buying one share of stock? The point is that it opens the door to buying more stock later at lower costs to you through the company's dividend reinvestment plan (DRP).

DPPs give investors the opportunity to get involved with little upfront money (usually enough to cover the purchase of one share) and usually no commissions. Why do companies do this? For their sake, they want to encourage more attention and participation from investors. For your purposes, however, a DPP gives you what you may need most: a low-cost entry into that particular company's DRP (which you can read more about in the section "Dipping into DRPs," later in this chapter).

Investing in a DPP

If you have your sights set on a particular company and have only a few bucks to start out with, a DPP is probably the best way to make your initial investment. The following steps can guide you toward your first stock purchase using a DPP:

1. **Decide what stock you want to invest in. (This whole book is about that topic.)**

   Say that you did your homework and you decide to invest in Yumpin Yimminy Corp. (YYC). Contact the company directly and request to speak to someone in the shareholder services department. You can get YYC's contact information through the stock exchange YYC trades on. For example, if YYC is traded on the New York Stock Exchange, you can call the NYSE or visit its Web site (www.nyse.com) and ask for the contact information for YYC. So you can contact NYSE to reach YYC for its DPP ASAP. OK?

2. **Find out whether YYC has a DPP.**

   Call YYC's shareholder services department and ask whether it has a DPP. If it does, great; if it doesn't, ask if it plans to start one.

3. **Ask about enrolling.**

   The company will send you an application along with a prospectus — the program document that serves as a brochure and, hopefully, answers your basic questions.

4. **Fill in the application and return it with the minimum investment amount specified (usually enough to cover at least one share).**

   The processing is typically handled by an organization that the company designates, an entity called the plan administrator (which can also be referred to as the transfer agent). From this point forward, you're in the dividend reinvestment plan. (See the section "Dipping into DRPs," later in this chapter.)

Finding DPP alternatives

Although several hundred companies offer DPPs, the majority of companies don't. What do you do if you want to invest in a company directly and it doesn't have a DPP? The following sections present some alternatives.

Buy the first share through a broker to qualify for DRPs

Yes, buying your first share through a broker will cost you a commission; however, after you make the stock purchase, you can contact that company's shareholder service department and ask about its DRP. (See the section "Dipping into DRPs," later in this chapter. After you're an existing stockholder, qualifying for the DRP is a piece of cake.

To qualify for the DRP, you must be on the books of record with the transfer agent. A *book of record* is simply the database that the company uses to track every single outstanding share of stock and the owner of the stock. The *transfer agent* is the person responsible for maintaining the database. Whenever stock is bought or sold, the transfer agent must implement the change and update the records on stock ownership. In many cases, you must have the broker issue a stock certificate in your name once you own the stock. This is the most common way to get your name on the books of record, hence qualifying you for the DRP.

Sometimes, simply buying the stock isn't enough to get your name on the books of record, because brokers often keep the stock in your account under a *street name*. Having a street name means that although you technically own the stock, your broker may keep it registered under a different name for ease of transaction. Having the stock in a street name really doesn't mean much to you until you want to qualify for the company's DPP or DRP. Remember to address this point with your broker.

Get started in a DRP directly through a broker

These days, more brokers are able to offer the features of the DRP (like compounding interest) right in the brokerage account itself, making it more convenient than having to go to the trouble of setting up a DRP with the company. This service is most likely a response to the growing number of long-term investors who have fled traditional brokerage accounts for the benefits of direct investing that DPPs/DRPs offer. The main drawback of a broker-run DRP is that usually it doesn't allow you to make optional cash purchases (a big negative!). See the section "Optional cash payment (OCP)," later in this chapter, for more on this topic.

Purchase via alternate buying services

Organizations have set up services to help small investors buy stock in small quantities. The primary drawback to these middlemen is that you will probably pay more in transaction costs than if you approach the companies directly. The most prominent services are the following:

- ✔ **Money Paper:** You can read more about this newsletter publisher at `www.moneypaper.com`.

- ✔ **National Association of Investors Corporation:** Find out more about this nonprofit group by checking out its Web site, `www.better-investing.org`.

Recognizing that every pro has a con

As beneficial as DPPs are, there are some minor drawbacks. (Aren't there always some drawbacks?) Keep the following points in mind when considering DPPs as part of your stock portfolio:

- ✔ Although more and more companies are starting to offer DPPs, still relatively few companies have them.

- ✔ Some DPPs require a high amount to invest (as much as $250 or more) or a commitment of monthly investments. In any case, ask the plan administrator about the investing requirements.

- ✔ A growing number of DPPs have some type of service charge. Usually this charge (if there is a charge) is very modest and lower than typical brokerage commissions. Ask about all the incidents, such as getting into the plan, getting out, and so on, that may trigger a service charge.

Don't invest in a company just because it has a DPP or DRP. DPPs and DRPs are simply a means for getting into a particular stock with very little money. They shouldn't be a substitute for doing diligent research and analysis on a particular stock.

Dipping into DRPs

Sometimes dividend reinvestment plans (DRPs) are called "DRIPs," which makes me scratch my head. *Reinvestment* is one word not two, so where does that *I* come from? But I digress. Whether you call them DRIPs or DRPs, they're great for small investors and for investors who are truly long-term investors in a particular stock. A DRP is a program that a company may offer to allow investors to accumulate more shares of its stock without paying commissions.

A DRP has two primary advantages:

- ✔ **Compounding:** The dividends get reinvested and give you the opportunity to buy more stock.

- ✔ **Optional cash purchases:** Most DRPs give participants the ability to invest through the plan to purchase more stock, usually with no commissions.

To be in a dividend reinvestment plan, here are the requirements:

- ✔ You must already be a stockholder for that particular stock.

- ✔ You must already have a dividend reinvestment plan set up.

- ✔ The stock must be paying dividends.

Compounding

Because dividends are reinvested, this offers a form of compounding for the small investor. Dividends buy more of the shares, in turn generating more dividends. Usually the dividends generated don't buy entire shares, so what they do purchase are fractional shares.

Say, for example, that you own 20 shares of Fraction Corp. at $10 per share for a total value of $200. Fraction Corp.'s annual dividend is $1.00, meaning that a quarterly dividend of 25 cents is issued every three months. What happens if this stock is in the DRP? The 20 shares generate a $5.00 dividend payout in the first quarter, and this amount is applied to the stock purchase as soon as the amount is credited to the DRP account. If you presume for this example that the stock price hasn't changed, the total shares in the DRP are 20.50 shares valued at $205 (20.50 shares × $10 share price). The dividend payout wasn't enough to buy an entire share, so it bought a fractional share and credited that to the account.

Say that, in the preceding example, three months have passed and that no other shares have been acquired since your prior dividend payout. Fraction Corp. issues another quarterly dividend for 25 cents per share. Now what?

- ✔ The original 20 shares of Fraction Corp. generate a $5.00 dividend payout.

- ✔ The .50, or half share, in the account generates a 12.5 cent dividend (half the dividend of a full share because it is only .50 of a share).

- ✔ The total dividend payout is $5.125 (rounded to $5.13), and the new total of shares in the account is 21.125 shares (the former 20.50 shares plus .625 shares purchased by the dividend payout). Full shares generate full dividends, and fractional shares generate fractional dividends.

To illustrate my point, the preceding example uses a price that doesn't fluctuate. Stock in a DRP acts like any other stock; the share price changes constantly. Every time the DRP makes a stock purchase, whether it is monthly or quarterly, the purchase price will likely change each time.

Optional cash payment (OCP)

Most DRPs give the participant the opportunity to make optional cash payments (OCPs). DRPs usually establish a minimum and a maximum payment. The minimum is typically very modest, such as $25 or $50. A few plans even have no minimum. This feature makes it very affordable to regularly invest modest amounts and build up a sizeable portfolio of stock in a shorter period of time, unencumbered by commissions.

DRPs also have a maximum investment limitation, such as specifying that "DRP participants cannot invest any more than $10,000 per year." For most investors, the maximum is not a showstopper. However, consult with the administrator of the plan because all plans are a little different.

OCPs are probably the most advantageous aspect of a DRP. If you can invest $25 to $50 per month consistently, year after year, at no (or little) cost, you may find that doing so is a superb way to build wealth.

Cost advantages

In spite of the fact that more and more DRPs are charging service fees, DRPs are still an economical way to invest, especially for small investors. The big savings come from not paying commissions. Although many DPPs/DRPs do have charges, they tend to be relatively small (but keep track of them because the costs can add up).

Some DRPs actually offer a discount of between 2 percent and 5 percent (a few are higher) when buying stock through the plan. Still others offer special programs and discounts on the company's products and services. Some companies offer the service of debiting your checking account or paycheck to invest in the DRP. One company offered its shareholders significant discounts to its restaurant subsidiary. In any case, ask the plan administrator because any plus is . . . well . . . a plus.

Weighing the pros with the cons

When you're in a DRP, you reap all the benefits of stock investing (along with the risks and responsibilities). You get an annual report, and you qualify for stock splits, dividend increases, and so on.

Before you start to salivate over all the goodies that come with DRPs, be clear-eyed about some of the negative aspects to them as well:

- ✔ You need to get that first share. But you knew that.

- ✔ Even small fees cut into your profits.

- ✔ Many DRPs may not have some types of services, such as Individual Retirement Accounts (IRAs). (Chapter 19 offers more information on IRAs.)

- ✔ DRPs are designed for long-term investing. Although getting in and out of the plan is easy, the transactions may take weeks to process because stock purchases and sales are typically done all at once on a certain day during the month (or quarter).

- ✔ Read the prospectus. You may not consider this a negative point, but for some people, reading a prospectus is not unlike giving blood by using leeches. Even if that is your opinion, you need to read the prospectus to avoid any surprises, such as hidden fees or unreasonable terms.

- ✔ Understand the tax issues. There, ya see? I knew that I'd ruin it for you. The point is that you should understand the tax consequences. Chapter 19 goes into greater detail. Just know that dividends, whether or not they occur in a DRP, are usually taxable (unless the DRP is in an IRA, which is a different matter).

Perhaps the biggest headache of DRPs is the need to keep good records. Keep all your statements together and use a good spreadsheet program or accounting program if you plan on doing a lot of DRP investing. These records will become especially important at tax time, when you have to report any subsequent gains or losses from stock sales. Because capital gains taxes can be complicated as you sort out short term versus long term, DRP calculations can be a nightmare without good record keeping.

DRPs offer a great way to accumulate a large stock holding over an extended period of time. However, think about what you can do with this stock. Say that you accumulate 110 shares of stock, valued at $50 per share, in your DRP. You can take out $5,000 worth (100 shares at $50 per share) and place it in your brokerage account. Why do that? Brokerage accounts still have plenty of advantages, such as, in this example, the use of margin (a topic I discuss in detail in Chapter 16). You can borrow up to 50 percent of the $5,000, or $2,500, as a margin loan and use it, for example, to pay off $2,500 worth of credit card debt. Because you're replacing unsecured debt (credit card debt that may be charging 15 percent, 18 percent, or more) with secured debt (borrowing against stock in a brokerage account is cheaper than credit card debt), you can save a lot of money. Additionally, ask your tax consultant about potential tax benefits. Investment interest expense is deductible, while consumer credit card debt is not.

The One-Two Punch: Dollar Cost Averaging and DRPs

Whoa! Have I veered away from DRPs into a brand-new topic? Actually, no. Dollar cost averaging (DCA) is a splendid technique for buying stock and lowering your cost for doing so. DCA works especially well with DRPs.

DCA is a simple method for acquiring stock. It rests on the idea that you invest a fixed amount of money at regular intervals (monthly, usually) over a long period of time in that particular stock. Because a fixed amount (say, $50 per month) is going into a fluctuating investment, you end up buying less of that investment as it goes up in price and more of it when it goes down in price. As Table 17-1 illustrates, your average cost per share is usually lower than if you buy all the shares at once.

DCA is best presented with an example. Presume that you decide to get into the DRP of the company Roller Coaster Inc. (RC). On your first day in the DRP, RC's stock is at $25, and the plan allows you to invest a minimum of $25 through its optional cash purchase program. You decide to invest $25 per month and assess how well (hopefully) you're doing six months from now. Table 17-1 shows how this technique works:

Table 17-1		Dollar Cost Averaging (an example)		
Months	Investment Amount	Purchase Price	Shares Bought	Accumulated Shares
1	25	25	1	1
2	25	20	1.25	2.25
3	25	17.5	1.43	3.68
4	25	15	1.67	5.35
5	25	17.5	1.43	6.77
6	25	20	1.25	8.02
Totals=	150	N/A	8.02	8.02

TIP

To assess the wisdom of your decision to invest in the DRP, ask yourself some questions:

✔ How much did you invest over the entire six months?

Your total investment is $150. So far, so good.

✔ What was the first share price for RC, and what was the last share price?

The first share price is $25, but the last share price was $20.

✔ What is the value of your investment at the end of six months?

The value of your investment is easily calculated. Just multiply the number of shares you now own (8.02 shares) by the most recent share price ($20). The total value of your investment is $160.40.

✔ What was the average share price you bought at?

The average share price is also easy to calculate. Take the total amount of your purchases ($150) and divide it by the number of shares that you acquired (8.02 shares). Your average share price becomes $18.70.

✔ Is that your final answer? (Do your best Regis Philbin voice.)

Yes, these are my final answers (look Ma, no lifelines!), but you should take note of the following:

• Even though the last share price ($20) was lower than the original share price ($25), your total investment value is still higher than your purchase amount ($160.40 compared to $150)! How could that be?! Dollar cost averaging is the culprit here. Your disciplined approach (using DCA) was able to overcome the fluctuations in the stock price to help you gain more shares at the lower prices of $17.50 and $15.

- Your average cost per share was only $18.70. The DCA method helped you buy more shares at a lower cost, which ultimately helped you make money when the stock price made a modest rebound.

- DCA works in helping you invest with small sums, all the while helping you smooth out the volatility in stock prices. This helps you make more money in your wealth-building program over the long haul.

Chapter 18

Corporate Hijinks: Looking at What the Insiders Do

In This Chapter

▶ Deciphering the signals of insider trading

▶ Understanding the reasons for corporate buybacks

▶ Splitting stocks

*I*magine that you're boarding a cruise ship, ready to enjoy a hard-earned vacation. As you merrily walk up the plank, you notice that the ship's captain and crew are charging out of the vessel, flailing their arms, and screaming at the top of their lungs — some are even jumping into the water below. Quiz: Would you get on that ship? You get double credit if you can also explain why (or why not). What does this scenario have to do with stock investing? Plenty. The behavior of the people running the boat gives you important clues about the near-term prospects for the boat. Similarly, the actions of company insiders can provide important clues into the near-term prospects for their company.

Company *insiders* are individuals who are key managers or investors in the company. Insiders may be the president of the company, the treasurer, or other managing officer. It can be someone who owns a large stake in the company or someone on the board of directors. In any case, insiders usually have a bird's-eye view of what's going on with the company. They have a good idea of how well (or how poorly) the company is doing.

Keep tabs on what insiders are doing because their buy/sell transactions do have a strong correlation to the near-term movement of their company's stock. However, don't buy or sell stock only because you heard that some insider did it. Use the information on insider trading to confirm your own good sense in buying or selling stock. Insider trading sometimes can be a great precursor to a significant move that you can profit from if you know what to look for. Many shrewd investors have made their profits (or avoided losses) by tracking the activity of the insiders.

Tracking Insider Trading

Fortunately, we live in an age of disclosure. Insiders who buy or sell stock must file reports that document their trading activity with the Securities and Exchange Commission (SEC), which makes the documents available to the public. You can view these documents either at the SEC office or at the Web site of the SEC, which maintains the EDGAR (Electronic Data Gathering, Analysis, and Retrieval) database (www.sec.gov/edgar.shtml). Just click on the "Search for company filings" button. Some of the most useful documents you can view there include the following:

- ✔ **Form 3:** This is the initial statement that insiders provide. Insiders must file Form 3 within ten days of obtaining insider status. This report is filed even if the insider hasn't made any purchase yet; the report establishes the insider's status.

- ✔ **Form 4:** Form 4 is the document that shows the insider's activity, for example, a change in the insider's position as stockholder — how many shares the person bought and sold or other relevant change. Any activity in a particular month must be reported on Form 4 by the 10th of the following month. If, for example, an insider sells stock during January, the SEC must get the report by February 10.

- ✔ **Form 5:** This annual report covers transactions that are small and not required on Form 4. It may include minor, internal transfers of stock or other transactions.

- ✔ **Form 144:** This form serves as the public declaration by an insider of the intention to sell restricted stock. This is stock that the insider received from the company as compensation, was awarded, or bought as a term of employment. Insiders must hold restricted stock for at least one year before they can sell it. Once an insider decides to sell, he files Form 144 and then must sell within 90 days or else must submit a new Form 144. The insider must file the form on or before the stock's sale date. When the sale is finalized, the insider is then required to file Form 4.

Companies are required to make these documents public. The SEC's Web site offers limited access to these documents, but for greater access, check out one of the many companies that report insider trading data, such as www.marketwatch.com and www.bloomberg.com.

The SEC has enacted the short-swing profit rule to protect the investing public. This rule prevents insiders from quickly buying their stock that was just sold at a profit. The insider must wait at least six months before buying it again. This rule is intended to prevent insiders from using their privileged knowledge to make an unfair profit, while the investing public can't react fast enough. The rule is also true if an insider sells stock. An insider can't sell it at a higher price within a six-month period.

Looking at Insider Transactions

The classic phrase "Actions speak louder than words" was probably coined for insider trading. Insiders are in the know, and keeping a watchful eye on their transactions — both buying and selling their company's stock — can provide you with very useful investing information. Analyzing insider buying versus insider selling can be as different as day and night. Insider buying is simple, while insider selling can be complicated. In the following sections, I present both sides of insider trading.

Learning from insider buying

Insider buying is usually an unambiguous signal about how an insider feels about his company. After all, the primary reason that all investors buy stock is because they expect it to do well. If one insider is buying stock, that's generally not a monumental event. But if several or more insiders are buying, those purchases should certainly catch your attention.

Insider buying is generally a positive omen and beneficial for the stock's price. Also, when insiders buy stock, that means that less stock is available to the public. If this decreased supply is met with increased demand by the investing public, then the stock price will rise. The following sections present some factors to keep in mind when analyzing insider buying.

A little (insider) knowledge is a dangerous thing

When an investor gets material, relevant inside information — anything that's not available to the public — on a stock and then uses that information to buy or sell that stock, this is considered illegal insider trading. Imagine that your uncle is the vice president of finance for Wizbang Inc. and he tells you that Wizbang is on the verge of announcing a new pharmaceutical product. That product, he says, cures the common cold, wipes out halitosis, removes wrinkles, and guarantees longevity to the age of 150. Armed with this knowledge, you buy stock in the company, knowing that when everyone else finds out about this product, the stock will surely skyrocket. Because you profit as a result of an unfair advantage, the transaction is considered illegal.

Identify who's buying the stock

The CEO is buying 5,000 shares. Is that reason enough for you to jump in? Maybe. After all, the CEO certainly knows how well the company is doing. But what if that CEO is just starting her new position? What if before this purchase she had no stock in the company at all? Maybe the stock is part of her employment package.

The fact that a new company executive is making her first stock purchase isn't as strong a signal urging you to buy as the fact that a long-time CEO is doubling her holdings. Also, if large numbers of insiders are buying, that sends a stronger signal than if a single insider is buying.

See how much is being bought

In the example in the previous section, the CEO bought 5,000 shares, which is a lot of stock no matter how you count it. But is it enough for you to base an investment decision on? Maybe, but a closer look may reveal more. If she already owned 1 million shares at the time of the purchase, then buying 5,000 additional shares wouldn't be such an exciting indicator of a pending stock rise. In this case, 5,000 shares is a small incremental move and doesn't offer much to get excited about.

However, what if this particular insider has owned only 5,000 shares for the past three years and is now buying 1 million shares? Now that should arouse your interest! Usually, a massive purchase tells you that particular insider has strong feelings about the company's prospects and that she is making a huge increase in her share of stock ownership. Still, a purchase of 1 million shares by the CEO isn't as strong a signal as 10 insiders buying 100,000 shares each. Again, if only one person is buying, that may or may not be a strong indication of an impending rise. However, if lots of people are buying, consider this a fantastic indication.

An insider purchase of any kind is a positive sign. But it's always more significant when a greater number of insiders are making purchases. "The more the merrier!" is a good rule for judging insider buying. All these individuals have their own, unique perspectives on the company and its prospects for the foreseeable future. Mass buying indicates mass optimism for the company's future. If the treasurer, the president, the vice-president of sales, and several other key players are putting their wealth on the line and investing it in a company that they know intimately, that's a good sign for your stock investment as well.

Notice the timing of the purchase

The timing of insider stock purchases is important as well. If I tell you that five insiders bought stock at various points last year, you may say, "Hmm."

But if I tell you that all five people bought substantial chunks of stock at the same time and right before earnings season, that should make you say, "HMMMMM!"

Picking up tips from insider selling

As I note in the previous section, insider buying either bodes well for the stock or is a neutral event at worst. Insider stock buying is rarely a negative event. But how about insider selling? When an insider sells his stock, the event can either be neutral or negative. Insider selling is usually a little tougher to figure out because insiders may have many different motivations to sell stock that may have nothing to do with the company's future prospects. (See the next paragraph for a list of some common reasons.) Just because the president of the company is selling 5,000 shares from his personal portfolio, that doesn't necessarily mean you should sell, too.

Insiders may sell their stock for a couple reasons: They may think that the company will not be doing well in the near future — a negative sign for you — or they may simply need the money for a variety of personal reasons that may have nothing to do with the company's potential. Some typical reasons why insiders may sell stock include the following:

- ✓ **To diversify their holdings.** If an insider's portfolio is heavily weighted with one company's stock, a financial advisor may suggest that he balance his portfolio by selling some of that company's stock and purchasing other securities.

- ✓ **To finance personal emergencies.** Sometimes an insider may need money for medical, legal, or family reasons.

- ✓ **To buy a home or other major purchase.** An insider may need the money to make a down payment or perhaps to buy something outright without having to take out a loan.

How do you find out about the details regarding insider stock selling? Although insiders must report their pertinent stock sales, as well as purchases, to the SEC, the information isn't always revealing. As a general rule, consider the following questions when analyzing insider selling:

- ✓ **How many insiders are selling?** If only one insider is selling, that single transaction doesn't give you enough information to act on. However, if many insiders are selling, you should see a red flag. Check out any news or information that is currently available. Web sites such as www.insiderscores.com, www.marketwatch.com, and www.cnnfn.com can help you get that information (along with other sources in Appendix A).

✔ **Are the sales showing a pattern or unusual activity?** If one insider sold some stock last month, that sale alone isn't that significant an event. However, if ten insiders have each made multiple sales in the past few months, those sales are cause for concern. See whether there are new developments at the company that are potentially negative. If massive insider selling has recently occurred and you don't know why, consider putting a stop-loss order on your stock immediately. I cover stop-loss orders more fully in Chapter 16.

✔ **How much stock is being sold?** If a CEO sells 5,000 shares of stock but still retains 100,000 shares, that's not a big deal. But if the CEO sells all or most of his holdings, that's a possible negative. Check to see whether other company executives have also sold stock.

✔ **Do outside events or analyst reports seem coincidental with the sale of the stock?** Sometimes, an influential analyst may issue a report warning about a company's prospects. If the company's management pooh-poohs the report but most of them are bailing out anyway (selling their stock), you may want to do the same. Frequently, when insiders know that damaging information is forthcoming, they sell the stock before it takes a dip.

Similarly, if the company's management issues positive public statements or reports that are contradictory to their own behavior (they're selling their stock holdings), the SEC may investigate to see whether the company is doing anything that may require a penalty. The SEC regularly tracks insider sales.

Considering Corporate Stock Buybacks

When you read the financial pages or watch the financial shows on television, you sometimes hear that a company is buying its own stock. The announcement may be something like, "SuperBucks Corp. has announced that it will spend 2 billion dollars to buy back its own stock." Why would a company do that, and what does that mean to you if you own the stock or are considering buying it?

When companies buy back their own stock, doing so is generally an indication that, all things being equal, they believe that their stock is undervalued and that it has the potential to rise. If a company shows strong fundamentals (for example, good financial condition and increasing sales and earnings) and it is buying more of its own stock, it's worth investigating — it may make a great addition to your portfolio.

Just because a company announces a stock buyback doesn't always mean that one will happen. The announcement itself is meant to stir interest in the stock and cause the price to rise. The stock buyback may be only an opportunity for insiders to sell stock, or it may be needed for executive compensation recruiting and retaining competent management is a positive use of money.

If you see that the company itself is buying back its stock while most of the insiders are selling their personal shares, that's not a good sign. It may not be necessarily a bad sign, but it's not a positive. Play it safe and invest elsewhere.

The following sections present some common reasons why a company may buy back its shares from investors as well as some ideas on the negative effects of stock buybacks.

Boosting earnings per share

By simply buying back its own shares from stockholders, a company can increase its earnings per share (see Chapter 10 and Appendix B for more on earnings per share) without actually earning extra money. Sound like a magician's trick? Well, it is, kind of. A corporate stock buyback is a financial sleight of hand that investors should be aware of. Here's how it works: Noware Earnings Inc. (NEI) has 10 million shares outstanding, and it's expected to net earnings of $10 million for the fourth quarter. NEI's earnings per share (EPS) would be $1.00 per share. So far so good. But what happens if NEI buys 2 million of its own shares? Total shares outstanding would shrink to 8 million. The new EPS becomes $1.25 — the stock buyback artificially boosts the earnings per share by 25 percent!

The important point to remember about stock buybacks is that actual company earnings don't change — no fundamental changes occur in company management or operations — so the increase in EPS can be misleading. But the marketplace can be obsessive about earnings, and because earnings are the lifeblood of any company, an earnings boost, even if it's cosmetic, can also boost the stock price.

If you watch a company's price to earnings ratio (see Chapter 9), you know that increased earnings usually mean an eventual increase in the stock price. Additionally, a stock buyback will affect supply and demand. With less available stock in the market, demand will necessarily send the stock price upward.

With all this great stuff that could happen, is anything wrong with boosting EPS with a stock buyback?

Whenever a company makes a major purchase, such as buying back its own stock, think about how the company is paying for it and whether it seems like a good use of the company's purchasing power. In general, companies buy their stock for the same reasons any investor buys stock — they believe that the stock is a good investment and will appreciate in time. Companies generally pay for a stock buyback in one of two basic ways: funds from operations or borrowed money. Either method has a downside. For more details see the section "Exploring the downside of buybacks," later in this chapter.

Beating back a takeover bid

Suppose that you read in the financial pages that Company X is doing a hostile takeover of Company Z. A hostile takeover doesn't mean that Company X sent storm troopers armed with mace to Company Z's headquarters to trounce its management. All a *hostile takeover* means is that X wants to buy enough shares of Z's stock to effectively control Z (and Z is unhappy about being owned or controlled by X). Because buying and selling stock are done in a public market or exchange, companies can buy each other's stock. Sometimes the target company prefers not to be acquired, in which case it may buy back shares of its own stock to give it a measure of protection against unwanted moves by interested companies.

In some cases, the company attempting the takeover already owns some of the target company's stock. In this case, the targeted company may offer to buy those shares back from the aggressor at a premium to thwart the takeover bid. This type of offer is often referred to as *greenmail*.

Takeover concerns generally prompt interest in the investing public, driving the stock price upward and benefiting current stockholders.

Exploring the downside of buybacks

As beneficial as stock buybacks can be, they have to be paid for, and this expense has consequences. If a company pays for the stock with funds from operations, it may have a negative effect on the company's ability to finance current and prospective operations. When funds from operations are used for the stock buyback, that means less money for other activities, such as upgrading technology or research and development. In general, any misuse of money, such as using debt to buy back stock, affects a company's ability to grow its sales and earnings — two measures that need to maintain upward mobility in order to keep stock prices rising.

Even greater dangers are posed when a company uses debt to finance a stock buyback. If the company uses borrowed funds, it has less borrowing power for other uses (such as upgrading technology or making other improvements). In addition, the company has to pay back the borrowed funds with interest, thus lowering earnings figures.

Say that NEI (introduced in the "Boosting earnings per share" section, earlier in this chapter) typically pays an annual dividend of 25 cents per share of stock and wants to buy back shares with borrowed money with a 9 percent interest rate. If NEI buys back 2 million shares, it won't have to pay out $500,000 in dividends. That is money saved. However, NEI is going to have to pay interest on $20 million it borrowed to buy back the shares over that same time frame to the tune of $1,800,000 (9 percent of $20,000,000). The net result from this rudimentary example is that NEI sees an outflow of $1,300,000 (the difference between the interest paid out and the dividends savings). Using debt to finance a stock buyback needs to make economic sense — it needs to strengthen the company's financial position. Perhaps NEI could have used the stock buyback money toward a better purpose, such as modernizing equipment or paying for a new marketing campaign. Because debt interest ultimately decreases earnings, companies must be careful when using debt to buy back their stock.

Stock Splits: Nothing to Go Bananas Over

Frequently, management teams decide to do a stock split. A *stock split* is the exchange of existing shares of stock for new shares from the same company. Stock splits don't increase or decrease the capitalization of the company. They just change the number of shares available in the market and the per-share price.

In a typical stock split, a company may announce that it will do a 2-for-1 stock split. For example, a company may have 10 million shares outstanding, with a market price of $40 each. In a 2-for-1 split, the company would then have 20 million shares (the share total would double), but the market price would be adjusted to $20 (the share price would be halved). Companies do other splits, such as a 3-for-2 or 4-for-1, but 2-for-1 is the most common split.

Why do companies split their stock? Usually, management believes that the stock's price is too high, thus possibly discouraging investors from purchasing it. The stock split is a strategy to stir interest in the stock, and this increased interest frequently results in a rise in the stock's price.

Qualifying for a stock split is similar to qualifying to receive a dividend — you must be listed as a stockholder as of the date of record. (For information on date of record, see Chapter 6.)

A stock split is technically a neutral event because the ultimate market value of the company's stock doesn't change as a result of the split. The following sections present the two most basic types of splits: ordinary and reverse stock splits.

Ordinary stock splits

Ordinary stock splits — when the number of stock shares is increased — are the ones we usually hear about. (For example, a 2-for-1 stock split doubles the number of shares.) If you own 100 shares of Dublin Inc. stock (at $60 per share) and a stock split is announced, what happens? If you own the stock in certificate form, you receive in the mail a stock certificate for 100 shares of Dublin Inc. Now, before you cheer over how your money just doubled, check the stock's new price. Each share is adjusted to a $30 value.

Not all stock is in certificate form. Stocks held in a brokerage account are recorded in book entry form. Most stock, in fact, is in book entry form. Stock certificates are issued only when necessary or requested by the investor. If you keep the stock in your brokerage account, check with your broker for the new share total to make sure that you are credited with the new number of shares after the stock split.

If a stock split is primarily a neutral event, why does a company bother to do it? The most common reason is that management believes that the stock is too expensive, so it wants to lower the stock price to make the stock more affordable and therefore more attractive to new investors. Studies have shown that stock splits frequently preceded a rise in the stock price. Although stock splits are considered a non-event in and of themselves, many stock experts see them as bullish signals because of the interest they generate among the investing public.

Reverse stock splits

A *reverse stock split* usually occurs when a company's management wants to raise the price of its stock. Just as ordinary splits can occur when management believes that the price is too expensive, a reverse stock split means that the company feels that the stock's price is too cheap. If a stock's price looks too low, that may discourage interest by individual or institutional investors (such as mutual funds). Management wants to drum up more interest in the stock for the benefit of shareholders (some of whom are probably insiders).

The company may also do a reverse split to decrease costs. When you have to send an annual report and other correspondence regularly to all the stockholders, the mailings can get a little pricey, especially when you have lots of investors who have only a few shares each. A reverse split helps to consolidate the shares to lower overall management costs.

A reverse split can best be explained with an example. TuCheep Inc. (TCI) is selling at $2 per share on the Nasdaq. At that rock-bottom price, it may be ignored by the investing public. So TCI announces a 10-for-1 reverse stock split. Now what? If an existing stockholder had 100 shares at $2 (the old shares), the stockholder would now own 10 shares at $20.

Technically, a reverse split is considered a neutral event. However, just as investors may infer positive expectations from an ordinary stock split, they may have negative expectations from a reverse split because a reverse split tends to occur for negative reasons.

If, in the event of a stock split, you have an odd number of shares, the company will not produce a "fractional share." Instead, you'll get a check for the cash equivalent. For example, if you have 51 shares and the company announces a 2-for-1 reverse split, the odds are that you will end up with 25 shares and a cash payout for the odd share (or fractional share).

Keep good records regarding your stock splits in case you need to calculate capital gains for tax purposes. (See Chapter 19 for tax information.)

Chapter 19

Tax Benefits and Obligations

A h, yes . . . taxes. After you're making gobs of money as a result of all the work you've done as a diligent investor thrilled at your masterful choices, now you have a new challenge — holding on to that money! Some people will tell you that taxes are brutal, complicated, and counterproductive. Other people will tell you that they're a form of legalized thievery, while still others will say that they're a necessary evil. They're all right. But regardless of philosophy, the bottom line is that taxes are a stark reality. I wrote this chapter to help you keep more of the fruits of your hard-earned labor.

Keep in mind that this chapter isn't intended to give you complete details on taxes (see *Taxes For Dummies,* written by Eric Tyson and David J. Silverman and published by Hungry Minds, Inc., for more-complete information), but it does cover the most relevant points for stock investors. As a stock investor, you need to know the tax treatment for dividends and capital gains and losses, along with common tax deductions for investors and some simple tax-reduction strategies.

You must take tax planning seriously because taxes are the single biggest expense during your lifetime. The average taxpayer pays more in taxes than in food, clothing, and shelter combined! I agree with radio and television entertainer Arthur Godfrey, who said, "I'm proud to be paying taxes to the U.S. The only thing is, I could be just as proud for half the money."

Paying through the Nose

This section tells you everything you need to know about the tax implications you'll face when you start investing in stocks. Profit you make from your stock investments can be taxed in one of two ways: as ordinary income or as capital gains, depending on the type of profit. *Ordinary income* means that the profit you make from stock investments is taxed at the same rate as wages — at your full, regular tax rate. If your tax bracket is 27 percent, then that's the rate your ordinary income investment profits will be taxed at. Two types of investment profits get taxed as ordinary income:

- **Dividends:** When you receive dividends from your stock (either in cash or stock), these get taxed as ordinary income. This is also true if those dividends are in a dividend reinvestment plan. If, however, those dividends occur in a tax-sheltered plan, such as an IRA or 401(k) plan, then they're exempt from taxes for as long as they are in the plan. Retirement plans are covered in the section "Tax-Advantaged Retirement Investing," later in this chapter. In January, investors receive a 1099-DIV statement from the issuer of the dividends that includes information on the amount of dividends earned the previous year.

- **Short-term capital gains:** If you sell stock for a gain and the time frame is one year or less, the gain is considered ordinary income. If you buy a stock on August 1 and sell it on July 31 of the following year, that is less than one year. To calculate the time, you use the trade date or date of execution. This is the date that you executed the order rather than the settlement date. (For more on important dates, see Chapter 6.) However, if these gains occur in a tax-sheltered plan, such as a 401(k) or an IRA, no tax is triggered.

Ordinary income is the ugliest tax concept stock investors need to know. Long-term capital gains are much better for you taxwise. Because the tax on capital gains is the most relevant tax for stock investors, don't forget to read the section "Minimizing the tax on your capital gains," later in this chapter.

Managing the tax burden from your investment profits is something that you can control. Gains are taxable only if a sale actually takes place. (In other words, the gain is "realized.") If your stock in GazillionBucks Inc. goes from $5 per share to $87, that $82 appreciation is not subject to taxation unless you actually sell the stock. Until you sell, it's an "unrealized" gain. Time your stock sales carefully — hold on to them at least a year — to minimize the amount of taxes you have to pay on them.

When you buy stock, record the date of purchase and the *cost basis* (the purchase price of the stock plus any ancillary charges, such as commissions). This information is very important come tax time should you decide to sell your stock. The date of purchase helps to establish the *holding period* (how long you've owned the stocks) that determines whether your gains are to be considered short term or long term.

Say that you buy 100 shares of GazillionBucks Inc. at $5 and pay a commission of $18. Your cost basis is $518 (100 shares times $5 plus $18 commission). If you sell the stock at $87 per share and pay a $24 commission, the total sale amount is $8,676 (100 shares times $87 less $24 commission). If this sale occurred less than a year after the purchase, it's a short-term gain. In the 27 percent tax bracket, the short-term gain of $8158 is also taxed at 27 percent. (Short-term gains are taxed as ordinary income.) Read the following section to see the tax implications if your gain is a long-term gain.

Any gain (or loss) from a short sale is considered short term regardless of how long the position is held open. For more information on selling short, check out Chapter 16.

Minimizing the tax on your capital gains

Long-term capital gains are taxed at a more favorable rate than ordinary income. To qualify for long-term capital gains treatment, you must hold the investment for over one year (in other words, for at least one year and one day).

Recall the example in the previous section with GazillionBucks Inc. As a short-term transaction at the 27 percent tax rate, the tax would have been $2,343 ($8,676 × 27 percent). After you revive, you say, "Gasp! What a chunk of dough. I better hold off a while longer." You hold on to the stock for at least a year to achieve the status of long-term capital gains. How does that change the tax? For anyone who is in the 27 percent tax bracket or higher, the long-term capital gains rate of 20 percent would apply. In this case, the tax would be $1,735 ($8,676 × 20 percent), resulting in a tax savings to you of $608 ($2,343 less $1,735). Okay, it's not a fortune, but it is a substantial difference from the original tax.

Don't sell a stock just because it qualifies for long-term capital gains treatment, even if the sale would ease your tax burden. If the stock is doing well and meeting your investing criteria, then hold on to it.

Capital gains taxes *can* be lower than the tax on ordinary income, but they're never higher. If, for example, you're in the 15 percent tax bracket for ordinary income and you have a long-term capital gain that would normally bump you up to the 27 percent tax bracket, the gain is taxed at your lower rate of 15 percent rather than a higher capital gains rate.

Coping with capital losses

Ever think that having the value of your stocks fall could be a good thing? Perhaps the only real positive regarding losses in your portfolio is that they can reduce your taxes. A *capital loss* means that you lose money on your

Debt and taxes: Another angle

If you truly need cash, but you don't want to sell your stock because it's doing well and you want to avoid paying capital gains tax, consider borrowing against it. If the stock is a listed stock (as in listed on the New York Stock Exchange, for example) and is sitting in a brokerage account, you can borrow up to 50 percent of the value of marginable securities at favorable rates. (Listed stocks are marginable securities.) This is considered a margin loan, and the interest you pay is low (compared to credit cards or personal loans) because it's considered a secured loan (your stock acts as collateral).

investments. This amount is generally deductible on your tax return, and you can claim a loss on either long-term or short-term stock holdings. This loss can go against your other income and lower your overall tax.

Say that you bought Worth Zilch Co. stock for a total purchase price of $3,500 and sold it later at a sale price of $800. Your capital loss would be $2,700. This loss is tax deductible.

The one string attached to investment losses is that the most you can report in a single year is $3,000. On the bright side, though, any excess loss is not really lost — you can carry it forward to the next year. If you had net investment losses of $4,500 in 2002, then you can deduct $3,000 in 2002 and carry the remaining $1,500 loss over to 2003 and deduct it on your 2003 tax returns.

Before you can deduct losses, the IRS states that the capital losses from your investments must first be used to offset any capital gains. If you realize long-term capital gains of $7,000 in stock A and $6,000 of realized long-term capital losses in stock B, then you have a net long-term capital gain of $1,000 ($7,000 gain less the offset of $6,000 loss). Whenever possible, see whether losses in your portfolio can be realized to offset any capital gains to reduce any potential tax.

Here's your optimum strategy: Where possible, keep losses on a short-term basis and push your gains into long-term capital gains status. If a transaction can't be tax free, then at the very least try to defer the tax to keep your money working for you.

Gains and losses scenarios

Of course, any investor can come up with hundreds of possible scenarios. For example, you may wonder what happens if you sell part of your holdings now as a short-term capital loss and the remainder later as a long-term capital gain. You must look at each sale of stock (or potential sale) methodically to calculate the gain or loss you would realize from it. Figuring out your gain or loss isn't that complicated. Here are some general rules to help you wade through the morass:

✔ If you add up all your gains and losses and *the net result is a short-term gain,* it is taxed at your highest tax bracket (as ordinary income).

✔ If you add up all your gains and losses and *the net result is a long-term gain,* it's taxed at 20 percent if you're in the 27 percent tax bracket or higher. If you're in the 15 percent tax bracket or lower, the tax rate on long-term capital gains is 10 percent.

✔ If you add up all your gains and losses and *the net result is a loss,* it's deductible as follows: If your loss is $3,000 or less, it's fully deductible against other income. If you're married filing separately, then your deduction limit is $1,500.

✔ If you add up all your gains and losses and *the net result is a loss that exceeds $3,000,* then you can deduct up to $3,000 in that year, and the remainder goes forward to future years.

Sharing Your Gains with the IRS

Of course, you don't want to pay more taxes than you have to, but as the old cliché goes, "Don't let the tax tail wag the investment dog." You should buy or sell a stock because it makes economic sense first, and consider the tax implications as secondary issues. After all, taxes consume a relatively small portion of your gain. As long as you experience a *net gain* (gain after all transaction costs, including taxes, brokerage fees, and other related fees), consider yourself a successful investor — even if you have to give away some of your gain to taxes.

Hold on to stocks over the long term to keep transaction costs and taxes down. Remember that you don't pay tax on a stock profit until you sell the stock.

Try to make tax planning second nature in your day-to-day activities. No, you don't have to consume yourself with a blizzard of paperwork and tax projections. I simply mean that when you make a stock transaction, keep the receipt and maintain good records. When you make a large purchase or sale, pause for a moment and ask yourself whether there are any tax consequences. (Refer to the section "Paying through the Nose," earlier in this chapter, to review various tax scenarios.) Speak to a tax consultant beforehand to discuss the ramifications.

Filling out forms

Most investors report their investment-related activities on their individual tax returns (Form 1040). The reports that you will likely receive from brokers and other investment sources include the following:

- **Brokerage and bank statements:** Monthly statements that you receive
- **Trade confirmations:** Documents to confirm that you bought or sold stock
- **1099-DIV:** Reporting dividends paid to you
- **1099-INT:** Reporting interest paid to you
- **1099-B:** Reporting gross proceeds submitted to you from the sale of investments, such as stocks and mutual funds

You may receive other, more obscure forms that are not listed here, but you should retain all documents related to your stock investments.

The IRS schedules and forms that most stock investors need to be aware of and/or attach to their Form 1040 include the following:

- **Schedule B:** For reporting interest and dividends
- **Schedule D:** To report capital gains and losses
- **Form 4952:** Investment Interest Expense Deduction
- **Publication 17:** Guide to Form 1040

You can get these publications directly from the IRS at 800-TAX-FORM, or you can download them from the Web site www.irs.gov.

If you plan to do your own taxes, consider using the latest tax software products, which have become inexpensive and easy to use. These programs usually have a question-and-answer feature to help you do your taxes step-by-step, and they include all the necessary forms. Consider getting either TurboTax or H&R Block's TaxCut at your local software vendor.

Playing by the rules

Some people get the smart idea of "Hey! Why not sell my losing stock by December 31 to grab the short-term loss and just buy back the stock on January 2 so that I can have my cake and eat it, too?" Not so fast. The IRS puts the kibosh on maneuvers such as that with something called the "wash-sale rule." This rule states that if you sell a stock for a loss and buy it back within 30 days, the loss isn't valid because you didn't make any substantial investment change. The wash-sale rule applies only to losses. The way around the rule is simple: Wait at least 31 days before you buy that identical stock back again.

Some people try to get around the wash-sale rule by doubling up on their stock position with the intention of selling half. Therefore, the IRS makes the 30-day rule cover both sides of the sale date. That way an investor can't buy the identical stock within 30 days just before the sale and then realize a short-term loss for tax purposes.

The Softer Side of the IRS: Tax Deductions for Investors

In the course of managing your portfolio of stocks and other investments, you will probably incur expenses that will be tax deductible. The tax laws allow you to write off certain investment-related expenses (as itemized expenses on Schedule A — an attachment to IRS Form 1040). Keep records of your deductions and retain a checklist to remind you of what deductions you normally take for future tax years. The following sections explain common tax deductions for investors.

Investment interest

If you have paid any interest to a stockbroker, such as margin interest or any interest to acquire a taxable financial investment, that is considered investment interest and is usually fully deductible as an itemized expense. Keep in mind that not all interest is deductible. Consumer interest or interest paid for any consumer or personal purpose is not deductible.

Miscellaneous expenses

Most investment-related deductions are reported as miscellaneous expenses. Here are some common deductions:

- ✔ Accounting or bookkeeping fees for keeping records of investment income.
- ✔ Any expense related to tax service or education.
- ✔ Computer expense. You can take a depreciation deduction for your computer if you use it 50 percent of the time or more for managing your investments.
- ✔ Investment management or investment advisor's fees. (Fees paid for advice on tax-exempt investments are not deductible.)
- ✔ Legal fees involving stockholder issues.
- ✔ Safe-deposit box rental fee or home safe to hold your securities, unless used to hold personal effects or tax-exempt securities.
- ✔ Service charges for collecting interest and dividends.
- ✔ Subscription fees for investment advisory services.
- ✔ Travel costs to check investments or to confer with advisors regarding income-related investments.

You can deduct only that portion of your miscellaneous expenses that exceeds 2 percent of your adjusted gross income.

Givin' it away

What happens if you donate stock to your favorite (IRS-approved) charity? Because it's a noncash charitable contribution, you can deduct the market value of the stock.

Say that last year you bought stock for $2,000 that is worth $4,000 this year. If you donate it this year, you can write off the market value at the time of the contribution. In this case, you have a $4,000 deduction. Use IRS Form 8283, which is an attachment to Schedule A, to report noncash contributions exceeding $500.

To get more guidance from the IRS on this matter, get its free Publication #526, "Charitable Contributions," by calling 800-TAX-FORM.

Knowing what you can't deduct

Just to be complete, here are some items that you may have thought you could deduct but, alas, you can't:

- ✔ Financial planning or investment seminars
- ✔ Any costs connected with attending stockholder meetings
- ✔ Home office expenses for managing your investments

Are you having fun yet? Yeah, I know, taxes can be intimidating. They really shouldn't be such a complicated matter. Write your U.S. congressional representative to make this stuff easier. After all, it is your money!

Tax-Advantaged Retirement Investing

If you're going to invest for the long term (investing for retirement is the best example of this), then you may as well maximize your usage of tax-sheltered retirement plans. Many different types of plans are available, but I touch on only the most popular ones. Although retirement plans may not seem relevant for investors who buy and sell stocks directly (as opposed to a mutual fund), there are plans, called self-directed retirement accounts, that allow you to invest directly.

IRA's

Individual Retirement Accounts (IRA's) are accounts that you can open with a financial institution, such as a bank or a mutual fund company. An IRA is available to almost anyone who has earned income, and it allows you to set aside and invest money to help fund your future retirement. Opening an IRA is easy, and virtually any bank or mutual fund can guide you through the process. Two basic types of IRA's include traditional and Roth.

Traditional Individual Retirement Account (IRA)

The traditional Individual Retirement Account (also called the deductible IRA) was first popularized in the early 1980s. The basic point of the traditional IRA is that you can put in up to $3,000 per year (for tax years 2002–2004) and write off that amount as a tax deduction. (Technically, it's taken as an adjustment to your gross income and reported on page one of your Form 1040.) The tax act of 2001 allows individuals who are at least age 50 to make additional investments of $500 (from 2002 to 2005).

The money can then grow in the IRA account unfettered by current taxes because the money isn't taxed until you take it out. Because IRA's are designed for retirement purposes, you can start taking money out of your IRA in the year you turn 59½. (Hmmm. That must really disappoint those who want their money in the year they turn 58¾.) The withdrawals at that point are taxed as ordinary income. Fortunately, you'll probably be in a lower tax bracket then, so the tax shouldn't be as burdensome.

If you take out money from an IRA too early, the amount is included in your taxable income, and you may be zapped with a 10 percent penalty. You can avoid the penalty if you have a good reason. (The IRS provides a list of reasons that qualify the premature withdrawal of money as being exempt from the penalty.)

To put money into an IRA, you must earn income equal to or greater than the amount you're contributing. *Earned income* is money made either as an employee or a self-employed person. Although traditional IRA's can be great for investors, the toughest part about them is qualifying.

Wait a minute! You may be thinking that IRA's usually are done with mutual funds or bank investments. How does the stock investor take advantage of an IRA? Stock investors can open a self-directed IRA with a brokerage firm. This means that you can buy and sell stocks in the account with no taxes on dividends or capital gains. The account is tax deferred, so you don't have to worry about taxes until you start making withdrawals. Also, many dividend reinvestment plans (DRPs) have IRA's as well. See Chapter 17 for more about DRPs.

Roth IRA

The Roth IRA is a great retirement plan that I wish had existed a long time ago. Here are some ways to distinguish the Roth IRA from the traditional IRA:

- ✔ The Roth IRA provides no tax deduction for contributions.
- ✔ The Roth IRA can grow tax free and be withdrawn tax free when you, again, turn 59½.
- ✔ The Roth IRA doesn't have any early distribution penalties.

The maximum contribution per year is $3,000, and you can open a self-directed account with a broker as well. Also, qualifying for participation in a Roth IRA is a lot easier because the limitations aren't as stringent.

401(k) plans

Company-sponsored 401(k) plans (named after the section in the tax code that allows them) are widely used and are very popular. In a 401(k) plan, companies set aside money from their paychecks that the employees can use to invest for retirement. Generally, you can invest as much as $11,000 (in 2002) of pretax earned income and have it grow tax deferred. Usually, the money is in a mutual fund through a mutual fund company or an insurance firm. Although 401(k) plans don't give you the opportunity to be self-directed, I mention them in this book for good reason.

Because your money is in a mutual fund that may invest in stocks, take an active role in finding out the mutual funds in which you're allowed to invest. Most plans allow you several types of stock mutual funds. Use your growing knowledge about stocks to make more informed choices about your 401(k) plan options.

Keep in mind that a mutual fund is only as good as what it invests in. Ask the plan administrator some questions about the funds and the types of stocks it invests in. Are the stocks defensive or cyclical? (For more information on defensive and cyclical stocks, see Chapter 12.) Are they large cap or small cap? If you don't make an informed choice about the investments in your plan, someone else will — someone who doesn't have as much interest in your financial success as you do.

Part V
The Part of Tens

The 5th Wave   By Rich Tennant

In a bizarre mix up, Ken takes a look at a bus schedule instead of the company's balance sheet then books a seat for him and Laverne in one of the company's file drawers.

*From that time forward, Laverne handled their financial affairs.

In this part . . .

This wouldn't be a *For Dummies* book if I didn't include a Part of Tens. Here you find quick reference lists to many of the most basic stock investing concepts and practices. Check the information in this part when you don't have time to read the denser parts of the book or when you just need a quick refresher on what to do before, after, and even during your stock investing pursuits.

Chapter 20

Ten Things to Think About Before You Invest

In This Chapter

▶ Planning and saving for emergencies

▶ Taking charge of your career

▶ Educating yourself about the stock market

▶ Using a disciplined approach

T hrough the years, I've seen the good, the bad, and some of the ugly of investing, so I'm aware of some common mistakes and oversights by investors. Many people start investing before they're really ready. These same people would probably never leave on vacation without filling up the gas tank or shutting off the oven. Yet these people often don't prepare as thoroughly when they're investing thousands of their hard-earned dollars.

Before you invest in anything, you first must make sure that you have a strong economic foundation. If you don't, your situation is like building a brick house on shifting sand. You need to ensure that your debts are under control, your assets exceed your liabilities, you spend less money than you earn, and you regularly save a portion of what you earn. If you need help with any of these areas, seek a financial advisor who can help you locate and remedy the weak spots in your investment program's foundation.

A second prerequisite to investing is a complete understanding of the types of investments that are appropriate for your current situation in life. For example, if you're retired or near retirement, you need more safety and stability in your investments than people in their 30s do.

Finally, you must take the time to educate yourself about financial and investment matters. The average person spends more than 80,000 hours during a typical working lifetime yet may spend an average of less than 15 minutes a month finding out how his money can work for him.

The following sections offer specific ways to get your house in order before you begin investing.

Have Adequate Insurance

Do you have proper coverage for potential problems, such as disability or the death of a breadwinner in your family? Many stock portfolios get liquidated pretty fast when the dependents of the deceased need money for daily living expenses. You may work a lifetime to build your stock portfolio. If you don't have appropriate insurance, it could be wiped out very quickly and needlessly. See an insurance professional to guarantee that you and your family are protected.

Update Your Career Skills

Do you keep your skills and expertise up-to-date so that you can continue to be employable regardless of how uncertain the economy is? No matter how secure your job or company is, you should periodically update your resume and job skills to maintain your employability. At least once every two years, bring your most current resume to an employment agency and ask, "How quickly can you get me a job?" If your question is met with hesitation or a grimace, update your skills and expertise immediately, while you're still employed.

Take Care of Estate Planning

In case of death, do you have a will, trust, or other vehicle that will take care of your estate for the benefit of your family? Even if you already have a will or trust in place, ask an estate planning specialist to make sure that it complies with changing laws.

Establish an Emergency Fund

An emergency fund is a critical component of your financial well-being. Investors make a huge mistake by not having one. They assume that their stock portfolio and/or mutual fund investment will do, but they're wrong. Your stocks and mutual funds are meant for long-term growth, not short-term cash needs. Set up an emergency fund by putting at least three to six months' worth of gross living expenses in a safe, interest-bearing bank account or money market mutual fund.

Set Up a Budget

Budgeting is a crucial part of your financial foundation. Budgeting is the act of regularly monitoring and controlling what you make (income) and what you spend (expenses). Are you keeping your spending under control? Does income meet or exceed your expenses? The bottom line is that if you can't (or won't) budget, then you probably won't succeed as an investor. Fortunately, budgeting is easy, and many resources are available to help you set up a budget that suits your needs and goals. See Appendix A for resources on budgeting help.

Understand Basic Economics

The average citizen is incredibly ill informed about economics. Yet a knowledge of economics is extremely important to everyone's investment goals. In fact, plenty of financial advisors and stock experts have lost a lot of money for themselves and their clients because they were woefully uninformed about basic economics. Concepts such as supply and demand aren't distant, arcane abstractions; they affect your money and financial success every day.

If you do read up on economics, look for authors who are well versed in free market principles, which lie at the heart of sound investment decisions. Economics based on socialist or communist reasoning will do more harm than good. In other words, if you're going to read Marx, make sure that it's Groucho and not Karl. Some of the best economists that the serious stock investor should read are Ludwig von Mises (www.mises.org), Mark Skousen, and Kurt Richebacher. Some Web sites that offer excellent economic research are www.financialsense.com (Puplava Securities Inc.) and www.aier.org (American Institute for Economic Research).

Learn the Language

If you move to Croatia, it would behoove you to learn Croatian. Sure, you probably could function in that society without knowing the language, but you would be at a great disadvantage. The same advice applies to the language of stock investing.

Because stock investing means putting your money into businesses, you need to have a basic knowledge of accounting and business terminology. For example, you should know what words such as "earnings," "debt," and "equity" mean, and you also should become familiar with documents such as balance sheets and income statements. Check Appendix A for resources and Web sites that help you quickly and easily become acquainted with accounting — even if you're not an accountant. Okay? *Dobro* (which means "good" in Croatian).

Read About Investing

If I had to mention only one behavior that separates successful investors from unsuccessful ones, it would be reading. Just as in almost every discipline, people who read more learn more and gain more benefit.

Become an avid reader of stock investing publications and books. Browse investment newspapers, such as *The Wall Street Journal* and *Investor's Business Daily*. Read books written by (and on) the great investors in history and the strategies they employed. Read commentaries from financial writers and advisors that present both bullish and bearish opinions on the market. Look for different points of view on the stock market to develop and challenge your ability to be a logical and independent financial thinker.

Be Independent-Minded

When the legendary billionaire J. Paul Getty was asked about successful investing, he said that "buy low and sell high" was more than just a catchy phrase; it was the essence of successful investing. If you look deeper into this almost too-simple advice, you come away with the greater point: Do the opposite of what the crowd is doing.

More often than not, the herd mentality is wrong. Think as a contrarian investor. Contrarians usually make a fortune on the simple premise of buying when others are selling and vice versa. Contrarians look for stocks that are generally ignored by the market at large. They look for stocks that are hidden values that the public hasn't yet discovered. If the contrarian hears a dozen high-profile stock experts say, "Buy Quagmire Inc.," he won't buy it, because the public has already bought up the stock and there's usually little growth left in it.

However, if you do your own research (which is what this book is about), you can find great stocks before the market does and then watch the stock price rise when experts and the public start to notice your stock. As the public bids up the price of your shares, look for great opportunities to sell and lock in a handsome profit.

Discipline Yourself

Successful investors do their homework on a stock, stick to their principles, and use a disciplined approach to stock buying (and selling). At the very least, they invest by using disciplined techniques that will help ensure a profit or limit loss. (Techniques such as trailing stops are a great example of a disciplined approach. See Chapter 16 for more information.)

Discipline is your ally in stock investing. Frequently, investors lose money or destroy their wealth as they let their emotions rule. Fear and greed are emotions that have driven bad investment decisions throughout history. Develop a rational and disciplined approach, and your long-term investment success will be more assured.

Chapter 21

Ten Things to Remember After You Invest

*Y*ou did the research and planning, and you finally bought your stock. Can you sit back and relax? Of course not! Successful investing involves actively monitoring your stocks for as long as you have them. Your house is an investment, and you didn't stop your due diligence on the closing date. If anything, the work increased; the chores are never done! For stock investors, the same type of diligence applies.

Diversify Your Portfolio

Diversify your investments. That doesn't mean that you simply purchase a batch of different stocks, although I do hope that you have a batch of different stocks. Diversification for the successful investor happens at more than one level. An investor with five different stocks is, all things being equal, more diversified (hence safer) than an investor with all her stock money in a single stock. Strong diversification also means spreading your money among the following places:

▸ **Stocks in different industries:** What if you have five stocks but all of them are with companies in the same industry? Well, if that industry gets into trouble, then your stock portfolio will suffer.

✔ **Stocks in different segments of the economy:** Owning stocks in different industries doesn't necessarily mean that you're diversified. Sometimes different industries are dependent on each other and can affect each other. As a good example, consider airlines, cruises, and resorts. Each may be considered a different industry, but all of them are in the same segment or sector of the economy.

✔ **Other types of financial investments:** Besides investing in stocks, consider other investments that help you minimize your risks and maximize the return on your money. Examples include mutual funds, bonds, and real estate.

Recognize That You're in for the Long Haul

Stocks are most appropriate for long-term considerations. If you jump into a stock but then jump out of it in a few days or weeks, you're not investing; you're speculating. Short-term price movements always seem to act irrationally and actually work against you. However, the longer the time frame, the greater the chance of success. Now don't get me wrong; I'm not an automatic "buy and hold" or "get it and forget it" aficionado. "Buy and hold" can be financial suicide at the start of a long-term bear market. However, studies have shown that stocks are the top performing category of financial investments (as opposed to bank accounts and bonds, for example) when compared over long periods of time, such as ten years or longer.

Know the Business

Always ask yourself, "What kind of business am I investing in?" A stock is a representative piece of a company and its future prospects. The stock is ultimately only as good as the company you invest in. Because you invest in a stock for the long term, you should consider yourself a business owner. Make an effort to understand the company, its management, and its products and services. What does the company sell? Does it consistently earn a profit? Does it offer new, innovative products or technologies? Is it among the leaders in its industry?

Know the Industry

What industry is your stock in? The more you know about what's happening in the industry and its prospects for future growth, the more money you'll make with that particular company. If an industry is doing well, that bodes well for your stock. You can see that the saying "A rising tide lifts all boats" certainly applies to stock investing.

Judging the strength and growth of an industry is easier than judging an individual company. Therefore, you increase your chances of success by investing in the best companies that are in the forefront of healthy, growing industries.

Plan for Taxes

Are you planning your stock investing and general finances with tax planning in mind? According to the Tax Foundation, taxes take a bigger bite out of the average consumer's budget than food, clothing, and shelter combined. You will pay more in taxes in your working lifetime than you would for a mortgage or an automobile. If the average taxpayer reduced his taxes by even a few percentage points over his career, this money could easily add up to $100,000 to a quarter of a million dollars. If this extra money were properly invested, even a low-salaried individual could accumulate wealth exceeding a million dollars.

Do tax reduction and tax deferral strategies make a significant difference to your wealth-building program? Absolutely. If you're seeking to build wealth through stock investing, this is especially important. After you make some profitable stock investment purchases, check with a tax advisor about the implications of your investment decisions before you make a sale. Maximizing your success means more than making money; it also means keeping more of it.

Stay informed about the ongoing changes in the tax code. Investors keep a watchful eye on capital gains tax rates. Usually, long-term capital gains receive more favorable tax rates than short-term capital gains. This advantage makes long-term investing that much more attractive for your financial success.

Keep track of your expenses because some investment-related expenses are tax deductible. Also check with your tax advisor about the latest rules on Roth IRA's and other tax-advantaged programs. The name of the game is to keep more of the fruits of your labor.

Stay Informed

Are you an avid reader about current events and how they affect your stock portfolio? Do you watch the evening news with a critical eye for investment opportunities? Staying informed helps you see how your company and/or industry may suffer or benefit from current or pending laws, regulations, and societal trends. Whether the news media are warning about mad cow disease in Great Britain or about stringent energy regulations in California, astute investors always look for the ripple effects. When you watch the news or read the newspapers, make it second nature to ask yourself the following questions:

- Will any stocks be impacted, either positively or negatively, by this piece of news?

- If a particular country or region of the world is experiencing problems, will the company you plan to invest in be affected adversely?

- If a major event has caused my company's stock price to fall, should I sell it or view it as a chance to buy more stock at a bargain price?

- If the media report the passage of a new law or the enactment of a tough government policy, will that news be good or bad for my stock?

Alert investors know that stocks don't exist in a vacuum. All types of events can affect your portfolio and its future prospects for success.

Know What's New with the Company

Stock investors have an obligation to stay informed about the companies in which they invest. Doing so can protect you against losses and may even help you reap some profits. Here are some points to keep in mind:

- Check to see whether the company is making major purchases and how it is paying for them. Is it buying new equipment or another company? Is it using cash or debt?

✔ Watch the management of the company. Are difficulties with the company forcing the CEO to resign? Are the company's earnings strong and growing? Are the company's insiders, as a group, buying or selling the company's stock in recent months?

✔ Is the company being investigated by the SEC or other regulatory agencies for fraud or malfeasance?

Even in the best of times, a company's stock can suffer because of negative events happening within the company.

Compare and Profit

When anyone asked comedian Henny Youngman, "How is your wife?" his typical response was, "Compared to what?" Stock investors need to regularly see how are their stocks are doing compared to some objective benchmark. The fancy term for this process is *comparative analysis*. Ask yourself the following questions regarding the company's progress:

✔ How is the company doing this year compared to last year?

✔ What are the expectations for the company next year compared to this year?

✔ How is the company doing compared to its industry peers?

✔ Is the company doing well compared against popular indexes, such as the S&P 500 index?

Employ Investing Techniques

Investment success depends not only on what you invest in but also on how you invest. Use investing techniques that will maximize your financial progress. Here are some points to keep in mind:

✔ Use trailing stops (which I describe in Chapter 16) and other stock orders where available and appropriate. If you bought a stock at $10 a few years ago and it's now $95, be protective about your gain. Put that stop-loss order in and give yourself peace of mind by knowing that if the market goes against you, the worst that happens is that you're forced to take a profit instead of watching your gains (or worse, your original principal) get wiped out in a bear market.

✔ Are you using dollar cost averaging (DCA) to purchase your stock over an extended period of time? Dollar cost averaging helps you get the stock at various prices so that ultimately you can buy your stock at a lower average cost. (For more information on DCA, see Chapter 17.)

✔ Are you using limit orders to buy stocks at a good price? Perhaps you think that a particular stock would be a great addition to your portfolio, but it's too expensive. If the stock is at $50 and you want to buy it at $45 or lower, put in a limit order with your broker. (For more on limit orders and other orders, see Chapter 16.)

The bottom line is that certain investment techniques can make your stock investing more profitable and less risky.

Stay Focused

Are you staying focused on your short-term and long-term goals? A stock, like any investment, is simply a tool to help you achieve a particular end result, such as funding college or reaching financial independence. In other words, stock investing should be seen as a means to an end and not an end in itself.

As you approach your retirement years, the long-term focus on stocks should start to change. Once you get into your 60s and 70s, a greater portion of your investable funds should shift away from stocks and into more stable, income-producing investments, such as bonds and bank certificates of deposit. Until you get there, stay focused on your stocks and continuously ask yourself the following questions:

✔ Are my stocks continuing to perform satisfactorily to help me achieve my financial goals?

If, for example, your target goal is to accrue enough assets to reach a million dollars in net worth, are you tracking your total portfolio value and performance to expedite your progress toward that target amount?

✔ Am I getting too attached to a particular stock and losing focus on why I have that stock at all? Perhaps you had a winning stock for years and now that stock is losing steam. Will you continue to hold on to it as a sentimental favorite, or will you be disciplined enough to get rid of it?

Chapter 22

Ten Signals of a Stock Price Increase

*I*f you have a stock that has all ten signals listed in this chapter, back up the truck and load up. The odds are that you won't need all ten to indicate that it's a stock worth a closer look. Probably five or more signals are enough to merit further consideration. In any case, the more signals, the better your chances of choosing a winning stock.

Regardless of market conditions and investor sentiment (how investors "feel" about stocks and the economy), remember the three rules of stock investing success: profits, profits, profits, also known as earnings, earnings, earnings. This advice is as important as real estate's location, location, location. It's that important . . .uh . . . important, important.

Rise in Earnings

If a company earned $1 per share for the past three years and its earnings are now $1.20 per share (a 20 percent increase), consider this increase a positive harbinger. As the saying goes, "Earnings drive the market," so you need to pay attention to the company's profitability. The more a company makes, the greater the chance that its stock price will increase.

Some people wonder whether to invest in a company that was losing money and then finally turns a profit. Perhaps you're considering the stock of a company involved in new, untested technology. My advice is that you need to be careful in this situation. In such a case, it's hard to predict whether a second year of profits will show up, but of course, that's what investors are hoping.

For the serious investor, a track record of positive earnings is important. Several years of earnings (especially growing earnings) are crucial in the decision-making process. As earnings rise, make sure that the growth is at a rate of 10 percent or higher.

Say that you're looking at the stock Buckets-o-Cash Inc. (BOC). BOC had earnings of $1.00 per share in 1999, $1.10 in 2000, and $1.21 in 2001. First, you can see that the company is a profitable enterprise. Second (and more importantly), you can see that the earnings grew 10 percent each year. The fact that earnings are growing consistently year after year is important because it indicates that the company is being managed well. Effective company management has a very positive effect on the stock price as the market notices the company's progress.

Growing earnings are important for another reason — inflation. If a company earns $1.00 per share in each year, that's, of course, better than earning less or losing money. But inflation erodes the purchasing power of money. If earnings stay constant, the company's ability to grow decreases because the value of its money will decline as a result of inflation.

Increase in Assets as Debts Are Stable or Decreasing

Increasing assets while decreasing debts (or at least stabilizing them) is key to growing the book value of a company. *Book value* refers to the company's value as it appears on a balance sheet — equal to total assets minus liabilities. Book value usually differs significantly from market value (or market capitalization) because market value is based on supply and demand of the company's stock in the marketplace. For example, a company may have a book value of $10 million dollars (assets of $15 million less liabilities of $5 million) but a market value of $19 million (if, for example, it has 1 million shares that are currently trading at $19 per share). Usually, market value is higher (sometimes much higher) than book value.

Rising book value has a positive impact on market value, which, in turn, tends to drive the stock price up as well. Therefore, it pays to watch book value. Rising book value can be accomplished in one of two basic ways:

✔ Debt stays level as assets rise.

✔ Assets stay level as debts decline.

At the most basic level, total assets should exceed total debt. Preferably, the company should have a ratio of at least 2-to-1 or better in terms of assets to debt. A ratio of 3-to-1 is better and so on. The less debt, the better.

A company with $1 million in total assets and $800,000 in total debt is in okay shape. The company's condition could be better, but, hey, it could be worse, too. In recent years, it has indeed been worse; many corporations drowned in a sea of debt and subsequently filed for bankruptcy.

The best way to figure out a company's asset to debt ratio is to look at the company's most recent balance sheet and compare it to its balance sheet from the previous year. If possible, look at the balance sheet from the year before that as well. By comparing the figures over a period of time, you can see a trend developing. If the asset to debt ratio has been stable or improving over these three balance sheets, the company is showing growing financial strength, which will help the company's stock price increase in value.

Positive Publicity for Industry

When the media report that a company is doing well financially or that its products and services are being well received by both the media and the market, that news lets you know that this company's stock may be going places. This positive publicity ties in nicely with the other point made in this chapter about consumer acceptance for the company's products and services.

Positive press and consumer acceptance are important because they mean that the company is doing what's necessary to please its customers. The positive media coverage also may attract new customers to the company. Gaining customers means more sales and more earnings. This translates into a higher price for the stock.

Heavy Insider or Corporate Buying

Company insiders (such as the CEO and the treasurer) know better than anyone else about the health of a company. If insiders are buying stock by the boatload, then these purchases are certainly a positive sign for investors. Chapter 18 thoroughly covers insider trading, but I highlight the main points here. Insiders can do one of two things:

✔ **Buy stock for themselves:** If individuals such as the CEO or the treasurer are buying stocks for their personal portfolios, you can assume that they think the stock is a good investment.

✔ **Buy stock as a corporate decision:** When the corporation buys its own stock, it's usually a positive move. The corporation may see its own stock as a good investment. Additionally, corporate stock buying reduces the supply of stocks available in the market, potentially pushing the stock price higher.

All things being equal, either one will have a positive impact on the stock price. The odds are that you won't see a stampede of insiders buying the stock in a day or week, but you will see it over a period of months. This is generally true simply because each insider has different circumstances and insider buying is usually done on an individual basis. An accumulation of purchases tells you that members of the management team believe so strongly that the company will do well that they're willing to put their own money at risk.

More Attention from Analysts

In recent years, analysts have been criticized for being overly optimistic about stock investing. I never advise people to invest (or not invest) because of analysts' views, but they're important nonetheless. Many good analyst reviews, and the public's opinion of a single influential analyst, can make a stock's price move dramatically.

Analyze the stock according to its own merits first. Then watch the stock's price as more and more analysts start to direct the public's attention to it. In a sense, they're promoting your stock, an action that tends to boost the stock's price. Don't let the analyst's views sway you, though, because analysts may tout a stock for unsavory reasons. Perhaps the company is a client of the brokerage firm, or maybe the brokerage firm owns a lot of the company's shares and wants to unload it.

Rumors of Takeover Bids

I never want anyone to base an investment decision on a rumor of a takeover bid, but it doesn't hurt if you were considering the stock anyway — basing your decision on a variety of other solid factors, of course, such as strong fundamentals, earnings growth, popular products or services, and so on. A company that is rumored to be a takeover candidate (a company that may be potentially bought out by another company) may have an attractive aspect, such as a promising new patent or exclusive rights to certain properties, that could make it worthy for investors as well.

A good example is American Water Works, Inc. (AWW), a water utility with strong fundamentals, which serves a prosperous geographic area. Rumor or not, takeover bid or not, a strong utilities company like this is probably a safe investment. Investors who bought stock in AWW early in 2001, in the $30–$33 stock price range, were rewarded when rumors about a takeover bid took the price near $40. The rumor turned out to be true, and the subsequent takeover price hit $46 per share. Even investors who bought the stock because of rumors at $40 per share were rewarded.

Rumors of a buyout are always welcome, but the bottom line is that it should alert you to a good value. Regardless of whether the buyout rumor proves true, you shouldn't even consider the stock if it isn't worth owning on its own merits. If it's a good stock, the rumor tends to increase its visibility so that the chances of a takeover do, in fact, increase. Rumor or not, the attention does tend to increase the stock's price.

Praise from Consumer Groups

A company is only as good as the profit it generates. The profit it generates is only as good as the revenues that the company generates. The revenues are based on whether customers are accepting (and shelling out money for) the company's products or services. Therefore, if what the company offers is popular with consumers, it bodes well for profits and consequently higher stock prices.

When you're ready to invest in stocks, look for high consumer satisfaction. Review consumer publications and Web sites and read the surveys and consumer feedback information. Good publicity and word-of-mouth consumer satisfaction are things that investors should be aware of. Stock-picking expert Peter Lynch (formerly of Fidelity Magellan fund fame) sees this as very valuable stock-picking information. He likes to see what consumers buy because that's where the company's success starts.

Strong or Improving Bond Rating

In Chapter 9, I point out that a poor or deteriorating bond rating is a warning sign for the company. The creditworthiness of a company is a critical factor in determining the company's strength. Most people presume that the bond rating is primarily beneficial for bond investors, and they're correct. However, because the bond rating is assigned according to the company's ability to pay back the bond plus interest, it stands to reason that a strong bond rating (usually a rating of AAA, AA, or A) indicates that the company is financially strong.

The work of independent bond rating firms, such as Standard & Poor's and Moody's, is invaluable for stock investors. For more about bond ratings, turn to Chapter 9.

Powerful Demographics

If you know that a company generates lots of profit from the teenage market and you find out that the teenage market is going to expand by 10 percent per year for the foreseeable future, what would you do? Exactly — you'd buy the stock of that company. If a company has strong fundamentals and appealing products or services and its market is expanding, that company has a winning combination.

Stay alert to growing trends in society. How are demographics changing? Which sectors of the population are growing? Shrinking? What shifts are expected in society in terms of age or ethnicity? Check out the data freely available at the Department of Commerce's Web site for the U.S. Census Bureau (www.census. doc.gov).

A market that is growing in size is not an indicator all by itself (in fact, no indicator gives you the green light all by itself anyway), but it should alert you to do some research. The fact that a strong company sees improving demographic shifts in its marketplace is a big plus.

Low P/E Relative to Industry or Market

The price to earnings (P/E) ratio is a critical number for investors. Value investors in particular scrutinize it. Because the stock price's future ability to rise is ultimately tied to the company's earnings (profits), you want to know that you're not paying too much for the stock. A low P/E ratio (low relative to some standard, such as the industry's average or the average P/E for the S&P 500) is generally considered safe, and the stock is a potential bargain.

If the industry's P/E ratio is 20 and you're looking at a stock that has a P/E of 15, all things being equal, that's great. There's room for growth, and you would have a good value.

Chapter 23

Ten Warning Signs of a Stock's Decline

In This Chapter

▶ Slowdown in earnings and sales

▶ Reduced dividends

▶ Industry or political troubles

▶ Questionable accounting practices

Have you ever watched a movie and noticed that one of the characters coughs excessively throughout the entire film? To me, that's a dead giveaway that the character is a goner. Or maybe you've seen a movie in which a bit character annoys a crime boss, so right away you know that it's time for him to "sleep with the fishes." Stocks are not that different. If you're alert, you can recognize some definite signs that your investment may be ready to kick the bucket.

Let the tips in this chapter serve as an "insurance policy" on your stock investment. The signs in this chapter can help you avoid — or at least minimize — costly losses.

Earnings Slow Down or Head South

Profit is the lifeblood of a company. Of course, the opposite is true as well. The lack of profit is a sign of a company's poor financial health. Watch the earnings. Are they increasing or not? If they aren't, find out why. If the general economy is experiencing a recession, stagnant earnings are still better than robust losses — everything is relative. Earnings slowdowns for a company may very well be a temporary phenomenon. If a company's earnings are holding up better than its competitors and/or the market in general, you don't need to be alarmed.

Nonetheless, a company's earnings are its most important measure of success. Keep an eye on the company's P/E ratio. It could change negatively (go up) because of one of two basic scenarios:

- The stock price goes up as earnings barely budge.
- The stock price doesn't move, yet earnings drop.

Both of these scenarios will result in a rising P/E ratio that will ultimately have a negative effect on the stock price.

A P/E ratio that is lower than industry competitors' P/E ratios makes a company's stock a favorable investment.

Don't buy the argument "Although the company has losses, its sales are exploding." This is a variation of "The company may be losing money, but it'll make it up on volume." For example, say that Sweet Patootee, Inc., (SPI) had sales of $1 billion in 2001 and that sales expect to be $1.5 billion in 2002, projecting an increase at SPI by 50 percent. But what if SPI's earnings were $200 million in 2001 and the company was actually expecting a loss for 2002? The company wouldn't succeed, because sales without earnings isn't enough — the company needs to make a profit.

Sales Slow Down

Before you invest in a company, make sure that sales are strong and rising. If sales start to decline, that downward motion will ultimately affect earnings. (See the previous section, "Earnings Slow Down or Head South.") Although the earnings of a company may go safely up and down, sales should consistently rise. If they cease to rise, a variety of reasons may be to blame. Perhaps the company is having marketing problems, or a competitor is eating away at its market share. Maybe a new technology is replacing its products and services. In any case, falling sales raise a red flag you shouldn't ignore.

Exuberant Analysts Despite Logic

Too often, stocks that any logical person with some modest financial acumen would avoid like the plague receive glowing praise from analysts. Why is this? In many instances, there is, alas, a dark motive. Analysts are, after all, employed by companies that earn hefty investment banking fees from the very companies the analysts tout. Can you smell a rat?

Conflict of interest was a primary factor in a SEC survey taken in 2000 showing that brokers overwhelmingly give glowing recommendations on stocks ("strong buy," "buy," and "market outperform"). The SEC noticed only an outright "sell" recommendation in less than 1 percent of all the recommendations that it reviewed, even though 2000 witnessed crashing stock prices in most of the popular stocks that were analyzed. Analysts, no matter how objective they may sound, are still employees of companies that make money from the same companies that the analysts analyze.

In fact, you should be wary of analysts' views, especially the analysts who make positive recommendations even when the company in question has worrisome features, such as no income and tremendous debt. It seems like a paradox: Sell a stock when all the pros say to buy it? How can that be? Remember, the merits of any stock should speak for themselves. When a company is losing money, all the great recommendations in the world will not reverse its fortunes. Also, keep in mind that if everybody is buying a particular stock — the current analysts' favorite — who's left to buy it? When it turns out to be a dud, you won't be able to sell it off because all the other suckers already own it (thanks to analysts' recommendations). And, if they already own it, they're probably already aware of the company's flaws. What happens then? You got it: More and more people will end up selling it. When more people are selling rather than buying a stock, its price declines.

Insider Selling

Heavy insider selling is to a stock what garlic, sunrises, and crosses are to vampires: an almost certain sign of doom! If you notice that increasing numbers of insiders (such as the president of the company, the treasurer, and the vice-president of finance, for instance) are selling their stock holdings, you can consider it a red flag. In recent years, massive insider selling has become a telltale sign of a company's imminent fall from grace. After all, who better to know the company's prospects for success (or lack of) than the company's high-level management? What management does (selling stock, for example) speaks louder than what management says. For more information on insider trading, see Chapter 18.

Dividend Cuts

For investors who own income stock, dividends are the primary consideration. But, income stock or not, dividend cuts are a negative sign. Of course, if a company is having modest financial difficulty, perhaps a dividend cut is a good thing for the overall health of the company. However, usually a dividend cut is seen as a sign that a company is having trouble with its earnings or cash flow. In either case, a dividend cut is a warning sign that trouble may be brewing for the firm as it becomes . . . uh . . . less firm.

If your stock announces a dividend cut, find out why. The cut may be simply a temporary measure to help the company out of some minor financial difficulty, or it may be a sign of deeper trouble. Check the company's fundamentals and then decide. (Refer to Chapter 11 to find out how to read and interpret company financial documents.)

Increased Negative Coverage

You may easily recognize unfavorable reports of a company's stock as a sign to unload that stock. Or you may be a contrarian and see bad press as an opportunity to scoop up some shares of a company victimized by negative reporting. In any case, take the negative reports as a signal to further investigate the merits of holding on to the stock or as a sign for selling it so that you can make room in your portfolio for a more promising stock choice.

Industry Problems

Sometimes being a strong company doesn't matter if that company's industry is having problems; if the industry is in trouble, the company's decline is probably not that far behind. Tighten up those trailing stops. (See Chapter 16 to find out how.)

Political Problems

Political considerations are always a factor in investing. Be it taxes, regulations, or other government actions, politics can easily break a company and send its stock plummeting. If your company's stock is sensitive to political developments, be aware of potential political pitfalls for your stock (or industry) of choice. Reading *The Wall Street Journal* and regularly viewing major financial Web sites can help you stay informed. (I give you lists of sources in Appendix A.) In recent years, drug and tobacco stocks in general suffered because of prevailing political attitudes. Also, certain stocks in particular (Microsoft and IBM come to mind) have seen their stock prices drop drastically because they were targets of government actions for reasons ranging from antitrust concerns to public safety issues.

Debt Is Too High or Unsustainable

Excessive debt is the kiss of death for a struggling company. During 2000 and 2001, many companies that experts thought were invincible went bankrupt. In 2001, a record 255 companies filed for bankruptcy. A good example is the now-bankrupt Global Crossing, Ltd. Most analysts gave positive recommendations on the stock ("Buy it!"), but the company's financial data showed billions of dollars of debt. Chapter 11 and Appendix B can help you read and understand a company's financial data clearly so that you can make an informed decision about buying or selling its stock.

Funny Accounting: No Laughing Here!

Throughout this book, I discuss the topic of accounting as an important way to see how well (or how poorly) a company is doing. Understanding a company's balance sheet and income statement and making a simple comparison of these documents over a period of several years can give you great insights into the company's prospects. You don't have to be an accountant to grasp key concepts. Enron is a perfect example of how you can avoid a stock investing disaster with some rudimentary knowledge of accounting.

Many investors and analysts were caught by surprise by Enron's bankruptcy — the biggest in U.S. history. The financial media reported that the company's collapse battered many portfolios and caused many people (including company employees) to see their retirement funds wiped out. Even experts and auditors who worked with the company didn't appear to see the disaster coming. What's the average investor to do? A lot!

Despite the fact that Enron hid many of its financial problems from public view, the information that was available made the message clear: "Big problems coming! Stay away!" If investors had done their homework, they would have plainly seen the following revealing points in 2000, over a year and a half before the collapse:

- ✔ **Enron's price to earnings (P/E) ratio hit 90 in 2000.** This stratospheric P/E kept most value investors (including myself) away.

- ✔ **Its price to book (P/B) ratio hit 12.** For investors, this meant that the market value of the company, compared to the company's book value (also called "accounting value"), was 12 to 1 — for every $12 of market value, investors were getting only $1 in book value. When you consider that a P/B ratio of 3 or 4 is considered nosebleed territory for value investors, you can see that Enron's P/B ratio was screaming, "Watch out!"

✔ **The price to sales (P/S) ratio hit an incredible 221.** This means that investors paid $221 in market value for every $1 of sales the company generated. When a P/S of 5 or 10 is considered too high, 221 is astronomic!

I culled the information in the preceding list from Enron's public filings that anyone could have seen. To understand these points more fully (along with other equally incisive and lucid accounting and financial points), and to know how to use the information to avoid similar mistakes in the future, see Chapter 11 and Appendix B.

Chapter 24

Ten Ways to Protect Yourself from Fraud

. . . .

In This Chapter

▶ Looking to the SEC for help

▶ Adopting a skeptical attitude

▶ Steering clear of scams

. . . .

*M*aking money is tough enough without worrying about who is out to get your money. The usual suspects, such as the IRS and other government agencies, are trying to take your money legally. Fortunately, most of that money goes to beneficial pursuits. However, others are out to take your money by illegal methods. Fraud and theft schemes have always been there. Scammers were there during the heady days of the Roaring Twenties as well as during the Great Depression that followed. The scammers were working overtime during the '90s, and they're still here today. Be alert. This chapter also includes tips on what to do if you are scammed.

Be Wary of Unsolicited Calls

Phone calls out of the blue to solicit money from you are always a bit questionable, but if they offer investments, you need to be particularly careful. But you knew that, right? You've read countless consumer reports warning you about investing through telemarketers. If the investment that's being pitched is so good, why is someone calling to sell you on it? Hasn't the financial press reported it? It probably has, but only as an advisory warning you to turn down any such offers.

The bottom line is that you should be the one looking for great investments, not the other way around. As for the unsolicited telephone call or e-mail touting a fantastic investment, either politely decline the offer or ask the caller how much he invested and whether he would mind sending literature with full details so that your attorney or financial advisor can review it. Or ask the caller for the company name and telephone number and say that you'll get back to him. The odds are that nine times out of ten the caller will probably hang up on you. Great! Who needs that annoying call at dinnertime anyway?

Get to Know the SEC

Long before you invest your first dollar, whether in stocks or any other financial investment, get to know the Securities and Exchange Commission (SEC). It's there primarily to protect investors from fraud and other unlawful activity designed to fleece them. The SEC was created during the early 1930s by the federal government to crack down on abuses that continued to linger from the speculative and questionable trading practices that were in high gear during the 1920s. It continues to this day to be the most important watchdog of the investment industry.

The SEC has an excellent Web site at `www.sec.gov`. The site offers plenty of great articles and resources for both novice and experienced investors to help you watch out for fraud and better understand the financial markets and how they work. Look up the telephone numbers for regional offices and feel free to call with your questions about dubious investments and broker/dealers. The SEC carries on a number of activities designed to help you invest with confidence. It maintains a database on file about complaints lodged against brokers and companies that have committed fraud or other abuses against the investing public.

Your tax dollars pay for this important agency. Find out about its free publications, services, and resources before you invest. If you've already been victimized by unscrupulous operators, call the SEC for assistance.

Don't Invest If You Don't Understand

Investments frequently can come in complicated forms that promise a great return but can be hard to understand. The premise of the investment — how it works and how it will create a great return on your money — may be hard to figure out. Scammers count on people being overwhelmed by the details to the point that they ignore the mechanics of the deal. Don't fall for such approaches. You should understand exactly what you're investing in, how it makes money, and what the risks are. If you still can't understand the investment (even if it is legitimate), then you're better off not plunging in with your hard-earned money.

If the investment still sounds intriguing, then at the very least get a second opinion by reviewing the details with advisors you trust.

Question the Promise of Extraordinary Returns

In good times and bad, people want to make as much money as possible with their investments. Hey, who doesn't? If your money is in a bank account earning a paltry 2 percent, what's wrong with putting some of it into some investment earning 17 percent compounded hourly? The extraordinary returns promised either end up being illusory or the result of great risk.

Misrepresenting or inflating promises of a great return on your money is common; sometimes even good brokers can unwittingly make them. Higher returns mean more exposure to loss.

If the investment is bona fide and is quoted as having a high rate of return (either in income or capital gains potential), then you can expect commensurate risk. The risk may not be immediately apparent, but it is there. As the Johnny-one-note that I am in this chapter, I recommend that you seek independent third parties for an informed second opinion. Appendix A has an extensive list of places and people to turn to.

A notable investment pro once remarked, "Sometimes, a return *on* your money is not as important as a return *of* your money." In other words, until you pick up more investing knowledge, keeping your original investment safe is better than risking it for questionable, pie-in-the-sky promises.

Verify the Investment

If anyone asks you to invest, first verify that the investment exists. Sounds weird, huh? Not really. Yes, many people have lost money in a bad or dubious investment, but you'd be surprised at how many people have been willing to fork over hard-earned money for phantom investments.

A man was prosecuted for fleecing millions from investors who were quick to jump into a dot-com IPO that he was peddling. After the SEC and other authorities investigated, they found that no such dot-com IPO existed at all. (Does that make it a dot-gone?) Sometimes, you can't even trust a con man to be even partially truthful.

When someone offers you an investment and you're not certain what type of investment it is or where it's traded, ask questions of the person presenting the investment and of third parties who can offer verification. Here are some questions to ask:

- What exchange or market is this investment traded or sold on?

- What governmental agency oversees this investment, and how can I contact that agency?

- Have articles on this investment been published by major media sources, such as *The Wall Street Journal* and *Money* magazine?

- What literature do you have that I can present to my accountant and attorney?

Check Out the Broker

Sometimes the investment is legitimate, but the broker or dealer isn't. Scammers don't let the absence of a license stop them. When an unfamiliar financial products marketer contacts you, do some homework first. Contact one of the following to check the status of a broker or dealer:

- **Professional associations:** Do you want to know whether a marketer is a member in good standing? Associations help the public deal with unethical parties in the industry.

- **The National Association of Securities Dealers (NASD):** Visit one of its great Web sites at www.nasdr.com. This site informs the public about brokers and dealers who have been convicted or have complaints against them.

- **The SEC:** Are these marketers properly registered? The SEC can inform you about whether these marketers have been penalized or banned from further activity.

Beware of the Pump-and-Dump

The pump-and-dump is a classic scam that usually shows up in bull markets. The scam works best with small cap or (even better) microcap stocks — in other words, small companies that have relatively few shares or small capitalization. Scams are at their most effective when they can play on the two most overworked emotions in the financial markets: greed and fear. In the pump-and-dump, greed is the operative emotion. In this example, the investor to be plucked is called Walter Pidjun (no relation to the actor Walter Pidgeon).

The insiders at the dubious company first try to promote the stock as a "hot investment." The company activates the "pump" when insiders and/or stock-broker, in cahoots with the insiders, call up investors such as Mr. Pidjun to tout this fantastic opportunity. They promise an opportunity to get into a profitable stock that will skyrocket in value. As a result of the high-pressure sales tactics, investors start buying the stock. This demand pushes up the price easily because so few shares are available on this thinly-traded stock. Perhaps Mr. Pidjun didn't bite the first time the broker called, but the broker calls again.

"Hello again, Mr. Pidjun! This is Barry Kuda, account representative from the brokerage firm of Fleece, Peeples, & Scram. Do you remember that stock investment I brought to your attention last week? That's right . . . Titanic Bio-Tech, Inc. Have ya seen the way its price has zoomed since then? When I last spoke to you, it was at $3 a share. Now it's already at $47! Our respected research department tells me it should be at $93 by lunchtime and will proba-bly triple again before the weekend. You don't want to miss this opportunity of a lifetime! Now how many shares would you like?"

Indeed, the price certainly went up dramatically as Mr. Kuda said it would. Mr. Pidjun puts the order in immediately while dollar signs dance in his head. The "pump" is working very well. After the fraudulent operators see that the stock has gone as high as possible, they immediately sell their stock at grossly inflated prices. The "dump" is complete, and they disappear into the wood-work. Mr. Pidjun and the other investors watch as their "hot" investment turns stone cold and the stock plummets to pennies on the dollar. Investors were so blinded by their greed that the pump-and-dump scam was success-fully done even in cases when there was no stock at all!

The SEC has been working overtime in recent years on cases similar to this example. Stock fraud was so lucrative that even organized crime got in on the action.

How can I do a warning about something legal in a chapter about fraud? Actually, isn't this entire chapter a warning? Yes, but sometimes you need a warning for things that aren't immediately apparent. As odd as this sounds, I want to warn you about something that is technically not fraud. What is it? Well, there is a legal version of the pump-and-dump scheme. It is not unusual for brokers and analysts to "pump" up a stock in the media. For example, a celebrated market strategist or high-profile CEO may talk up the wonderful potential of XYZ stock on a financial show. Then later you find out (through SEC filings, for instance) that while that these people were recommending that people buy the stock, they had actually been furtively selling their holdings in the stock! You were hearing "buy, buy," yet they were really saying "bye-bye."

Watch Out for Short-and-Abort

Short-and-abort works on the same premise as pump-and-dump. The difference is that instead of playing on the greed emotion, the con works on the fear emotion. To understand this scam, you should keep in mind that one can profit even when a stock falls in price by "going short." Chapter 16 goes into detail about making money from going short on a stock, but here I want to briefly describe it.

Going short is a strategy that an investor can utilize in a margin account with just about any broker. An investor may consider going short on a stock if she expects the stock's price to fall. Say that you think the stock of the company Plummet Inc. (at $50 per share) will sink fast. When you tell the broker that you want to go short on 100 shares of Plummet Inc., the broker will borrow 100 shares from the market, sell those shares, and credit $5,000 to your account (100 shares at $50 per share). Because this transaction is based on "borrowed stock," sooner or later you'll have to return the stock. Say that the stock price falls to $30; you could then instruct your broker to "close out the position." This directive means that the broker will debit your account for $3,000 (to buy 100 shares at $30 and return the stock to the source). In this case, you would make a $2,000 profit (the original $5,000 less the $3,000).

In the case of short-and-abort, the scammers want to make money from a stock's plummeting price. They may contact shareholders directly or plant phony stories or press releases in the media to cause concern and panic over a company's prospects. Naturally, shareholders in that particular company get anxious over their investment and decide to sell. The sudden, mass selling causes the stock's price to fall. The scammer then closes out the short position, takes the money, and runs.

Remember That Talk Is Cheap (Until You Talk to an Expert)

A fertile area for misleading investors is in the world of independent, third-party information sources. As the bull market reached its zenith in late 1999, some people were selling expensive stock-investing seminars and newsletters that promised get-rich-quick results. One promoter sold basic information (some of which was inaccurate) in a $5,000 seminar program. After many complaints, the authorities investigated and found out that the presenters made a lot of money from their seminars, but they actually lost money on their investment strategies!

Another information marketer published an expensive newsletter that promised lucrative stock picks. It was discovered that he was not recommending stocks found through diligent and honest research; he recommended the stocks because the companies paid him to tout their stocks.

Even though I make a good part of my living from giving seminars and writing articles on financial matters, I want you to be aware of the charlatans in the stock-investment industry. Seminars and newsletters are excellent sources of information and expertise on a given topic, but you should stay away from marketers that use hard-sell approaches for outrageously priced seminars and other information products. If you're considering expensive seminars and information products, check with such sources as the Better Business Bureau and www.fraud.org for registered complaints.

Recovering (If You Do Get Scammed)

If, despite your best efforts to invest wisely, you have that sinking feeling that you've been conned, it's time to gain assistance from securities enforcement authorities. The SEC is a good place to start, but you can turn to other agencies, too.

If a scheme was promoted through the postal service, contact the postal service. File a complaint with the postmaster in your town. Provide complete details in writing, including your account of what happened and copies of literature you received from the offending organization.

Also contact the appropriate state government securities department and state attorney general's office. If a scam originated in Florida, for example, then contact the Florida attorney general. Appendix A has a detailed listing to help you if you believe that you were a victim of fraud.

Appendix A

Resources for Stock Investors

- -

*G*etting and staying informed is an ongoing priority for stock investors. The lists in this appendix represent some the best information resources available.

Financial planning sources

To find a financial planner to help you with your general financial needs, contact the following organizations:

Certified Financial Planner Board of Standards
1700 Broadway, Suite 2100
Denver, CO 80290-2101
888-237-6275
www.CFP-Board.org
Get a free copy of the CFP Board's pamphlet *10 Questions to Ask When Choosing a Financial Planner.* Be sure to ask for one that specializes in investing.

Financial Planning Association (FPA)
1615 L Street, N.W.
Washington, DC 20036
800-322-4237
www.fpanet.org

National Association of Personal Financial Advisors
355 West Dundee Road
Suite 200
Buffalo Grove, IL 60089
888-333-6659
www.napfa.org

The language of investing

Dictionary of Financial Terms
By Virginia Morris and Kenneth Morris
Published by Lightbulb Press Inc.
Comments: A nicely laid out A-to-Z publication for investors mystified by financial terms. It explains the important investing terms we come across every day.

Investor Words
www.investorwords.com
One of the most comprehensive sites on the Internet for beginning and intermediate investors on learning words and phrases unique to the financial world.

Periodicals and magazines

Barron's
www.barrons.com

Forbes magazine
www.forbes.com

Investor's Business Daily
www.ibd.com

Kiplinger's Personal Finance magazine
www.kiplinger.com

Money magazine
www.money.com

SmartMoney
www.smartmoney.com

The Wall Street Journal
www.wsj.com

Books and pamphlets

At the Crest of the Tidal Wave: A Forecast for the Great Bear Market
By Robert Prechter
Published by New Classics Library

Austrian Economics for Investors
By Mark Skousen
Published by Pickering & Chatto Ltd.

Common Stocks and Uncommon Profits
By Philip Fisher
Published by John Wiley & Sons, Inc.

Elliott Wave Principle: Key to Market Behavior
By Robert Prechter and A.J. Frost
Published by New Classics Library

Forbes Guide to the Markets
By Marc Groz
Published by John Wiley & Sons

How to Buy Stocks
By Louis Engel and Henry Hecht
Published by Little, Brown and Company

*How to Pick Stocks Like Warren Buffett: Profiting from the Bargain Hunting
Strategies of the World's Greatest Value Investor*
By Timothy Vick
Published by McGraw-Hill Professional Publishing

The Intelligent Investor: A Book of Practical Counsel
By Benjamin Graham (preface by Warren Buffett)
Published by HarperCollins

*One Up on Wall Street: How to Use What You Already Know to Make Money
in the Market*
By Peter Lynch (contributor John Rothchild)
Published by Simon & Schuster

Secrets of the Great Investors (audiotape series)
Published by Knowledge Products
800-876-4332
www.knowledgeproducts.net

Security Analysis: The Classic 1934 Edition
By Benjamin Graham and David Dodd
Published by HarperCollins

Standard & Poor's Stock Guide (available in the library reference section)
Ask your reference librarian about this excellent reference source, which
gives one-page summaries on the major companies and has detailed financial
reports on all companies listed on the American Stock Exchange.

Unofficial Guide to Stock Investing
By Paul Mladjenovic
Published by Hungry Minds, Inc.
www.hungryminds.com
My shameless plug for another great book. Seriously, the book has several hundred resources and tips that add tremendously to your stock investing knowledge.

The Wall Street Journal Guide to Understanding Money and Investing
By Kenneth Morris, Virginia Morris, and Alan Siegel
Published by Fireside Press

"Invest Wisely: Advice From Your Securities Regulators" (pamphlet)
www.sec.gov/consumer/inws.htm
This publication provides basic information to help investors select a brokerage firm and sales representative, make an initial investment decision, monitor an investment, and address an investment problem.

General investing Web sites

Bloomberg
www.bloomberg.com

CNBC
www.cnbc.com

CNNFN
www.cnnfn.com

MarketWatch
www.marketwatch.com

Money Central
www.moneycentral.msn.com

Motley Fool
www.fool.com

Thomson Financial Network
www.thomsonfn.com

Stock investing Web sites

10-K Wizard
www.10kwizard.com

Allexperts Stock Market Q and A
www.allexperts.com/invest/stocks.shtml

Allstocks.com
www.allstocks.com

Quote.com
www.quote.com

Blue Chip Success
www.bluechipsuccess.com

Contrarian Investing.Com
www.contrarianinvesting.com

Daily Stocks
www.dailystocks.com

Disclosure-Investor.com
www.disclosure-investor.com

FinancialWeb
www.financialweb.com

FreeEDGAR
www.freeedgar.com

Investools
www.investools.com

Investor.Net
www.investor.net

InvestorPackages.com
www.InvestorPackages.com

Market Guide Investor
www.marketguide.com

Market Mavens
www.marketmaven.com

MoneyBrief
www.moneybrief.com

Multex Investor Network
www.multexinvestor.com

RagingBull.Com
www.ragingbull.com

Simply Stocks
www.simplystocks.com

Standard and Poor's
www.standardandpoors.com

Stock and Mutual Fund Evaluator
www.stockevaluator.com

Stock Consultant
www.stockconsultant.com

Tech Stock Investor
www.techstockinvestor.com

Wall Street Links
www.wallstreetlinks.com

Investor associations and organizations

National Association of Investors Corp. (NAIC)
810-583-6242
www.better-investing.org

American Association of Individual Investors (AAII)
625 North Michigan Ave.
Chicago, IL 60611-3110
312-280-0170
ww.aaii.org

Stock exchanges

American Stock Exchange
www.amex.com

Boston Stock Exchange
www.bostonstock.com

Chicago Stock Exchange
www.chicagostockex.com

Nasdaq
www.nasdaq.com

New York Stock Exchange
www.nyse.com

OTC Bulletin Board
www.otcbb.com

Pacific Stock Exchange
www.pacificex.com

Philadelphia Stock Exchange
www.phlx.com

Helping you choose brokers

Gomez & Associates
www.gomez.com
This firm acts like the J.D. Power & Associates for consumers in the broker-age industry.

How to Choose Your Online Broker
www.sonic.net/donaldj

Mercer, Inc.
379 West Broadway
Suite 400
New York, NY 10012
800-582-9854
This firm does a directory of discount brokers and compares their fees, services, and so on.

Brokers

A.B. Watley
888-229-2853
www.abwatley.com

Accutrade
800-494-8949
www.accutrade.com

Ameritrade
800-326-7507
www.ameritrade.com

Brokerage America
866-BATRADE
www.gruntal.com

Brown & Company
800-776-6061
www.brownco.com

Charles Schwab & Co.
800-540-9874
www.schwab.com

Credit Suisse First Boston
800-825-5723
www.csfbdirect.com

Datek Securities Online
888-GO-DATEK
www.datek.com

E*TRADE
800-STOCKS-5
www.etrade.com

Fidelity Brokerage
800-544-3063
www.fidelity.com

Merrill Lynch
877-653-4732
www.ml.com

Muriel Siebert & Co.
800-USA-0711
www.siebertnet.com

My Discount Broker
888-882-5600
www.mydiscountbroker.com

Quick and Reilly
800-533-8161
www.quick-reilly.com

Salomon Smith Barney Access
800-221-3636
www.salomonsmithbarney.com

Scottrade
800-619-SAVE
www.scottrade.com

TD Waterhouse Securities, Inc.
800-934-4448
www.waterhouse.com

Vanguard Brokerage Services
800-992-8327
www.vanguard.com

Wall Street Access
800-WALL-ST1
www.wsaccess.com

Wall Street Discount Corporation
888-4WALLST
www.wsdc.com

Sources for growth investors

The Elliott Wave Theorist
707-536-0309
www.elliottwave.com

Fleet Street Letter
508-368-7492
www.fleetstreetletter.com

Hulbert Financial Digest
1-866-428-6568
www.hulbertdigest.com

The IPO Reporter
40 West 57th St.
New York, NY 10019
800-455-5844

John Dessauer's Investor's World
800-804-0942
www.dessauerinvestorsworld.com

Louis Rukeyser's Wall Street
800-892-9702
www.rukeyser.com

Martin Weiss's Safe Money Report
407-625-3300
www.safemoneyreport.com

Outstanding Investments
508-368-7492
www.outstandinginvestments.com

Richard Russell's Dow Theory Letters
P.O. Box 1759
La Jolla, CA 92038
619-454-0481
www.dowtheoryletters.com

Strategic Investments
508-368-7492
www.strategicinvestments.com

The Value Line Investment Survey
800-634-3583
www.valueline.com

Sources for income investors

Income Stocks
P.O. Box 476
South Bend, IN 46624-0476
219-291-3823

Investing For Income
290 Eliot St.
Ashland, MA 01721-9104
800-343-5413

Utility Forecaster
1101 King St. #400
Alexandria, VA 22314
800-832-2330

Dividend reinvestment plans

Buy and Hold, Inc.
800-646-8212
www.buyandhold.com

DRIP Central
www.dripcentral.com

First Share
800-683-0743
www.firstshare.com

Netstock Direct Corporation
888-638-7865
www.netstockdirect.com

Share Builder
888-638-7865
www.sharebuilder.com

Earnings and earnings estimates

First Call
www.firstcall.com

Zacks Summary of Brokerage Research
www.zacksadvisor.com
Zacks tracks analysts' earnings estimates for major companies. Typically, it records over 15,000 such changes, made by over 3,500 analysts at 210 brokerage firms covering 5,000 companies.

Industry analysis

Hoover's
www.hoovers.com

MarketWatch
www.marketwatch.com

Standard & Poor's
www.standardandpoors.com

Factors that affect market value

Economics and politics

American Institute of Economic Research (AIER)
Box 100
Great Barrington, MA 01230
www.aier.org
Note: AIER also has a great little booklet on budgeting for consumers.

Economy.com, Inc.
600 Willowbrook Lane
West Chester, PA 19382
866-275-3266
www.economy.com
www.dismal.com
www.freelunch.com

Federal Reserve Board
www.federalreserve.gov

Financial Sense
Box 1269
Poway, CA 92074
858-486-3939
www.financialsense.com

Foundation of Economic Education
30 South Broadway
Irvington, NY 10533
800-960-4FEE
www.fee.org

Le MetroPole Café
www.lemetropolecafe.com

Ludwig von Mises Institute
518 West Magnolia Ave.
Auburn, AL 36832
334-321-2100
www.mises.org

Securities and Exchange Commission (SEC)
www.sec.gov
The SEC has tremendous resources for investors. In addition to information on investing, the SEC also monitors the financial markets for fraud and other abusive activities. For stock investors, it also has EDGAR (Electronic Data Gathering, Analysis, and Retrieval system), which is a comprehensive, searchable database of public documents that are filed by public companies.

Federal laws

Thomas legislative search engine
www.thomas.loc.gov

U.S. House of Representatives
www.house.gov

U.S. Senate
www.senate.gov

Go to any of these sites to find out about new and proposed laws. The on-site search engine will help you find laws either by their assigned number or a keyword search.

Technical analysis

Big Charts (Provided by www.Marketwatch.com)
www.bigcharts.com

Stockcharts.com, Inc.
www.stockcharts.com

Elliott Wave Theorist
www.elliottwave.com

Insider trading

Insider Scores
www.insiderscores.com

Securities and Exchange Commission (SEC)
www.sec.gov

Street Insider
www.streetinsider.com

Tax benefits and obligations

J.K. Lasser's series of books on taxes
By J.K. Lasser
John Wiley & Sons
www.wiley.com

Taxes For Dummies
By Eric Tyson and David J. Silverman
Hungry Minds, Inc.
www.hungryminds.com

Americans for Tax Reform
www.atr.org

Fidelity Investments
www.401k.com

National Taxpayers Union
www.ntu.org

Roth IRA
www.rothira.com

Social Security analysis & views
www.socialsecurity.org

Fraud

Consumer Information Center
www.pueblo.gsa.gov
Investing publications for consumers from the Consumer Information Center catalog are available for downloading at this Web site at no charge.

National Association of Securities Dealers
1735 K Street, N.W.
Washington, DC 20006
1-800-289-9999
1-202-728-8000
www.nasdr.com
This Web site gives you information and assistance on reporting fraud or other abuse by brokers.

The National Fraud Center
www.fraud.org

North American Securities Administrators Association
1-888-846-2722
www.nasaa.org

Securities and Exchange Commission (SEC)
www.sec.gov
The government agency that regulates the securities industry.

Securities Industry Association
1401 I Street, N.W.
Washington, DC 20005
202-296-9410
www.sia.org

Financial Ratios

• •

As dull or cumbersome as the topic sounds, financial ratios are indeed the "meat" of analyzing stocks. Sadly, most investors don't exercise their due diligence when it comes to doing some relatively easy things to make sure that the company they're investing in is a good place for their hard-earned investment dollars. This appendix lists the most common ratios that investors should be aware of and use. A solid company doesn't have to pass all these ratio tests with flying colors, but at a minimum, it should comfortably pass a few key ones regarding profitability and solvency.

Keep these points in mind about ratios:

✔ Not every company and/or industry is the same. A ratio that seems problematic in one industry may be just fine in another. Investigate.

✔ A single ratio is not enough on which to base your investment decision. Look at several ratios covering the major aspects of a company's finances.

✔ Look at two or more years of a company's numbers to judge whether the most recent ratio is better, worse, or unchanged from the previous year's ratio. Ratios can give you early warning signs regarding the company's prospects.

You can look at literally dozens of key ratios. No, you don't have to look at all of them. Just look at enough to comfortably answer some questions on these basic issues:

✔ **Profitability:** Is the company making money? Is it making more or less than it did in the prior period? Are sales growing? Are profits growing?

✔ **Survivability:** Is the company keeping debts and other liabilities under control? Are the company's assets growing? Is the company's net equity (or net worth or stockholders' equity) growing?

Liquidity Ratios

Liquidity means the ability to quickly turn assets into cash. Liquid assets are simply assets that are easier to convert to cash. Real estate, for example, is certainly an asset, but it's not liquid because it could take weeks, months, or even years to convert it to cash. Current assets such as checking accounts, savings accounts, marketable securities, accounts receivable, and inventory are much easier to sell or convert to cash in a very short period of time.

Paying bills or immediate debt takes liquidity. Liquidity ratios help you understand a company's ability to pay its current liabilities. The most common liquidity ratios are the current ratio and the quick ratio; the numbers to calculate them are located on the balance sheet.

Current ratio

The current ratio is the most commonly used liquidity ratio. It answers the question "Does the company have enough financial cushion to meet its current bills?" It is calculated as follows:

> Current ratio = total current assets ÷ total current liabilities

If Holee Guacamolee Corp. (HGC) has $60,000 in current assets and $20,000 in current liabilities, the current ratio is 3 because the company has three dollars of current assets for each dollar of current liabilities. As a general rule, a current ratio of 2 or more is desirable. A current ratio of less than 1 is a red flag that the company may have a cash crunch that could cause financial problems.

Quick ratio

The quick ratio is frequently referred to as the "acid test" ratio. It's a little more stringent than the current ratio in that it is calculated without inventory. I'll use the current ratio example discussed in the preceding section. What if half of the assets are inventory ($30,000 in this case)? Now what? First, here's the formula for the quick ratio:

> Quick ratio = (Current assets less inventory) ÷ current liabilities

In the example, the quick ratio for HGC is 1.5 ($30,000 divided by $20,000). In other words, the company has $1.50 of "quick" liquid assets for each dollar of current liabilities. This amount is okay. *Quick liquid assets* include any money in the bank, marketable securities, and accounts receivable. If quick liquid assets at the very least equal or exceed total current liabilities, that amount is considered adequate.

The acid test that this ratio reflects is embodied in the question "Can the company pay its bills when times are tough?" In other words, if the company can't sell its goods (inventory), can it still meet its short-term liabilities? Of course, you must watch the accounts receivable as well. If the economy is entering rough times, you want to make sure that the company's customers are paying invoices on a timely basis.

Operating Ratios

Operating ratios essentially measure the company's efficiency. "How is the company managing its resources?" is a question commonly answered with operating ratios. If, for example, a company sells products, does it have too much inventory? If it does, that could impair the company's operations. The following sections present common operating ratios.

The return on equity (ROE)

Equity is the amount left from total assets after you account for total liabilities. The net equity (also known as shareholders' equity, stockholders' equity, or net worth) is the bottom line in the company's balance sheet, both geographically as well as figuratively. It is calculated as

Return on equity (ROE) = net income ÷ net equity

The net income (from the company's income statement) is simply the total income less total expenses. Net income that is not spent or used up increases the company's net equity. Looking at net income is a great way to see whether the company's management is doing a good job growing the business. You can check this out by looking at the net equity from both the most recent balance sheet and the one from a year earlier. Ask yourself whether the current net worth is higher or lower than the year before? If it is higher, by what percentage is it higher? Use the ROE in conjunction with the ROA ratio (see the following section) to get a fuller picture of a company's activity.

Return on assets (ROA)

The ROA may seem similar to the ROE, but it actually gives a perspective that completes the picture when coupled with the ROE. The formula for figuring out ROA is

Return on assets = net income divided by total assets

The ROA reflects the relationship between a company's profit and the assets used to generate it. If the company HGC makes a profit of $10,000 and has total assets of $100,000, the ROA is 10 percent. This percentage should be as high as possible, and it should generally be at the same rate as the ROE.

Say that the company has an ROE of 25 percent but an ROA of only 5 percent. Is that good? It sounds okay, but there is a problem. If the ROA is much lower than the ROE, this indicates that the higher ROE may have been generated by something other than total assets — debt! The use of debt can be a leverage to maximize the ROE, but if the ROA doesn't show a similar percentage of efficiency, then the company may have incurred too much debt. In that case, investors should be aware that it could cause problems (see the section, "Solvency Ratios," later in this appendix).

Sales to receivables ratio (SR)

The sales to receivables ratio (SR) gives investors an indication of a company's ability to manage what customers owe it. This ratio uses data from both the income statement (sales) and from the balance sheet (accounts receivable, or AR). The formula is expressed as

Sales to receivables ratio = sales ÷ receivables

Say that you have the following data for HGC:

Sales in 2000 are $75,000. On 12/31/00, receivables stood at $25,000.

Sales in 2001 are $80,000. On 12/31/01, receivables stood at $50,000.

Based on this data, you can figure out that sales went up 6.6 percent, but receivables went up 100 percent! In 2000, the SR was 3 ($75,000 divided by $25,000). However, the SR in 2001 sank to 1.6 ($80,000 divided by $50,000), or nearly cut in half. Yes, sales did increase, but the company's ability to collect money due from customers fell dramatically. This information is important to notice for one main reason: What good is selling more when you can't get the money? From a cash flow point of view, the company's financial situation deteriorated.

Solvency Ratios

Solvency just means that the company will not be overwhelmed by its liabilities. Insolvency means "Oops! Too late." You get the point. Solvency ratios have never been more important than now. (I hope that you're reading this in 2002, but if not, ratios are still important.) Solvency ratios look at the relationship between what the company owns and what it owes. Here are two of the primary solvency ratios.

Debt to net equity ratio

The debt to net equity ratio is an indicator of the company's solvency. It answers the question "How dependent is the company on debt?" In other words, it tells you how much the company owes and how much it owns. You calculate it as follows:

Debt to net equity ratio = total liabilities ÷ net equity

If the company HGC has $100,000 in debt and $50,000 in net worth, the debt to net equity ratio is 2. The company has two dollars of debt to every dollar of net worth. In this case, what the company owes is twice the amount of what it owns. Whenever a company's debt to net equity ratio exceeds 1 (as in the example), that isn't good. In fact, the higher the number, the more negative the situation. If the number is too high and the company isn't generating enough income to cover the debt, the company runs the risk of bankruptcy.

Working capital

Technically, working capital isn't a ratio, but it does belong to the list of things that serious investors look at. *Working capital* means what the company has in current assets and its relationship to current liabilities. It is a simple equation:

Working capital = total current assets – total current liabilities

The point is obvious: Does the company have enough to cover the current bills? And, actually, you can formulate a useful ratio. If current assets are $25,000 and current liabilities are $25,000, that is a 1 to 1 ratio, which is cutting it close. Current assets should be at least 50 percent higher than current liabilities (say, $1.50 to $1.00) to have enough cushion to pay bills and have some money to finance continuing growth. Preferably, the ratio is better at 2 to 1 or higher.

Common Size Ratios

Common size ratios offer simple comparisons. There are common size ratios for both the balance sheet (where you compare total assets) and the income statement (where you compare total sales).

To get a common size ratio from a balance sheet, the total assets figure is assigned the percentage of 100 percent. Every other item on the balance sheet is represented as a percentage of total assets. For example, if Holee Guacamolee Corp. (HGC) has total assets of $10,000 and debt of $3,000, you know that total assets equal 100 percent, while debt equals 30 percent (debt divided by total assets or $3,000 ÷ $10,000, which equals 30 percent).

To get a common size ratio from an income statement (or profit and loss statement), you compare total sales. For example, if a company has $50,000 in total sales and net profit of $8,000, then you know that the profit equals 16 percent of total sales.

Keep in mind the following points with common size ratios:

- ✔ **Net profit:** What percentage of sales is it? What was it last year? How about the year before? What percentage of increases (or decreases) is the company experiencing?

- ✔ **Expenses:** Are total expenses in line with the previous year? Are any expenses going out of line?

- ✔ **Net equity:** Is this item higher or lower from the year before?

- ✔ **Debt:** Is this item higher or lower from the year before?

Common size ratios are used to compare the company's financial data not only with prior balance sheets and income statements but also with other companies in the same industry. You want to make sure that the company is not only doing better historically but also as a competitor in the industry.

Valuation Ratios

Understanding the value of a stock is very important for stock investors. The quickest and most efficient way to judge the value of a company is to look at valuation ratios. The type of value that you deal with throughout the book is the *market value* (essentially the price of the company's stock). You hope to buy it at one price and sell it later at a higher price — that's the name of the game. But what's the best way to determine if what you are paying for now is a bargain or is fair market value? How do you know if your stock investment is undervalued or overvalued? The valuation ratios in this appendix can help you answer these questions. In fact, they're the same ratios that value investors have used with great success for many years.

Price to earnings (P/E) ratio

The price to earnings ratio can also double as a profitability ratio because it is a common barometer of value that many investors and analysts look at. I cover this topic in Chapter 10, but because it is such a critical ratio, I also include it here. The formula is

P/E ratio = price (per share) divided by earnings (per share)

For example, if a company's stock price per share is $10 and the earnings per share are $1, the P/E is 10 (10 divided by 1).

The P/E ratio answers the question "Am I paying too much for the company's earnings?" Value investors find this to be a very, very important number. Here are some points to remember:

- Generally, the lower the P/E ratio, the better (from a financial strength point of view). Frequently, a low P/E ratio indicates that the stock is undervalued.

- A company with a P/E ratio significantly higher than its industry average is a red flag that its stock price is too high.

- Don't invest in a company with no P/E ratio (it has a stock price, but the company experienced losses). Such a stock may be good for a speculator's portfolio but not for your retirement account.

- Any stock with a P/E higher than 40 should be considered a speculation and not an investment. Frequently, a high P/E ratio indicates that the stock is overvalued.

When you buy a company, you're really buying its power to make money. In essence, you're buying its earnings. Paying for a stock that is priced at 10 to 20 times earnings is a conservative strategy that has served investors well for nearly a century. Make sure that the company is priced fairly and use the P/E ratio in conjunction with other measures of value.

Price to sales ratio (PSR)

The price to sales ratio (PSR) is another method for valuing the company. It helps to answer the question "Am I paying too much for the company's stock based on the company's sales?" This is a useful valuation ratio that I recommend using as a companion tool with the company's P/E ratio. You calculate it as follows:

PSR = stock price (per share) divided by total sales (per share)

This can be quoted on a per-share basis or on an aggregate basis. For example, if a company's market value (or market capitalization) is 1 billion dollars and annual sales are also 1 billion dollars, the PSR is 1. If the market value, in this example, is $2 billion, then the PSR is 2. For investors trying to make sure that they're not paying too much for the stock, the general rule is that the lower the PSR, the better. Stocks with a PSR of 2 or less are considered undervalued.

Be very hesitant about buying a stock with a PSR greater than 5. If you buy a stock with a PSR of 38, that means you're paying $38 for each dollar of sales — not exactly a bargain.

Price to book ratio (PBR)

The price to book ratio (PBR) is yet another valuation method. This ratio compares the market value to the company's accounting (or book) value. Recall that the book value refers to the company's net equity (assets minus liabilities). The company's market value is usually dictated by external factors such as supply and demand in the stock market. The book value is indicative of the company's internal operations. Value investors see the PBR as another perspective to valuing the company to determine if you're paying too much for the stock. The formula is

Price to book ratio (PBR) = market value divided by book value

An alternate method is to calculate the ratio on a per-share basis, which yields the same ratio. If the company's stock price is $20 and the book value (per share) is $15, then the PBR is 1.33. In other words, the company's market value is 33 percent higher than its book value. Investors seeking an undervalued stock like to see the market value as close as possible to (or even better, below) the book value.

Keep in mind that the PBR may vary depending on the industry and other factors. Also, judging a company solely on book value may be misleading because many companies have assets that aren't adequately reflected in the book value. Software companies are a good example. Intellectual property such as copyrights and trademarks are very valuable yet are not fully covered in book value. Just bear in mind that generally the lower the market value is in relation to the book value, the better for you.

Index

• E •